POLI
GIRL

In Pursuit Of The English Dream

Monika Wiśniewska

A MEMOIR

For My Mama,
the most loving and supportive friend throughout this 13-year
journey to self-discovery.

CONTENTS

TO THE READER

Take a comfortable seat, relax and join me on my journey of a
lifetime
towards spiritual awakening.
I need to warn you though.
You need to be brave.
But don't worry: if I could do it, so can you.
Ready?
Three…
Two…
One…

*'Men go abroad to wonder at the heights of mountains,
at the huge waves of the sea, at the long courses of the river, at
the vast compass of the ocean, at the circular motions of the
stars, and they pass by themselves without wondering.'*
-Saint Augustine

CHAPTER 1 - DIE BEFORE YOU DIE

'The path to paradise begins in hell.'
-Dante Alighieri

'The lorry's here!' Mama exclaimed from the kitchen on hearing Cezar, our German Shepherd, barking relentlessly in the garden.

I ran outside and saw two men climbing out of a white lorry while my stepdad was opening the gate.

'Come on; you can drive inside!' he exclaimed, waving his hand invitingly and once the lorry had backed into our driveway, the men opened the back door.

My whole life was in there.

I helped with unloading the boxes which contained most of my personal belongings. One of the men took out my white bike with a straw basket which had, when I last saw it, contained groceries and tulips. Next came boxes of different sizes, each labelled 'Monika—Poland.'

'It's over. My life is over.'

It was quiet. Nobody said anything, as if two surgeons were performing an autopsy to examine the cause of death. Only Cezar barked occasionally, running around the lorry and unaware of what was REALLY happening.

'Can you please sign here, ma'am?' one of the men asked, giving me a pen and a clipboard.

I didn't cry as I signed.

I had to be strong.

After the lorry's departure, I walked into my room which was now filled with stacks of boxes. Opening them one by one, I noticed the print canvas of John and me standing cheek to cheek, lovingly holding hands at the bottom of the white doorsteps of Schönbrunn Palace in Vienna. Then, in between randomly-thrown-in shoe boxes and my jackets, I noticed the book that John had designed shortly after we'd met. The cover featured a picture of us in a warm embrace outside Windsor Castle. The title said:

Monika and John
First Month Together

I ran out of the house and then through the back gate into the fields of barley, feeling sharp stalks cutting my bare legs, as if enemy swords were about to strike the final blow in my losing battle of the game of life. Breathless, I fell on my bleeding knees, gazed at the red sky of everlasting fire at the gates of Hades, the Hell on Earth I had found myself in, and I screamed out, crying, 'Why??'

The next morning, I woke up to the sound of the birds singing in the garden and a massive pain all over my body, letting me know that I was still alive.

'Why have I woken up?' I asked myself, 'I don't want this reality. This is not how I'm supposed to be living.

Sleeping was the only thing that stopped this excruciating pain, but only because it made me unconscious of the world around me. It wasn't so much about the pain being physical, even though it was, but because it tore my soul into pieces. The moment my consciousness came back from the sleep, telling me: 'Wake up, it's another day,' I could already feel needles pushed into my heart. My eyelids, swollen from crying for weeks, could hardly lift their own weight, making me want to stay buried in the darkness of my soul. The torturing muscle spasms, radiating from my back and squeezing my chest in a deadly embrace, made it hard for me to breathe. The beating of my heart, louder than the ticking of the clock, forced me to beg for one thing.

I yearned for it to stop.

And stop the agony of losing everything I had worked so hard for. But most of all, from losing the man who WAS the love of my life.

'What am I going to do now? It's over. My dream is over.'

I couldn't have failed more if I'd tried. It was the biggest downfall of my life, and I could not understand why it had happened. I'd trusted John with my whole life. I'd given him my beating heart on a silver tray, so he could lock it up in the safe of his heart and treasure it forever. I had surrendered, for the first time in my life, giving up my independence as a woman and letting a man, another human being, take full control of what would happen to me, just as I would have entrusted God: 'And I give you my heart and soul, I trust in your guidance, and that you will provide me with all I need in return.' The kind of prayer that shows faith in the Higher Power and its limitless ability to look after you. Just like the plants and trees blindly know the universe will provide them with enough nutrients, rain, and sunshine so they can grow effortlessly to become the masterpiece of God's creation. John was not God—far from it—nor any other deity. But he was part of my soul and I'd believed that he wouldn't have let me experience such an annihilation of my heart.

Staring, from my bedroom window at the garden immersed in twilight, I could hear nothing but the crickets, dogs barking across the fields, and millions of thoughts in my head, as if my brain was software infected by a vicious virus that was about to cause damage to the whole system. But I didn't hear *him* anymore. No calls. No text messages. The voice of the man I loved so much was the most wonderful sound in the world and its sudden absence now was deafening.

Only a year ago, we'd been squeezing each other's hands, listening to the most touching Strauss concert in the Great Gallery of Schönbrunn Palace.

'*Kocham Cię*,' I'd whispered, gently kissing the most wonderful man on Earth, tearful from this surreal experience.

'I love you more, baby! You're my beautiful princess!'

Only a few months ago, we'd danced on the marble floor of our million-euro villa in Holland, after walking in for the first time.

'Welcome home, baby!' he'd said, twirling me around and gluing me to his chest so he could kiss me.

'We can finally be happy now,' I replied, thrilled from this historic—for us—moment.

Only a few months ago, we'd been wrapped in the intimate embrace in the warm waters of the infinity pool, overlooking the snow-capped Alps, clinking Champagne glasses.

'Is this really happening?' I'd asked, kissing his warm, wet lips.

'Get used to it! This is our new life. I will always look after you.'

Only a few months ago, we'd gone skiing for the first time in Innsbruck.

'I can do it! Look!' I'd shouted with childlike enthusiasm, dressed in a white skiing outfit with a Russian-style hat with flaps over my ears, making me look like a Cocker Spaniel.

'That's great! Me too!' he'd replied, falling on his backside for the hundredth time, making me burst into laughter.

Only a few months ago in Austria, my neck had become home to the most exquisite, sparkling-with-a-million-crystals necklace, given to me by the most generous, loving man I'd ever met.

'It's for you. The most beautiful necklace in the store for the most beautiful woman!'

'Oh, thank you so much. You are too kind. How much? A thousand euros? Oh, no… It's too expensive!'

'You deserve it. Happy birthday!'

Only a few months ago, John had been shielding my back when standing on a boat, dressed in white, admiring the passing lights of the spectacular sights of Prague.

These and hundreds of other memories filled my mind, torturing my soul as if they were traumatic war flashbacks. They hurt me now, and I didn't know how to stop them. They were the most wonderful moments of my life and I wanted them to live with me forever.

My life abroad was over now, even though I still didn't want to believe it. My mind showered me with desperate images filled with hope that it was just a bad dream, that John would come back for me any day now. Just like he'd promised he would when I'd seen him for the last time.

'I'll come and get you when it's all over,' he'd said, kissing me gently on the forehead before driving off.

Since that day, I had waited to see his smiling face when he would get out of the car in front of our gate. Cezar, sensing his arrival quicker than any of us, probably because of the tractor noise of our super car's engine, would jump up and down from excitement, barking like a complete lunatic. Mama would rush to open the gate so he could run to me, lift me high up in the air and say:

'*Kocham Cię*, I'm sorry I hurt you, baby. I was so stupid. I've missed you! You are my life!'

My mind gave me this vision in the only hope of my salvation. But maybe I was not to receive my salvation just yet? Maybe I had to experience this spiritual crucifixion to awaken fully, stop letting my ego control my mind, and ultimately find the secret to happy life? Maybe I had to 'die before you die,' which according to Zen masters, would magically transform me into the human being who finally finds peace?

I woke up each morning, looking at the crystal chandelier, hoping that today would be the day when John would come and take me back to our home in Holland, where we would live the ultimate freedom from the anguish we had been going through for years. That we would finally be happy and enjoy our lives to the fullest.

My mama tried to help me as much as she could, trying to understand it all, just like I did, not knowing what to say, other than: 'Maybe it's for the best,' but with such little conviction in her voice that it made this statement suspiciously untrue to me.

'I got you your favourite cake!' she said, sitting next to me on my bed, distressed from the state I was in.

She had never expected this to happen. There had been no visible signs of it being possible. She had hoped that my loving relationship with John was so strong that we would live happily ever after in our villa in Holland, after having got married in the Gothic cathedral, whisked away into the sunset by a white horse-drawn carriage, kissing passionately under a shower of rice, thrown high up in the air by the cheering guests.

I had never thought our love would end, either. It just could not. It was the deepest, most powerful love any human being could experience in this physical dimension. Or maybe, I had had the premonition of this disaster, and if so, why was I surprised that I ended up imprisoned in my family home in Poland, losing everything I had worked so hard for in all those years abroad.

Lying on my heated amethyst mat, which gave my muscles a relief from turning into hard lumps of knots, excruciatingly painful even at the slightest attempts to massage them out, I stared at the walls, trying to understand.

'Is this the final message from God? Give up, Monika! It's over! Should I finally stop this silliness of pursuing "that thing," a better life and happiness in a foreign land? What do I want to achieve? Career? Money? Husband? Are those an achievement anyway? Is that all that can be achieved in life? Everyone can do that, with better or worse outcomes. And in any country. What is my soul so desperately searching for? Weren't my last few years abroad a big enough adventure to teach me what I needed to know about myself? Should I just live a peaceful, less adventurous, and "safer" life back in Poland? Should I accept the defeat? But how can this journey be over? Not now. Not yet. I'm not ready for the end of it. But can I do it again? Can I start all over, bruised emotionally and physically, with a heavy heart filled with pain? Do I have the strength to lift my body from this heated mat and face the petrifying world out there?'

True, I had already done it once before. I had gone to England a naive 25-year-old girl and started from zero. But it was different now. I was ill and I was defeated, even before I started. My body and soul had been wrecked to the ground by a bulldozer driven by the man of my dreams.

True, I had already taken that leap of faith and a two-hour flight to the 'dream island' where anything was possible. The country of endless opportunities, if only one were ready to work hard and not let any obstacles stop them along the way. But could I do it once more? How? Where would I go? Who could I ask for help, embarrassed about my biggest life failure?

I had always hated that horrible feeling of having to rely on other people, showing my total vulnerability of not being strong enough to look after myself. But over those years back in England, trusting others and counting on complete strangers' help and their good-will had been the only way for me to survive some of my biggest challenges. I will always thank God for sending them onto my path in the most unexpected ways, helping me to go through that journey, full of dangers lurking around the corner, some of which could have easily ended tragically.

'Should I try again? Should I take another leap of faith and go back to England, rising spectacularly like a phoenix from the ashes? Should I prove that I can do it once more? Should I reclaim my independence as a woman? But most of all, should I regain my dignity as a human being?'

One of John's last messages had said:

'YOU WILL NEVER MAKE IT WITHOUT ME.

CHAPTER 2 - LEAP OF FAITH

'Two there are who are never satisfied-
the lover of the world and the lover of knowledge.'
-Rumi

My plane had landed at London Stansted Airport, on a December evening in 2004, nine years before.

As a qualified English teacher, I could already speak the language of the 'natives', but my peaceful life with my mama, stepdad, Cezar and cat Miki, in my small town near Toruń, in northern Poland, had not prepared me for the journey I was about to embark on. I had learnt my first English words as a young girl from an American TV programme which I had watched over and over, relentlessly repeating words and the alphabet sung by animal puppets.

Over the years at school, I had become the 'smartie', lifting my hand high up in the air, ready to answer questions from the exercise book, even before the other children had a chance to read them. Mama, seeing my passion for English, spent every extra zloty for private lessons. We lived from one month to the next, but she always found a way to save up for them. As long as there was an English lesson that day, I would walk briskly to school, for two miles through the countryside at dawn, in minus ten degrees Celsius, with my boots squeaking in half a meter of deep snow and a thick scarf around my face, covered with frozen crystals from my breath. On other days, I wasn't that happy. In the evenings, I travelled two hours each way on the train to Toruń, to attend private lessons with a university professor. Walking back home in complete darkness along the train tracks, I prayed that nobody would hurt me. And nobody ever did. My angels always looked after me.

I studied to be an English teacher, but I had a strange feeling that once I could speak English fluently, the world would open up to me with vast opportunities. I soon realised that my biggest dream was to live in England and speak beautifully sounding English words, every single day.

***

Walking into the arrivals on that cold December day, I was astounded by the hustle and bustle of the airport. Wearing my white jacket and a scarf loosely thrown over my neck, dragging my pink suitcase full of clothes and only £100 in my wallet, I didn't know whether I would stay in England FOREVER. Just like I didn't know that what I was about to discover on my journey would turn out to be far greater than I could have ever imagined.

'If I find a job, I might stay,' I said jokingly to my tearful mama, hugging her tightly goodbye at Bydgoszcz Airport.

But it was only a joke. Or maybe that deep-rooted desire I'd always had to live in England? To experience the far more exciting world out there, rather than just my hometown? True, I was scared. Scared of the unknown. But my curiosity was stronger than fear. Besides, I was going to stay with my good friend Marta, who had invited me for Christmas. Hakim was picking me up to take me to her house and when I saw his smiling face, waving at me in the crowd of people, I knew I would be fine.

CHAPTER 3 - FRENCH RIVIERA

'Beauty awakens the soul to act.'
-Dante Alighieri

I had met Hakim on a beach in Cannes, two years before my arrival in England. Swimming in the warm, turquoise sea, together with my friend Ania, enchanted by the breathtaking beauty of the coast, I noticed the dark-haired man with goggles on his head, watching me.

'Hey gorgeous! Where are you from?' he said with a gummy smile, having swum closer in the crystal clear water.

'I'm from Poland,' I replied, surprised by his directness. 'I'm on a bus trip to Costa del Sol, and we are just stopping here for one night.'

'Lovely, and I'm French and I live in London. I'm a physics teacher,' he replied and when we sat down on the beach, we talked for over two hours.

'You are very beautiful, Monika! I'd like to see you again! I want to visit you in Poland. Would you like that?' he asked, making me blush from his compliments and feel flattered that a man like him had any interest in me.

Watching Ania swimming, I couldn't believe my luck. I had met this amazing man in a paradise of sun, sea, and the biggest wealth on Earth I had ever seen. I was 23 at that time and I'd been saving for this trip for years as a student, giving private English lessons in the evenings and weekends. I had always dreamt of travelling. Flicking through glossy pages of a travel magazine for hours, staring at the picturesque Greek, Italian or Spanish beaches, I'd imagined being there, despite having no idea how I would get the money to do it. But it hadn't stopped me from dreaming. After all, dreams are free! And travelling from Poland to Spain on the bus for four days didn't discourage me at all.

In the French Riviera, I stepped into the most magical place on Earth. Shiny super cars, looking like full-size boys' toys, speeded up the windy roads, making loud engine noises. The tall, palatial hotels, sprinkled with palm trees, had limousines parked outside, as if the rich and famous had just had another day in paradise. Sunny streets were lined with expensive boutiques and the harbours were filled with the most stunning gigantic yachts, furnished with white leather sofas on decks where I could see myself sunbathing and drinking Champagne with the other glamorous women, wearing the biggest hats and the smallest bikinis.

In Monaco, the second smallest independent state in the world and the home of the Formula One Grand Prix, I put €1 into the slot machine inside the Casino de Monte-Carlo. I lost. But at least I gambled, and I could brag about it ever after. Just not about my winnings! The changing of the guards, dressed in white uniforms and marching outside the Prince's Palace, a former home of Princess Grace, looked spectacular. Walking along the streets, lined with colourful houses, I was stunned by the flags which looked just like the Polish ones, only upside down. The postcard views of the sea from this 'heaven on the hill' made me gasp with astonishment.

'Am I dreaming? Is this world real? What a wonderful life it would be if I could see more places like this!'

In Cannes, I compared the size of my palms with celebrities' hand prints on the pavement of the walk of fame. Posing for a picture on the red carpet of the Palace des Festivals et des Congres, where the annual biggest film festival took place, made me feel like a movie star—at least, for a minute. Walking along the seaside promenade at twilight, I noticed a sign on the board outside an Italian restaurant. The cheapest pizza was €9, almost a fifth of my total budget, but I decided to be adventurous and order it. I ate it al fresco, buzzing from excitement. It was the most delicious, thin-crusted, juicy margarita pizza, so thin that it hardly filled me up. But I ate it in Cannes, overlooking the eternity of the turquoise sea, and that was all that mattered to me.

After this trip, my desire to live in England got even stronger. I knew England wouldn't be the same as Cote d'Azur, especially with regards to the weather, but getting a good job there would allow me to become financially independent and travel around the world. Yes, this was now officially my biggest dream.

The dream to live in England.

CHAPTER 4 - THE KING

'Cześć, Monika, *jak się masz?*' ('Hi, Monika, how are you?') Hakim said on the phone with a sweet Polish accent, right after my return home.

From then on, he called me every evening, expressing his adoration for my beauty, and just as he had promised on the beach in Cannes, he bought a plane ticket to visit me in Poland. It was an incredible event for my family. At that time, no foreigners came to my town. At least, I had never seen or met any.

'How wonderful! What a visitor to have!' said Mama, as if the King himself was honouring us with a visit.

French or not, he was coming from England. And who was I? Just a young Polish girl, a student, living in a small town. Hakim had arrived with his entourage of elegant clothes and heavenly perfumes. When he was explaining different brands and labels on his jeans that I had never heard of, I felt inferior to him. *Why does he want to be with me? I don't even wear designer clothes,* I thought, looking at his sartorial look.

'This is for your mama, to use in cooking,' he said, handing me jars with a thick orange paste. Mama was happy to receive such gifts, but we didn't really know what to do with them, so they stayed in the fridge for months. Later, I learnt they were jars of Indian curry, something completely alien to us at that time. Instead, we cooked Polish food, but it couldn't contain pork. For some reason, he didn't eat it.

I took Hakim for long walks around the countryside, through fields wrapped in a thick foggy blanket, with colourful leaves paving our way. I hoped to impress him with the Gothic cathedral in town, standing majestically by the lake, which reflected its stunning architectural beauty. Walking through the central nave, I shared the story of the precious robe kept in the treasury, supposedly made from the saddle of wezyr Mustafa, brought as a trophy by King Jan III Sobieski after the defeat of the Ottoman army in Vienna.

'My family is originally from Algeria and I don't practice any religion,' Hakim said when we had walked out.

As much as I had tried to entertain him, he wasn't too happy, even in Warszawa, where we had stopped overnight before his flight back. We went for a walk in Łazienki Park, the largest park in the city, to see the palace on the island which had been a bathhouse before the last Polish king, Stanisław August Poniatowski, had turned it into a residence.

'And this is the monument of our Polish composer Fryderyk Chopin, famous for his piano pieces such as mazurkas and nocturnes,' I explained, pointing at the large bronze statue of Chopin sitting under a willow tree, reminding me of a harp.

'Umm, I've never heard of him' he said, and looked away.

We then strolled through the Old Town, in a labyrinth of cobblestone streets and colourful medieval houses. I told Hakim that they had been rebuilt after Warszawa had been razed to the ground by Hitler in WWII, when an unbelievable 90 per cent of buildings had been destroyed during the 1944 Warsaw Uprising. It was one of the most tragic events in twentieth century history. The courageous resistance movement had fought the German occupation for 63 days in sewers and cellars, in hope of support from the Red Army. But the Red Army had only watched this hell on Earth from the other side of the Vistula River. And so did the Allies, who did not do much to help. When the massacre had finished, the Soviets' tanks rolled into the destroyed city. Almost 250,000 civilians had been slaughtered.

'Our dramatic history hasn't been paved with roses! If it wasn't for our spirit and bravery, we as a nation probably wouldn't even exist now,' I concluded, adding that Poland had fought for freedom over 40 times between 1600 and 1945, and had only become a democratic country recently, after the fall of Communism in 1989.

'I'd like to show you the Ghetto Heroes Monument, commemorating the martyrdom of Jews and their deportation to concentration camps.'

'Oh Monika, your Polish history is so sad. Can we have something to eat now?' he replied, so we found an Indian restaurant.

'Did you like it? I asked, looking at him finishing his meal.

'Yes, it's nice, but not as good as in London!' he replied.

'Why does he only want to eat his food rather than trying our cuisine? Who wouldn't like our *pierogi* or *bigos*?' I said to Mama on the phone later.

'I'll get you a plane ticket to London for Christmas! I want to show you the most amazing city in the world, my gorgeous! You haven't seen anything yet!' he'd said, hugging me goodbye at the airport.

'Oh, thank you, that's very kind of you,' I replied, grateful for his invite.

I had learnt a lot about English history and read Shakespeare, Emily Bronte and Jane Austin during my studies, so the thought of seeing more English heritage was very exciting. But I was also a bit scared. I had never been on a plane before.

***

Hakim's central London flat was cold, with old windows, always covered in condensation. He cooked the 'orange paste' with chicken and served it with some kind of flat bread that I had never tasted before. And cooking involved putting plastic containers into the microwave and then its contents on my plate.

'Nice?' he asked.

'Oh, yes, but can I have some more water, please?' I replied, not being used to such spicy food.

But the most important thing was that we could spend time together. Rushing through London, I got a glimpse of the main tourist attractions, the Tower of London, the Houses of Parliament, Big Ben and Buckingham Palace. We jumped on a red, double-decker bus to the busiest, longest street I'd ever seen in my life, lined with hundreds of shops. Oxford Street. We walked in and out of shops, passing people, running around like headless chickens, carrying piles of clothes and shoes, as if preparing for the apocalypse. Hakim bought a jumper and two pairs of jeans. I couldn't afford anything except a cosmetics set. But what else would one need from a trip to London anyway?

CHAPTER 5 - GONE

'When you meet a man, you judge him by his clothes,
When you leave, you judge him by his heart.'
-Russian proverb

'Do you want to attend a cabin crew course with me?' Marta asked on the phone one day.

When I finally got my master's degree in 2004, which I had been working so hard for, Marta, my good friend from university, decided to attend a cabin crew training course for an airline based in England. Poland had just entered the European Union in May, opening the silver cage door to a new-found freedom, letting us spread our wings and fly out, so that we could seek new opportunities and a better, more prosperous life. It was a true gift of freedom to be able to possibly earn more money, and travel without the need to apply for a visa which before, could have only been granted if family members had sent the invite. Remembering vaguely the times of Communism, I was excited about the opportunities of working in England, allowing me to live life to the fullest. I probably could have achieved a lot career-wise by staying in Poland, but in my heart I felt that through hard work and commitment, I could achieve much more in England. But I was hesitant about attending the course with Marta. After my last flight from London, my head almost exploded like a balloon from the pressure in my ears before landing, so I decided: best not to. Marta went to England, but we stayed in touch and I started to work as an English teacher in a special needs school, in a nearby town. I soon realised, however, that this career path was not for me.

'Miss, we know we are freaks,' the kids said repeatedly, swearing and throwing chairs at everyone, including me.

'We can't even speak Polish properly, so why are you telling us to learn English? What do we need it for?' said Karolina, one of my teenage pupils who scared everyone with her violent outbursts but was very polite to me, staring at me as if she was in love.

Having pondered on this profound statement, I had to admit that she was probably right. They simply wouldn't and couldn't do anything I asked them to do, and the only way for me to keep them calm and make them sit for 45 minutes of the lesson was writing very long English sentences on the blackboard, in the hope they would copy them into their notebooks. And it worked. Sometimes.

Jesus, it looks like nothing what I have written, I thought to my horror when Karolina showed me her notebook.

'Oh, super, *bardzo pięknie,*' I praised her, looking at her dreamy eyes, not knowing what else to say, slowly losing the will to live.

'Try drinking Melissa tea, it helps to relax,' my mama said, seeing me stressed every single day.

My adult life had begun!

One day, a 12-year-old boy, famous for terrorising both teachers and pupils, stood up in the middle of my lesson and just as I had turned around from writing on the blackboard, he jumped out of the window.

'Piotr! *Nieeeeeeeeeeeeee!!!!*' I protested with a near heart attack, seeing myself taken to prison, cuffed and sentenced for life but when he started running on top of the roof underneath the window, children burst out laughing and I sighed with relief.

'*Dzień dobry,* ('Good Morning') Sir. I must tell you that Piotr jumped out of the first floor window during my lesson,' I reported to the headmaster with a tremulous voice.

"Really? Did he kill himself?' he asked, looking straight into my eyes.

'*Nie.*'

'Oh, *szkoda!*' ('Oh, that's a shame') He replied with a grin that made it impossible for me to tell if he was being serious or not.

***

'Can you help me with getting a job as a teacher?' I asked when I arrived in the UK and Hakim was taking me in his car to Marta's house.

'You? A teacher? Impossible! You need a UK teaching qualification to teach in this country,' he replied, snorting with laughter.

Hakim had known about my dream to live in England, but he'd never suggested helping me with that first step, even though I'd always hoped he would. The following day, I called him but he didn't pick up. I tried again the day after but there was no reply.

'He will never call me back, will he? I can't count on his help,' I realised, sitting on Marta's bed, staring at my phone.

'Why doesn't he want to know me now? After years of calling me every day, tantalizing me with beautiful words of how much he missed, loved and adored me,' I said to Mama on the phone.

'I don't know, darling, but he obviously doesn't want to help you. You see, a friend in need is a friend indeed, and I have a feeling he is still probably married,' she replied, knowing that when I had visited him a few months before, I'd noticed a picture of him and a woman sitting next to two other people, wearing elegant clothes. 'It looks like a wedding day,' I'd thought.

When I'd confronted him, he admitted he had been married but he'd divorced her, and she was living in Algeria now.

One morning, I'd woken up and said, 'I dreamt that I talked to your wife.'

'Oh really? And what did she say?' he replied without looking at me, and continued to iron his shirt.

After these strange conversations, I knew that I probably wouldn't be with him for the rest of my life so I decided to find out about my future and if I would find true love and get married, just like everyone else. Arabella from Toruń seemed like the right person to ask. After all, who else would know better than a fortune teller? Her room in the old house was very dark. The colourful patchwork covered the sofa, and the heavy smell of incense filled the air. When I sat down in front of her, she asked me to shuffle her Tarot cards before doing the spread.

'I can see a man who lives abroad,' she said, making me think that she was very good, 'but he is married,' she added.

'He WAS married, but he got divorced,' I corrected her, knowing she was talking about Hakim.

'Oh no, he is still married,' she replied with calm confidence and satisfaction, as if she had just caught a thief of hearts.

'Will I get married soon? Can you see my soulmate?' I asked my burning question after hearing what I'd suspected anyway.

'I don't see it in the nearest future. And when you ask about a soulmate, well, there can be many soulmates in a lifetime. Some are only here to help you grow and prepare you for the one you are meant to be with,' she replied, 'but you will live abroad,' she added with a soothing, mysterious voice.

'Oh, really?' I replied, disappointed that my biggest dream to find love since I'd been a little girl wouldn't come true quickly—but at the same time, I was excited about living abroad.

'Let me tell you something, my dear. You see, some people want to be like weeds and some want to be roses. You are a rose and your soul wants to grow, learn and develop in this lifetime,' she added.

What does it mean that I'm a rose? Why can't I be just like everyone else? Just happy? And why do I need to learn so much? I thought, having left her house, unaware of what lessons were waiting for me in my adventure of a lifetime.

Hakim was gone from my life as soon as I came to England.

I never heard from him again.

CHAPTER 6 - NOW OR NEVER

'When are you going back to Poland, Monika?' asked Marta on a Boxing Day.

Marta lived in Bishop's Stortford, a small historic town in Hertfordshire, on the border with Essex, close to London Stansted Airport. She shared the flat with other cabin crew members who had to work crazy shifts, flying all over Europe.

'I'd like someone to stay with me overnight and it would be best if you just went back to Poland,' she continued, letting me know that I couldn't sleep with her in her bed anymore.

I was surprised to hear that she was seeing a pilot, not only because it was such a cliché, but because she had a boyfriend in America whom I had thought she genuinely loved. *What's got into her, now that she's moved to England?* I thought.

After that, I slept on the blanket on the floor in the corner of the living room. Marta woke me up at five every morning, because I, sleeping on the floor, was not a nice view for her and the pilot whilst they had breakfast. But my unflinching determination to find a job did not diminish because of it. Her ruthless behaviour agonised me, mainly because of the disappointment of how unrecognisable she'd become, compared to how I remembered her from Poland, but deep down I knew that this was my one and only chance to stay in England. My only chance. I had no idea how but I knew, that I had no other choice—even though I did have a choice. I could have gone back home the next day.

The first two things I bought in England were a sim card to call my mama, which quickly used all my money, and… an umbrella. Walking along the high street at night, cold heavy raindrops were slowly melting away my dream of living in England. 'What should I do? Do I go back? But I don't want to go back. I want to find a job. But how, where? Why is Marta so horrible now? Why? Why?' My internal battle had started.

'Just get the ticket and come back home, darling, please don't stay there,' Mama repeated as I stared at the colourful Christmas shop displays.

'*Nie* Mama, I'll stay another day. Maybe I'll find a job tomorrow,' I replied, adamant that I wanted to stay, despite the overwhelming fear of not knowing what might happen.

The following day, I went to a job centre close to the airport. I scanned the screen of vacancies on one of the stand-alone machines but I didn't know what jobs I could do. They all seemed challenging and serious.

Who would let me do such important jobs? I thought, as I walked out of the job centre.

'Are you looking for a job?' asked an Englishman, running after me. He was in his forties and looked like a construction worker.

'Yes I am, I would like to find a job. I've just come from Poland,' I replied.

'Follow me! I know someone who can help you!' he said, pointing towards the main airport building.

'Oh really? Who?'

'Come!' he replied.

'How did he know I needed help so much? Has he been sent by my angels?' I thought, walking alongside him.

When we approached the terminal building, he introduced me to a dark-haired man in a white shirt and black trousers, pushing a tall metal cage on wheels.

'This Polish girl is looking for a job. Have you got anything?' asked my new helper, sent by angels.

'Yes, I do have a job. Is that your CV you are holding? Come with me. I'll show you what the job is all about,' he replied, staring at me.

Bal, as that was his name, took me upstairs in a lift. We stopped in front of a restaurant.

'Your job will be to clean the tables. You will need to collect trays with dirty dishes and put them on the trolley. I'm a manager here so you will be working for me. You will be paid £4.25 per hour, and the shifts are usually ten hours a day, but could be more if required,' he said.

'Umm, that it's not really what I was looking for. I am a qualified teacher and I have a master's degree. I'm looking for at least an office job,' I replied.

'Without any references in this country you will not find a better job, and you need to start somewhere!'

'Ok, let me think about it,' I replied, feeling sad that after five years of studying, all I could do in England was work in a restaurant.

Bal called me persistently every other day.

'Hi Monika, so are you going to take it? It's a good job! It's a start for you!'

'Ok I'll take it. When can I start? 'I finally replied, desperate for money and stressed by Marta's pestering me to go back to Poland.

'Oh fantastic. Have you got anywhere to stay?' he asked with a cheerful voice.

'No, I don't.'

'We have a company house where you can rent a room and pay from your first salary,' he said. 'You can move in tomorrow. The door will be open,' he added.

'Ok, thank you, I'll go there tomorrow,' I replied, aware I only had £10 left in my wallet.

'Cześć I took that job. I'm staying in England,' I said to Mama on the phone.

'If that's what you want, darling. I hope it will work out fine for you. I would much prefer it if you came back home, but it's your choice.'

'I'll be fine, don't worry, and Bal seems like a nice man,' I replied and started to pack my suitcase, excited about what the next day was going to bring.

CHAPTER 7 - TAXI TO HOPE

'Are you sure you are going to be ok?' asked the taxi driver on the way to the company house.

'Yes, I will be ok. Why?' I replied.

Thomas was a friendly, chubby Englishman in his fifties. I told him about Marta and my new manager who had offered me a room in the house belonging to the restaurant. Thomas listened to my story, gazing at me with a concerned look on his face. When we stopped in front of the terraced house, he took out my bag from the boot.

'Why don't you give me your number and if I hear of any rooms for rent, I will let you know. I know lots of people. I take many cabin crew members to the airport every day,' he said.

'Oh, thank you very much! That would be great,' I replied.

I struggled to get my bag up the stairs, which were covered by a stained, blue carpet. To the right, and after what seemed like a climb to Mount Everest, there was a room with the door left ajar. Seeing the skeleton posters on the walls and black curtains, I knew it must have belonged to a man. *Could it be Bal's room?* I thought.

I opened the squeaky door to the room on the left, my new room, and I was hit by the obnoxious odour of a dead rat. It was freezing cold and empty, except the bed in the middle, or rather a wooden box, covered with a red, dirty cloth. The faded green wallpaper was coming off, close to the grey ceiling, which showed black marks of fungi.

Oh my God,' I thought.

I sat on my 'new bed', covered my face with palms and wept.

I can't do this. I can't stay here, it's not safe, God, I can't do it. I give up. I need to buy the ticket to Poland, I thought.

With a heavy heart, I picked up my phone and looked for the airline number. After about 15 minutes, but what had seemed like an eternity of an internal battle, my phone rang.

'Would you like to stay with me and my family in a single room for £300 a month?' Thomas asked in a cheerful voice.

'Oh, yes! I would love that! Thank you!'

'Listen, I'll pick you up in 20 minutes. Wait for me outside!'

'Ok, I will,' I replied and ran outside to wait for my saviour sent by my angels to rescue me from hell and making the final decision to go back to Poland.

I knew it was a sign. A clear sign from God that I should stay in England. Thomas and Rebecca, his wife, showed me a cosy, bright and clean room in their beautiful terraced house. The walls were snow white, the window framed by navy blue curtains and the floor covered in a soft cream carpet.

'Do you like it, Monika?' he asked.

'Of course, I love it!'

'After I take you to work tomorrow, we will buy you a bed and a cupboard. You will need to sleep on a mattress tonight—is that ok?' he asked, looking at me with his caring blue eyes as if he truly was my angel in disguise.

'Thank you so much. It's very kind of you,' I replied, feeling indescribable gratitude for having received such kindness from a complete stranger.

'It's unbelievable! Thomas and his family are amazing! How often do taxi drivers take someone home because they feel worried about them? Things like that do not normally happen in life, do they?' I said to Mama on the phone.

I loved the new house and the hospitality. But what I found strange was the separate taps in the sink, one for cold and one for hot water, unlike in Poland where I could wash my hands in a stream of warm water, running from one mixer tap. Now, I either burnt my fingers or froze them. The choice was always tough and I tried to make it warm by mixing the water from both taps in the air. Challenging indeed. I later found out that it was because of the way houses in Britain had been built after WWII, when the cold water tank had been usually placed in the attic, and was safe to drink from. Thomas said that if I was thirsty, I could simply pour cold water from the tap. The hot water tank had been separate and water from these two could not mix, for safety reasons. He also offered to take me to work and back every day. We enjoyed chatting and laughing in the car.

'Why did you want me to stay with you? You never had any lodgers before and you know lots of people who would need a room,' I asked in the car one day.

'I knew it wasn't safe for you to stay in that house after you had told me about your manager and the company house. I don't think it was a company house,' he replied.

'No, I don't think it was either. Bal lives there, in the room next door. Thank you for your help. If it wasn't for you, I would have had to go back to Poland. I knew I couldn't stay there,' I replied.

His wife, Rebecca, on the other hand, turned out to be rather petulant and never in a happy mood. One minute she was nice and friendly, the next minute, she exploded. It was hard to predict what would she would say next, so I avoided her as much as I could.

'Oh, shut up, you idiot,' she exclaimed to Thomas, in response to his attempts to make jokes.

Why did he marry her? I thought to my dismay.

He probably thought the same, but was never courageous to say it out loud, scared that his head would be pushed into a microwave by his opponent, skilled in ready-meal-cuisine.

CHAPTER 8 - WELCOME TO ESSEX

'Today he is dancing with you. Tomorrow he will go back to his wife,' said the sign on a poster in the ladies' toilet in a local pub that I had gone to on a Friday night with my new colleagues.

'Is this a joke? It can't be real,' I wondered, as I had never seen posters like that in Poland.

Dancing to eighties music, showing off my dance moves and forgetting about my worries, I noticed, from the corner of my eye, a tall, blond haired man, staring at me with a smile. When I'd stopped dancing, he approached me. 'Hi, I'm Ryan, what's your name?' he asked with a strong Essex accent, giving me a lascivious gaze.

'I'm Monika, nice to meet you,' I replied.

Ryan was a lorry driver, very friendly and with a quirky sense of humour.

'I must tell you something. I actually have a girlfriend, but it's not that serious and she can be really nasty at times,' he said when we sat down at the wooden table in a pub, a few days later.

'I'm sorry to hear that she isn't nice to you. Well, when you are single again, call me! I don't date men who are in relationships,' I replied, wondering why he would want to go out with me if he had a girlfriend.

He seemed surprised to hear my response, but I had my rules and I wanted to stick to them, even though I really liked him and his funny cheekiness. It was hard for me to say 'no' to him, but I did.

'It's over, I am single! I want to be with you! Can we meet in the pub?' he texted me on a Friday evening, two weeks later.

We met later that night and it felt wonderful to stand close to him, holding his hand, enjoying his flirtatious compliments and jokes, watching others dance. He tantalized me with his suave demeanour, making my heart pound fast.

'Do you want to come to my place tonight?' he asked.

'No Ryan, I am sorry, I can't. Thomas is picking me up at one and I have to keep my word to him.'

But I did promise to visit him in his house three days later, on Valentine's Day. I was excited to spend that special day with him and when I walked into his house, Ryan gave me a bouquet of red roses and had a table prepared for our dinner. We then cuddled on the sofa, watching a movie. I went upstairs to prepare a romantic atmosphere in the bedroom, lit candles and sprinkled red rose petals on the bed. Dressed only in my black underwear and a big red ribbon around my waist, I lay on the bed, waiting for him to unwrap me as his Valentine's gift. Seeing me, his eyes lit up.

'Happy Valentine's' I said, when he stood by the door speechless.

We met a few more times over the course of two weeks before he called me, asking me to come over. When he opened the door with a sad expression on his face, I instantly knew that something was wrong. I sat on the sofa and he hugged my knees, sitting on the floor, rambling.

'What is wrong? Tell me. What happened?' I asked, feeling my heart rate speeding up rapidly.

'I really don't want to hurt you, but I have something to tell you,' he finally mumbled. 'My ex-girlfriend called me and she wants to make up.'

I went quiet, trying to process what he had just said. 'After all that we have experienced together, you are considering going back to her? Do you want her back? Do you love her?' I bombarded him with questions a few minutes later.

He didn't reply, but looking into his teary eyes, I knew what the answer was. I stood up, shut the door behind me and wept walking back home, jilted by the first man I had met in England, who turned out to be mendacious. Even though it was only over a short period of time, this betrayal stuck in my memory. After only a few months in England, I quickly learnt that a man's intentions were not always what they had seemed. But how could I, as a woman, know if a man had good intentions? I could only find out myself once I decided to trust him and his commitment to a relationship.

Tying a red ribbon around my waist never crossed my mind again! Nor meeting a man in a bar! They never approached me anyway, as if I emanated a powerful deadly air, and they sensed they would perish once I ripped their head off for trying to play with my feelings. But it didn't turn me into a nun either—I was never inclined in that direction anyway. Despite the fact that my first school sweetheart became a priest. Pondering later about that poster in the toilet made me realise it was not a joke after all, but a warning for women not to fall into skilfully designed traps of local predators who had taken their wedding rings off for the night. Ryan didn't go back to his wife, but he did go back to his girlfriend. It was my welcome to Essex!

CHAPTER 9 - SURVIVAL GAMES

Cleaning tables at London Stansted Airport was not rocket science, nor what I would have predicted as my first job in England. Being paid just over £4 per hour, the minimum wage at that time—which, as I would find out months later, applied to under 21s, meaning I had earned even less than I should have, — I had to work really hard to earn a living. And what kind of living it was, with shifts of ten hours a day and only half an hour lunch break.

My uniform consisted of black trousers, black shoes, a white shirt and a knee-length blue apron, which looked very sexy on me—not really, but I was very excited for my first day at work. After all, I was officially working in England now. In England! My dreamland! I watched the happy faces of customers with due diligence, like an eagle, soaring in the sky, getting ready to catch my prey. As soon as they had finished their meal and left the table, I rushed to collect dirty dishes and pile them up efficiently onto the trolley. Once the trolley had been filled, I used my biceps strength to drag it through a slalom of suitcases and prams to the kitchen, where I exchanged it for an empty one. I then came back to my 'watching station', ready to begin the same process again.

'Only nine and a half hours more to go,' I sighed, looking at the luminous dial on my watch.

'Thank you, have a nice day!' I said to a leaving customer, who smiled back at me.

'You seem like a very nice girl. Why do you work here?' she asked.

'Well, I've just come to England and I had to start somewhere! But I would like to be a teacher, or work in an office one day.'

'You shouldn't be here. You are too intelligent and your English is very good,' she replied, and walked away without giving me a chance to explain that I could speak English because I was an English teacher, after all.

'What did you talk about with this woman?' Bal asked, approaching me straight after.

'She just said that I'm a nice and intelligent girl, that's all.'

'You are not allowed to speak to customers. Your job is to collect the dishes. That's it. Do you understand?'

'Yes, I do,' I replied.

'Now, clean those tables at the back. Customers are leaving,' he added and walked away as if he was a slave owner telling me off for trying to stand out.

'You are not allowed to sit down,' he said the following evening when I ducked onto the chair in the corner, when there were no customers around.

'But my legs really hurt. Please! Why can't I just sit for five minutes? There is nobody here anyway,' I begged, desperate for his compassion but his face remained merciless.

'You're not allowed to sit down. It's the company rules. Stand up,' he said, giving me another lash upon my back with his cold words.

My hopes that life would get better and good things would come to me still hovered in my head, but after only a week, the sad reality hit me with a large frying pan, making my head rattle from the powerful stroke, that things would not get better. Not here, not ever, making me feel exhausted—not only physically, from standing all day, but also mentally.

'Hey Monika, you know, when we saw you smiling when you started, we bet with the guys on when you would stop smiling. I won! I said it would be a week and I was right!' said Robbie, one of my colleagues at the counter, whom I'd asked for my daily pasta, glazed in the most tasteless cream sauce.

Soon, the painful and long-lasting cramps in my legs and feet from standing for inhuman hours tortured me daily. I was only allowed to sit for half an hour of my lunch break, but it obviously it wasn't enough for my body, which had started giving me clear signs that this job certainly wasn't a dream one. My slave salary was so small that after I had paid Thomas £300 for the room, I hardly had any money left for food. I could only get bread, butter, jam and pasta with a tomato sauce. Only enough to stop me from starving to death and collapsing from exhaustion on customers' luggage.

It looks so delicious. So full of chocolate, and the wafer seems so crispy, I thought, gazing longingly at a chocolate bar behind the counter, as if I had found myself again in the foreign shop in Communist Poland as a child, knowing it was only for special, rich people.

The anguish of realising that I couldn't afford it finally forced me to admit the saddest truth. I was officially POOR.

After two months, my spirit was almost broken. I couldn't see much beyond the walls of the restaurant, and I felt like a captive in there. I was extremely grateful to Thomas who took me to the airport and back every day. He looked after me, something I really needed after my first experiences with Marta, Hakim and Ryan. I couldn't afford bus tickets anyway. If it hadn't been for Thomas, I wouldn't have been able to get to work. Bu one day, he was very busy and I had to take a bus. Waiting at the bus stop, I wondered why the buses were passing me by. *Why aren't they stopping?* I thought, feeling more and more anxious. After half an hour, one finally stopped because someone was getting off. I managed to get to work but I was late and my oppressor, the boss, wasn't too happy.

'You need to wave your hand, otherwise buses won't stop!' said Thomas when I told him later about my strange experience. Now, that was something I had not been aware of. Buses always stopped in Poland without having to wave at them. If I had waved, the bus driver might have thought I had been a looney or I had fancied him. Why hadn't I been informed about this English custom upon my arrival in my 'Welcome to the Dream Island Guide'?

'Come with me. We need to get some boxes from the warehouse under the terminal. We'll take the industrial lift,' Bal said one day. It had never been part of my job to go to the warehouse, but I was afraid to refuse.

When we entered the storage room, Bal shut the metal door, came close to me and grabbed my waist, trying to kiss me on the lips. I turned my head away, avoiding to look into his dark piercing eyes. But being at his complete mercy, I knew had to be nice to him. He was my boss, and I needed this job to survive another day.

'Do you want to go to the cinema with me this weekend?' he asked, still not letting me get free from his embrace.

'Ummmm, I don't think I can. I'm sorry, I'm meeting with friends,' I replied, in hope he would finally give up and leave me alone.

It wasn't the first time he had asked me to go out with him. I had already rejected his invites for a drink in the past, which had only made him more angry and critical towards me.

'You are not the first girl he has tried this with. Be careful!' said Robbie, after I had come back from the toilet, where I had spent five precious minutes sitting on the toilet seat to relieve aches in my swollen legs.

After three months, I was worn to a frazzle. I could hardly get out of bed in the morning, dragging my legs as if they were being burnt by deadly flames at stake. They might as well have been. Maybe I had been a witch in my previous life, and now I was destined to suffer on English soil, for having thrown acne spells on court men in medieval times?

I had lost my liberty as a human being. I was poor and I didn't see any escape, other than: one, finding a new job; two, going back to Poland—something that my mama had been telling me to do every single day. I missed her very much, but I wanted to be strong and prove that I could look after myself and succeed— whatever succeeding meant to me then, which was mostly surviving another day with a roof over my head and some food.

I knew I couldn't live a happy, fulfilled life on this slave salary in a work camp which I had volunteered to work in. But that was my new reality. Bal had known I had just come from Poland, and I hadn't known how much I should have been paid or what the minimum wage was. He used my naivety and willingness to work in England with full awareness. With his hubristic belief in his own self-proclaimed superiority, he knew he could treat me badly, that I didn't know my rights as an employee, or that sexual harassment at work was a criminal offence. He knew. He knew. He knew. I knew it too—without knowing the law, because I could feel it in my heart that it wasn't right. But being vulnerable and at a complete mercy of my new Dream Life in England, I had to comply. Till I finally said to myself: 'Enough is enough.'

Plato, the Greek philosopher, had said that the income of the wealthiest employees should never exceed five times that of the poorest ones. My first salary in England indicated a rather higher salary ratio between the highest and lowest earners in global companies, which nowadays, according to experts, could even be a thousand to one. With my salary, I probably earned two thousand times less than some people. The survival of the fittest had started. And I wanted to win in this survival game of life, as if I were in the arena being watched by excited, merciless spectators: 'Will she make it? Will she make it not?'

I had to survive.

I had to win.

CHAPTER 10 - PRISON CELL

'There will be a new store opening soon on the airside, and we are looking for new sales assistants,' said Siobhan, one of Thomas's regular passengers, one day.

Thomas knew how much I hated the restaurant and that I wanted to get out of there as soon as possible. Siobhan, being one of the managers, agreed to invite me for an interview. I was ecstatic when I got the job as a beauty consultant in a shop, full of gorgeous smelling lotions and colourful make-up. It was Heaven on Earth, compared to my miserable existence in the restaurant. I was now selling and serving customers at the till. It was a big promotion for me and I was paid £1 more per hour!

My new manager, Jackie, trained me on how to demonstrate body creams, scrubs, make-up and the loyalty card. I soon discovered that selling was my talent. I always did my best to be polite and attentive to customers. I felt deeply obliged to serve them in the best possible way, using my personal charm. I was very good at encouraging them to buy the loyalty card. Not many refused my offer but my colleagues and my boss started to act strange after a while. They were not good at selling these cards, and I felt awkward hearing customers refusing to buy them. For me, it was a challenge. I wanted to be the best and to achieve. But it didn't mean I was appreciated. I noticed that being the best at work might not always be beneficial. Sarcastic comments towards me and teasing became more and more frequent. I had two choices again. One, find a new job; two, go back to Poland. I felt that life was forcing me to move forward. But why? Where? How?

***

'I'm very sorry, Monika, but you need to move out,' Thomas said with a sad voice as soon as I had started my new job.

'Oh, no! Why? Why do I need to move out?'

'I'm really sorry. I helped you, but it's time for you to go. You can't stay here,' he added.

'Do you really want me to move out? Do you really?' I asked, but he just left the kitchen, avoiding the answer.

Siobhan lived in a shared house and they had a spare room. Thomas used it as an opportunity to move me there. I was petrified because I didn't know what would happen to me from now on. The new job was a bit better, but I still had very little money. I enjoyed living with Thomas and his family. Rebecca invited me sometimes downstairs, so that I didn't have to sit alone in the room, and I joined them for Sunday dinner. Lamb with roast potatoes, mint sauce and peas. As much as I was grateful for the meal, it smelled of an old goat. I had not been used to eating lamb in Poland, and I wasn't a fan of eating someone's baby, either.

But it still wasn't as bad as when I had come to London for the first time on a bus trip during my studies. The lady of the house where we were staying prepared dinner, consisting of a black sausage, one potato and 15 peas—I know how many, because I counted them—as my only rescue from hunger. 'This is a traditional English meal. If you like it, eat it. If you don't like it, don't eat it. But there is nothing else for you,' she announced as soon as me and three other girls had sat at the table. She then walked out of the room, leaving us looking at each other, not knowing what to say. But after a 23-hour bus trip, I ate it all, even the tarmactasting sausage.

I didn't want to move out of Thomas's house, but I had known it was only a matter of time. 'When is she going move out? You said it was only going to be for a while!' I overheard Rebecca saying to Thomas, when I was walking downstairs to the kitchen one night.

'Thank you for everything, I appreciate it,' I said to Thomas, when he brought me to my new 'home.'

'Look after yourself, Monika. Good luck,' he replied with sadness in his eyes, and drove off.

My new room was very small and narrow, more like a prison cell than a bedroom, and unlike my spacious room back in Poland, which had furniture in it. The single bed took up the majority of the space, with no wardrobe or a chair. Having pushed my bag under the bed, I sat on it and became tearful. I was alone again. I already missed Thomas and I missed my family. *What will happen to me now?* I thought.

The rent was more expensive, so I spent most of my new salary on it. The Irish girls asked me for a deposit, but having just changed jobs, I had no savings yet. They knew about this but they still kept pestering me, standing at the door to my room as if they were prison guards demanding money.

'I'll give you the deposit once I get my first salary,' I explained with frustration but when I saw my first pay slip, my heart sunk. I knew I still couldn't give it to them because I had to pay rent and have some money for food and bus tickets. Thomas didn't take me to the airport anymore. Once again, I could only afford bread, milk, cornflakes and pasta. Each night I wept in the shower, lathering my stressed body, trying to wash away my worries about survival and living on the breadline. I earned a bit more now, but I also paid more for the room, feeling stuck like a hamster on a wheel, unable to get out of this vicious cycle. After only a few months in England, I fell into the complete darkness of my soul, consumed by sadness, fear and despair.

'Mama, I miss you, I can't even afford a ticket to Poland to see you with this salary. And the girls are horrible to me. All they care about is money and drinking parties. I don't want to be here anymore; I hate it, I hate them!' I said to her on the phone, lying on my bed every night, feeling so homesick that I didn't see anything good in my life anymore.

Should I just go back home? Why am I doing this? Is it worth it? Maybe I should give up and go back. It's too hard, I thought, feeling more and more depressed each day, tortured by thoughts of doubt and resignation.

'No, I can't give up. I've come so far. I will find a way. There must be a better way to live life. I don't know how, but there must be something good out there waiting for me. I need to be strong. I can't give up.'

I avoided the girls as much as I could, walking silently around the house like a mouse hiding from the cat. I didn't take part in their drinking parties in the living room, only heard them talking and laughing. I hid under my duvet to cover my pain. I missed Mama, Cezar, my friends and everyone else who cared about me back in Poland. I didn't have anyone who cared about me in England now. My feelings of angst were slowly killing my spirit.

'What is wrong with you? Why are you so serious? You are doing my head in! We will call the police and they will throw you out for not paying the deposit!' Siobhan, the prison guard, shouted, drunk again, having opened the door to my room.

'Leave me alone! Please! I beg you! Just leave me alone!' I exclaimed from under the duvet, weeping and losing the will to live, falling faster and faster into the dark realisation: 'I should just give up. Why am I doing this? I should just go back home.'

CHAPTER 11 - GUARDIAN ANGEL

'I saw the angel in the marble and carved until I set him free.'
-Michelangelo

My favourite place in the shop was at the very front, where the invisible line on the floor separated it from the rest of the airport surface.

That's how far I was allowed to go. Right up to the 'invisible border'. If I had crossed it, I would be in trouble with my manager. I had never pondered upon the importance of borders imposed on a human being that way. I had known about country borders, separating the humans speaking one language from the humans speaking another language, having to adhere to the rules imposed on them, but the new rules I had to adhere to included the invisible shop line on the floor where I long gazed at the busy airport life of passengers rushing to catch their planes and cleaners emptying the bins.

I wish I could pick up my bag and go somewhere nice, just like them, I thought, feeling an irresistible yearning to be somewhere else.

The airport business seemed like a giant computer game where all the characters had been given the instructions for their next move and direction. Being now part of this big game of life, I realised perfectly well what my place was, and what my duties were. Serving the customers, presenting lotions and scrubs on their hands, applying make-up on them, serving them at the till, dusting the shelves, getting new stock from the warehouse under the terminal and sweeping the floor on an evening shift. The next day, the same.

'Hello gorgeous, how are you today?' Abdu, the friendly cleaner asked me the usual daily question whilst passing by.

'I'm ok thanks, just not very busy. And you?

'Oh, I'm fine, darling. As always! I have to be,' he replied and continued to push the bin.

'See you tomorrow!' I shouted.

Meditating on my new dream life in England, gazing at the dancing rays of sunshine coning through the windows and filling me with hope, I noticed a man sitting on the bench, staring at my guileless face, still probably showing remains of hope for a change to come. I looked away and went back to the till.

'Hello! Have you got a massage oil?' asked that same man, tall and with dark chestnut hair, having walked into the shop, grinning from ear to ear.

'Yes, we do!' I replied, pointing at the shelf filled with different types of oils.

'Where are you from?' he asked with luminous eyes and a big smile that didn't want to leave his face.

'I'm from Poland.'

'Oh lovely! I like Poland!' he replied. 'So tell me… is it a good oil?'

'The very best! It contains relaxing lavender and ylang ylang,' I confirmed, nodding my head.

'Great, I'll take it then,' he said, handing it back to me.

'I'm going to France now to play golf but when I'm back, I'd like to take you out!' he continued with calm confidence as I was packing the oil into the bag.

'Have you got a piece of paper where I can write my number?' he added.

'Yes, there you go,' I said, giving him an empty page from my notebook.

'Send me a text message! My name is Adam, by the way! It was nice to meet you Monika!' he exclaimed, waving his hand for goodbye and rushing out of the shop.

'Ok, I will,' I exclaimed back, smiling to myself, thinking that he was just another man wanting to take me out just like many others passing by, giving me their numbers. I never called them. I had no energy, nor any reason why I should. I didn't plan to contact Adam either, wanting to stick to my rule—till one of my darkest moments. Lying in bed, with my tired swollen legs, and veins sticking out as if they were trying to show me I was still a human, staring aimlessly at the dirty-looking ceiling of my prison cell, I wanted to give up, buy a ticket and go back home. To my family, friends and Cezar. There was that prayer in the book I had taken from Poland on bringing miracles into one's life.

'Please, angels, please help me! Save me from this misery and suffering,' I silently finished my prayer every night, with a waterfall of tears, in the hope of finding solace by seeking angelic refuge.

And that was exactly what I needed then. A miracle. A positive change. And hope for a better day.

'I've decided to go back to Poland so I'm very sorry but I won't see you again.' I texted Adam as the voice inside me had told me to before making my final decision.

The phone rang a few seconds later.

'Hi Monika, I'll be back in a few days. Can you wait a bit longer? I'll come to you, I'll help you. Please, don't go back,' Adam said in a warm, caring and joyful voice, which wrapped my aching body and soul with a warm blanket of hope.

'Ok, I'll wait. I won't go to Poland yet,' I replied, smiling through my tears.

This comforting call from Adam was a clear sign to me that he had been sent by my guardian angel who had heard my prayers. I could now look forward to a new and better, more purposeful day. The day when I would see Adam.

CHAPTER 12 - KNIGHT IN SHINING ARMOUR

Adam came to the airport in his shiny armour, or rather, his luxury shiny silver car. Just like the knights in the shining armour of the court of Camelot, he came to rescue my soul in 21st century England. The Polish maiden in distress. Chivalry was not dead after all! Nor should it be—regardless of how much women wished to be portrayed as strong and independent nowadays, many, including me, still appreciated chivalrous men. Even though I was reluctant to admit it, and worried it would be a seen as a sign of a weakness. And 21st century men, often not wanting to show their bravery and kindness, worried it would show theirs.

It was a hot sunny August day and as soon as I had finished work, I changed into my pink skirt in the airport toilet and ran to the car park, as a thirsty person would run towards an oasis in a desert. Adam was standing by his car, showing off his gleaming white teeth with the most amazing smile. I fell straight into his arms, feeling shivers down my spine and pure euphoria. It was the biggest, warmest and most genuine hug I had ever felt. He opened the car door so that I could sit on the black leather seats. Just like a noble knight would do, helping a lady get on the white horse.

'How about I whisk you off to Cambridge for the day?' he asked, putting on his sunglasses.

'Oh, that would be amazing, I would love that!' I exclaimed, jumping from excitement.

Strolling through the cobblestone streets, we admired the famous college buildings and then stopped in an old pub where many college professors had been seen before, enjoying the English delicacy: fish and chips. As we were walking across the river bridge, he took my hand. Gazing at the sun, feeling Adam's warm energy, I smiled.

'Thank you, God, for that amazing moment,' I said to myself silently.

'Shall we go punting?' he suggested.

'Umm, I'm not sure,' I replied, having no idea what he had meant, but seeing people stepping aboard a narrow boat, I got very excited.

I could imagine Adam steering it, with a long wooden pole, while we drifted along the river and passed famous landmarks, including the enchanting Bridge of Sighs—a quintessential experience when I could finally sit back, relax and take in the astonishing beauty of this magnificent town and enjoy the courtship of a true English gentleman. But I only replied: 'Maybe next time.'

'Let's sit down in the shade, by the tree,' Adam suggested when we walked into the vastness of freshly cut grass, surrounded by college buildings, baking in the afternoon sun.

I sat in front of him, resting my back on his chest, wrapped by his arms, feeling like the most precious thing in the world to him, helping me forget about all my struggles and worries.

'I want to help you. Don't worry, everything will be fine,' he said with a warm, caring voice and kissed my forehead, making it the most comforting thing anyone could say or do for me after everything I'd gone through in the first months in England.

He then kissed me, passionately, for the first time, making my heart pound really fast. I was lifted from the grass by God's arms and taken to the fluffy white clouds. He made me feel so loved and special and when he'd driven me back to my 'prison cell', I yearned to see him again.

A few days later, my colleague told me about an organisation helping single people in a difficult situation by providing them with accommodation at a low cost. I told them about my troubles with the Irish girls, explaining how they wanted to throw me out for not paying the deposit.

'We have a flat for you, Monika. When can you move in?' asked the lady I had talked to a few days later.

Adam helped me move and settle into my new home, even though I could hardly call it 'home'. The flat was quite expensive and I spent most of my salary on it. I had to pay extra for electricity with a top-up card I put into the slot by the door. I often had to choose between buying food and having light. I was glad to be away from my prison guards but I was living in another horrible place, a small room with a tiny kitchenette to the side, with grey walls and a stained brown carpet, looking as if blood had been shed there in battles. The small bathroom had orange tiles which, no matter how much I tried to clean them, always looked dirty. At night, I heard the violent arguments of people living next door and above me, and an unbearable traffic noise and suffocating smell of fumes, forcing me to keep the window closed at all times, even thought it was the middle of a hot summer.

When Adam visited me a week later and took me to a romantic dinner on top of a roof terrace, I felt ashamed about the way I lived. But it didn't seem to matter to him, or the fact that I was poor, having paid all I had earned on rent and bills. My sad new existence had left me with no energy to get up to work in the morning and feel happy. Even though I could enjoy brief moments with Adam, I still stared at the dirty tiles in the shower each night.

'How much longer will I have to live like this? Will this ever end?'

Adam was in between jobs when I'd met him. He had just broken up from his girlfriend who was still living with him in the newly-built house they had bought together. They were now selling and it was only a formality, before they could go separate ways.

'Just to let you know, Mon, my ex is still living in the house and it's possible that you'll see her. But don't worry, we live in separate bedrooms now,' he said in the car, picking me up for the weekend.

'Hi,' I said, as soon as I saw her entering the house with Adam, confused about the situation.

'Hi, she replied and left the house.

Why did he want me to see her? And why did he want her to see me? Why would he want that for either of us? I thought, taking a shower in his en suite bathroom.

I put on a black dress and went downstairs for dinner, which Adam had prepared in a spacious and bright living room, filled with romantic music. It was then that I had tried prawns the first time in my life, served with avocados in large glasses.

Should I try them? Or not? I don't want to seem rude, I thought, gazing at them and Adam interchangeably but once I did, they turned out to be divine and unlike anything I'd ever tried before.

I enjoyed Adam's company and our conversations. For the first time since I had come to England, I felt safe. When I was with him, I could forget about all my troubles and I looked forward into the future with hope again. Adam also had a two bedroom flat in High Wycombe, a town surrounded by the picturesque countryside of Chiltern Hills in Buckinghamshire.

'I was offered a job for an IT company in London. I am starting next week,' he said whilst showing me around his flat.

'Oh, congratulations, I'm very happy for you!!' I exclaimed.

'Would you like to move in with me, Moni? I'll help you find a new, better job here. Just leave that shop at the airport where you are paid pennies and come to live with me!' he added.

'Really? You want me to do that? I would love that! Thank you!' I replied, giving him a big smooch, ecstatic about the prospect of our future together.

'So when can you move in?'

'Well, if I hand in my notice now, then in a week's time, I guess,' I replied, grinning from ear to ear and hugging him tightly.

CHAPTER 13 - TOGETHER FOREVER

Adam's chivalrous devotion to me could only mean that he was The One, or at least, I hoped he could be.

I quit my job at the airport, packed all my belongings in any bags I could find and we put them into Adam's car before we drove off to our new life. I'd fallen in love with him. I didn't care about the age difference, that he was in his forties, and neither did I care if it was right or wrong according to imposed social standards. All I knew, was that he had been sent by my guardian angel to love and care for me, always treating me with the outmost respect. In the first months, we went out to lovely restaurants, with him holding my hand and listening to me with deep care and understanding. Adam was a true gentleman and in return, I wanted to be the best woman I could be for him. I cooked dinners every day and waited for him to get back home from work, just like a good, caring wife would. It was my preparation to becoming a good wife one day in a committed relationship. Adam's favourite were *barszcz*, the beetroot soup and *pierogi*, dumplings with mushrooms.

'This was delicious, Moni, thank you!' he said after dinner, each time.

I started to look for a new job but in the meantime, cleaning and cooking were the only things I could do to show how much I cared for him. But my job search was taking longer than I'd expected. After applying for jobs every day for over a month, I still had no replies. I felt that Adam was getting a bit worried. And so was I.

One day, I decided to leave the flat, go into town and simply walk into shops. 'Do you have any vacancies? I've just moved into this area,' I asked one of the shop assistants at the beauty counter.

'Yes, I think we may do. Have a look at the announcements board,' replied a friendly blond lady.

I noticed a job advert for a French cosmetics company. I dialled the number and the lady asked me to email her my CV. To my delight, she invited me to an interview two days later. She listened with great interest about my master's degree, Bachelor's in English and my previous work experience which, at that point, was not that impressive—teaching English back in Poland and cleaning tables as my first job in England could be hardly called a valuable professional experience. However, working as a beauty consultant in the airport shop was very relevant.

'I'd like to offer you the role of account manager. Would you like that?' she asked when she called me the next day.

'Oh, thank you very much, yes, I'd love that!' I exclaimed and called Adam straight away to share the amazing news.

'Darling, I was offered the account manager position, even though the advert was for a beauty consultant! I'm so happy! Are you?' I asked.

'Well done, Moni, I have always believed in you,' he replied with a happy voice, clearly impressed by my new job.

I immediately felt that I had regained Adam's respect. Our relationship became even stronger and I felt good about myself and us again. Standing in the shop all day didn't bother me but soon, I discovered it was turning out to be a repeat of the 'work camp' experience at the airport, where I hadn't been allowed to sit down except for the half an hour lunch break, which made my back and legs turn into one physical exhaustion. Soon, painful cramps in my feet came back.

'You can't sit down, even when there are no customers,' said the store manager, every time I tried to duck onto a chair for a minute.

I even had to write daily reports standing. Being tall and bending forward at the low counter didn't help but, I didn't complain. I enjoyed selling, matching the right skincare products to customers' skin types and suggesting the most flattering make-up during makeovers. My sales rates were one of the highest in the country and the area manager who had hired me always praised me. I managed one girl, working part-time, but I couldn't help but observe that she wasn't very proactive, and was obsessed with her looks, staring in the mirror to check her own make-up, rather than reaching out to people passing by. I had to ask her repeatedly to approach customers, feeling a strong sense of duty to look after everyone stopping at the counter and asking them if they needed any help. It was the essence of good customer service after all.

CHAPTER 14 - SPANISH CASA

'I bought a house in Spain, Moni!' said Adam one day.

'Oh, I'm so happy for you! Are you going to show it to me??' I asked, amazed at the stunning pictures of the house.

'Of course—we are going there next month!' he replied.

As we were approaching the hill in the car, a white town at the very top appeared to be touching the fluffy clouds, as if it was floating in the air. The hill was so steep that I felt the altitude in my ears like in a submarine. When we got to the top, we got stuck in a narrow dead-end street and the locals helped us to reverse. I got out of the car on a cobblestone street, just outside the house and inhaled the fresh, evening breeze, touching my face.

'Moni, we are here!' Adam exclaimed.

The house was pure white, built in a typical old Spanish style, with a light and airy lounge but small, dark bedrooms and a spectacular rooftop terrace with breathtaking views, accessed via a spiral metal staircase. The town, nestled on top of the hill, with the remains of the medieval castle walls, perfectly blended with the built-in white houses, making it a perfect holiday postcard.

'Let's have breakfast here tomorrow, shall we?' Adam asked, kissing me passionately from excitement.

The town was full of traditional Spanish restaurants, playing loud flamenco music, and taverns serving fresh tapas. Since we were two of the few tourists there, we had to speak our broken Spanish to order food, which made the whole experience even more charming.

'*Hola! Buenos dias, senor!*' one of the locals greeted Adam when buying fresh croissants in the bakery every morning.

In the warm evening, we walked up the old steps to a bar built into the castle wall and admired the views of twinkling lights of the surrounding villages in the valley. We then sat by the colourful fountain in the middle of the town square and threw a coin, making a wish. My silent wish was to go back there, again and again, and again. With my beloved English gentleman, Adam.

Our visit to Gibraltar the next day, often called a piece of Britain in Spain, was unbelievable. When we got to the top of the Upper Rock, we waved hello to the cute monkeys living there, waiting to grab bags off tourists and look for food. The views of the blue sea were breathtaking. Walking along the mile-long high street, packed with busy boutiques, cafes and restaurants, made me feel as if I was back in England. Only, more sunny England.

'Since we are here, fancy visiting Morocco?' Adam asked me a question that he already knew the answer to.

The ferry from Tarifa to Tangier, in just over 30 minutes, transported us to a different world. A world I had never seen before. Walking along the old streets, baked in the hot sun, being stopped by the local sellers offering colourful scarves, gold jewellery and watches, we might as well have been on a movie set. It truly was a unique experience. But it also made me appreciate the world that I had lived in.

The next day, Adam was snoring on the sofa, having a siesta, and I, feeling a bit bored, got a brilliant idea to spray him with water, using the hose pipe from the patio.

A little bit of cool refreshment won't hurt, right? I thought, as I'd started, but Adam leapt up quicker than the speed of light and as soon as he'd realised what I'd done, he ran after me.

I quickly hid behind the balcony door and he didn't look very happy. But why? Cezar never minded it on hot summer days, just stood up, shook the water off his fur and ran around the garden, wiping his back on the grass, feeling wonderfully refreshed in the

35-degree heat. Seeing Adam retreat to the kitchen, I wasn't sure if it was safe for me to come out.

'Ahhhhhhh!' I screamed a few minutes later, feeling ice cold water landing on my head, and when I looked up, I saw him at the window holding a bucket, laughing at me.

'How could you? You are so cruel!' I shouted, furious, as I was only trying to refresh him a little bit in this Spanish heat and throwing ice cold water on my head was a different story.

'Sorry Moni, but you started!' he said.

I forgave him.

Three weeks later.

CHAPTER 15 - DIFFERENT PLANETS

A year since my arrival in England, and my life had finally started to feel balanced and peaceful.

I loved spending quality time with Adam and it made our relationship strong. On sunny days, Adam took me to an old English pub, driving through the lush, green and windy countryside roads in his white, sixties, British convertible. I often raised my hands up in the air to feel the strong cool wind on my palms. The fish served in that pub was the most delicious white, flaky cod with crispy batter. I loved Adam's company. On days like this, I could feel he loved me, even though he had never said it. But he didn't have to. We understood each other very well and showed that we loved each other.

Is he the one I've been looking for? Am I meant to be with Adam forever? I thought, holding his hand over the garden table in the hot afternoon sun.

One day, Zosia, a Polish girl with short, raven black hair in her late twenties, came to my counter with her four-year-old daughter. She was loquacious, telling me the story of how she'd just moved here from Poland to be with her husband who had been working in England for a year now. He had come here alone, so one day she'd decided to join him, together with her daughter. It seemed to me that she wanted to be with him more than he wanted to be with her, and she didn't seem too happy about her relationship. In return, I told her how I had met Adam at the airport and how much he cared for me.

'We should all meet for dinner one day,' she said.

'Oh, that's very nice of you, thank you. I will ask Adam if he would like that,' I replied.

He liked the idea and two days later, we visited them for dinner with lots of Polish food, laughing and telling stories of how we each met our partners. Zosia's husband was a tall, good-looking Polish man but he seemed a bit cold towards her and didn't show any form of affection. As a thank you, we invited them for dinner the next weekend. I cooked a traditional steak in breadcrumbs with potatoes and salad. For dessert, I served a creamy chocolate cake from the Polish shop. I was glad that we had found new friends. Adam and I often met with Zosia in a pub for lunch, watching her daughter play in the garden.

'Aren't you worried that Adam is older than you?' Zosia asked, during her visit to the store one day.

'No, why would I be?' I replied, surprised by her question. 'True, he is older, but why does it matter?'

'Do you think he will want to marry you? You are only in your twenties and he has already been married and has adult children. I doubt if he will want to do it again,' she added.

'Yes, you are right, maybe it will be an issue for us, but I don't want to think about it right now,' I replied and started tidying up the counter.

True, I was only 26 and Adam was in his early forties, but I didn't worry about it too much. Maybe a little bit, but it wasn't something that would stop me from loving him. I wasn't thinking about our future too far ahead and whether he would want to marry me or have a family. But I loved him. He was a fit, attractive and young-looking man with lots of energy, playing golf every Saturday. Sure, it sometimes bothered me, and we had stopped spending so much quality time together as we had in the beginning of the relationship, though I still thought we had something special. This was despite a huge argument, staying in a country hotel once: when Adam went to the golf shop, a young, blond-haired woman, standing close by, asked him to play with her and he agreed happily.

No worries, I'm not here! I'm invisible! I thought, standing by the door, watching her flirting with him and laughing.

'This is Monika, this is Elsa,' he introduced us to each other and started walking with her.

I was left walking behind them, seeing them laughing and having fun. *We were supposed to have a romantic weekend away and he just walks away with another woman to play golf,* I thought, sitting down on a bench, watching them move away. Adam didn't even check if I was still there. After what seemed like an hour, I noticed them playing in the distance. I stood up and with a sudden gush of fury, I stormed across the fields, risking my life by being hit by a golf ball.

'Can I please have the keys to the hotel room?' I asked Adam with a tremulous voice, reaching out my shaking hand.

'Sure, there you go!' he replied with a smirk, as if I were crazy for running across the middle of the golf course.

I grabbed the keys, looked at her and ran back to the hotel room where I stared at the walls for the next three hours of eternity.

'I was just playing golf!' Adam said when he finally got back to the room.

'Yes, playing golf with her, whilst I was left behind. You didn't even care if I was there. It was supposed to be some quality time for us and not for you and some woman you have just met. You hurt me!' I replied.

'I don't know what you want, really. I did nothing wrong,' he replied.

My explanations of how he had hurt me didn't seem to register with him. How could I be upset? Why was it so hard for him to understand my feelings? Why couldn't he just listen and have empathy for me? I knew we were from two different countries and even planets, but I had thought that we could talk about anything, not just the nice, happy things. I was wrong. We could not understand each other's point of view. I felt neglected and unloved when he walked off with her and didn't even apologise, saying he didn't do anything wrong, unable to admit that I had the right to feel hurt. It was the beginning of the end of our relationship, which was bound to fail without an honest, open communication about our feelings, wishes and desires, an insidious problem that eventually led to a disaster.

CHAPTER 16 - THE OTHER POLISH GIRL?

'Better to have loved and lost, than to have never loved at all.'
-Saint Augustine

A few days later, I argued with Adam for only God knows what reason.

I left the house to calm down and decided to walk to Zosia's house. Unannounced and unexpected, I knocked on her door which she opened with surprise on her face.

'Can I come in for a while, please?' I asked.

'Of course, you can. What happened?'

'We've just had a massive argument and I need to calm down,' and we sat at the table in the living room, chatting and drinking tea. Suddenly, I heard a loud knock on the door and Zosia went to check who it was.

'Heya, is Monika here? May I come in? I've brought some wine!'

Jesus, he actually followed me, and Zosia just let him in, I thought, seeing him walk in with a big smile, putting the bottle of Merlot on the table, talking to her as if nothing had happened, and ignoring me.

Zosia's husband was in Poland with their daughter, so she could take part in this show which she seemed to enjoy.

'I can see that you have argued. Can't you just make up?' she finally said with a smirk.

'I didn't do anything. It's Monika, she has got a problem,' he replied.

After an hour, I couldn't watch them anymore. 'I'm going back home,' I said, looking at Adam.

'I'm not going! You can go!' he replied, staring at his wine glass to avoid looking into my eyes.

'I said, I'm going home, are you coming with me?'

'No! I want to stay.'

'Ok, *cześć*, Zosia,' I said and left the house, feeling my pulse speeding up to 100 miles per hour, trying to understand what had just happened. After all, Adam had just stayed at my friend's house, alone, with her.

I lay the blanket on the floor in the spare bedroom but I couldn't calm down and fall asleep. Why did he stay there? How could he betray me like this? I thought, imagining the worst case scenario.

'Where are you? When are you coming back home?' I texted him past midnight, unable to calm down.

'I am here, with Zosia, we're having sex now!' he texted back, knowing it would annoy me even more.

I called him. 'What's wrong with you? Zosia and I are just friends!' he said with a relaxed voice as if he had drunk too much wine.

Was there something wrong with me? Feeling jealous about the man I loved? *'He that is not jealous, is not in love,'* said Saint Augustine. Maybe if Adam had been more emphatic I wouldn't have to feel jealous? But maybe, he was just being a man and didn't understand the language of love that would speak to me and my heart. What was wrong though, was that he stayed at my friend's house when I was home, alone and going through this nightmare.

I slept on the floor in the spare bedroom after that. On Saturday mornings, Adam sneaked into my room, only to get his golf clubs, shutting the door behind him with a big bang. We never spoke after that night. We didn't know how to and both avoided confrontation. We had loved and cared for each other so much, but where was that love now? How could love just evaporate? Only a year into our relationship? If only we'd had enough maturity to talk openly, we might have saved our relationship.

And Zosia? well, she was not my friend anymore. I'd thought I could trust her but I was wrong. Unhappy in her own marriage, she wanted to destroy my relationship. She succeeded. After all, why should I be happy when she wasn't? Human nature had always amazed me—unfortunately, in many ways I couldn't have predicted. Since then, I've always had a handful of true friends that I knew I could trust. And the others? Sometimes I felt it was best if they didn't know too much.

CHAPTER 17 - WE WILL MEET AGAIN

'The way of love is not a subtle argument. The door there is devastation.
Birds make great sky-circles of their freedom. How do they learn it?
They fall and falling, they are given wings.'
-Rumi

'I quit!' I exclaimed to the store manager after she'd told me off again for trying to sit down for five minutes, even though the store was completely empty.

I couldn't work like this anymore, being talked to as if she owned me. What about the health and safety of an employee, hurting my back and damaging my health by bending forward at the counter to write reports each day? The stress of silent days with Adam didn't help either. It took me half an hour to write a resignation letter and hand it in. I made up my mind right there and then. I'd had enough. It was a big risk because I didn't have a new job yet, but deep down I knew I had to do it. I couldn't stand being imprisoned behind that counter anymore, serving a life sentence for murdering two warehouse rats with my homemade trap made of a piece of cheese on a metal spike, for eating my spring collection make-up.

The next day, I went to all the recruitment agencies in the high street and handed in my CV. A week later, I was offered a new temporary job. The Canadian military base in a nearby town urgently needed a personal assistant to cover for a maternity leave for Major Lee. I was ecstatic about my new job. It was a new challenge in a completely different environment where I could learn more, and get trained on how to transfer calls and book appointments with senior military members. The Canadians turned out to be the most friendly people I had ever met, always chilled and re-laxed but at the same time, very professional. At lunchtime, Olivia, one of the officers, often shared delicious traditional pancakes with maple syrup.

Olivia often walked past my office to fill up her water bottle in the kitchen, and joked with me. One day, she invited me to her house, nicely decorated with modern furniture, with a massive lounge, three bedrooms and a huge garden. And Lou, her cutest little terrier, was to die for. Olivia dreamt of travelling around the world on a cruise ship as soon as she retired. After sleeping on the floor for weeks in the spare bedroom, I knew deep down that my relationship with Adam was over and I would have done anything to escape the feeling of loneliness in the flat. When Olivia, being aware of my situation, suggested I could rent a room from her, I agreed.

I packed my bags when Adam was not at home and Olivia picked me up in her car. She didn't charge much for the room and I knew I could afford it now, thanks to my job. I loved playing with Lou and having my own space with no bad atmosphere, but I missed Adam, who tried to contact me but I never picked up. I didn't want to tell him where I was. I felt heartbroken. After three months, I found out that my work contract couldn't be prolonged anymore so Olivia told me to move out, doubting that I could get another job quickly enough to pay rent.

'Hi Adam, how are you?' I asked on the phone.

'Moni, I decided to move back to Manchester so if you like, you can rent the flat from me,' he replied.

'Yes, I'd like that. Thank you,' I replied.

I then called a taxi and when I entered the flat with my bags, I saw Adam, standing in the kitchen.

'I can leave the car for you, if you like. I know you will need it for getting to work. I have just bought a new one, so I don't really need it now,' he said, offering me the car keys.

'Oh, really? Thank you, that's so kind of you. I interviewed for another temporary job in a nearby town, so if I get it, I will be starting next week,' I replied.

'Great, all the best, Moni! I will miss you,' he said, hugging me tightly with tearful eyes.

'Why are you going away? Why can't you stay?'

'I've been offered a good job in Manchester and besides, I'm too old for you.'

'No, you are not! Why do you say that?' I said with despair.

'I know you talked about it with Zosia. But it's ok, I get it.'

'I've never said you were too old! She asked me about the age difference, that's all,' I replied, feeling as if she had stabbed me in the back.

'Bye, Moni, good luck,' he said, releasing me from his hug, and left the flat.

Now I understood why our love had finished. It took me a while to forgive Zosia. And it took me a while to forgive Adam for leaving me, but he was a good man after all. Even though our paths went separate ways, we stayed friends for years.

The next day, on a Sunday afternoon, I decided to take the car for a drive as I had never driven on the left side of the road yet. This was it. My life depended on it. I had to be able to drive to work. I considered myself to be a good driver but all on the 'right side', back in Poland. I had to be brave now and simply get in the car and drive. On the left side. And I did just that. I could feel sweat creeping onto my forehead from the sheer adrenaline while concentrating on driving. I was doing quite well, turned around, and as I was going back down a steep hill, I approached the roundabout, but by the time I had thought about braking, due to being on the 'wrong' left side, I zoomed through it and ended up being beeped at by the car entering the roundabout from the right.

Jesus, this was so stressful! But I made it. Next time, I will know I need to stop there, I thought getting out of the car, happy as if I had just done bungee jumping.

Life seemed like a never-ending challenge and my next one was a month later. 'Ola, amigo, there is a light on the dashboard, indicating a low level of water in the radiator. I'm at my friend's house. What do I do?' I called him late in the autumn evening.

'Hi, Polska.' That's how Adam called me from now on. 'Just unscrew the black cap in the middle and add some water.'

'Ok, I will,' I replied and did just that, but on the way back home, the car stopped and I thought it had broken down for good. Luckily, I managed to start it again. 'Hey, amigo, I'm not sure what's happening, but the red light on the dashboard is still on, even though I poured in a litre of water,' I called him the next day.

'Which black cap did you open? I hope not this one?' he asked and sent me a picture of the engine.

'Yes, that's the one, you said the black one in the middle,'

'Oh my God, Polska, you put a litre of water in the engine!! You need to call for help and flush the system right now or the car will be dead!'

'Jesus Christ! Ok I will—you said black cap in the middle! Anyway, I'll call you later!' I replied, feeling my blood pressure rising.

Luckily, the oil mixed with water was removed by a very nice man who didn't laugh too much, and the car was saved. 'Well, I don't know all black caps in the car, do I? And besides, it was due to Adam's imperfect instructions!' I said, seeing his silly smirk.

Communication between me and Adam, as it had turned out, was really not our forte after all! Men, women, and cars! A perfect blend!

***

My breakup with Adam took its toll on my emotions and having decided that I needed to get away, I bought a ticket to a sunny Balearic Island in the Mediterranean, Majorca. A month later, I was sitting on a sandy beach at sunset, listening to the sea waves crashing against the shore, and music played on a guitar by an older man with a straw hat on.

'Do you like Majorca?' he asked, unexpectedly.

'Oh, yes, I do. I love it, it's beautiful. I wish I could live here! Do you?'

'Yes, I live here. I'm very lucky but I need to tell you one thing. It's because I'm happy with all I have in life. You see, I haven't got my own house, I haven't got a car and I haven't got a job, but I have much more than many other people that come here with money. I have peace of mind. I live on top of this mountain, looking after a house whose owners are often away. I play my guitar and it's enough for food and this shirt. Some people would say I have nothing. But I have more than them, looking at the most beautiful view of the sea at sunrise. And that's all I need to be happy. The key is to ask the universe for what you want, and God will give it to you. Trust me,' he replied.

It was as if he had been sent by God to me in the most unexpected moment of my life whilst crying over my lost relationship with Adam, here alone. This man with a guitar on the beach, teaching me about the essence of happiness in life, stayed in my memory forever, but it wasn't until many years later that I finally understood what he'd meant.

CHAPTER 18 - MR PRESIDENT

I had never made so much tea and coffee in my life.

My new temporary job, which I'd found from a newspaper advert, was for a personal assistant to Emma, a one star general at a nearby UK military base. There were 12 candidates per vacancy, so I was very happy they had chosen me, especially since I was now being paid £11 per hour. A bit of a pay rise from my first job in the restaurant. Because of the high-level security environment I was working in, I had to undergo a security clearance. However, my main duties as Emma's PA included making fresh tea and coffee every hour, for her and any visitors to the office, and sorting her inbox into the following folders: 'Read now', 'Read later' and 'Read next week'.

Shouldn't she just read all her emails as they come in? I wondered every day, often being wrong in my sorting judgements.

'Monika, you put that email in the wrong folder!' she said at least once a week.

Emma liked me, or at least I thought she did. She told me she organised Sunday meditation sessions in her house for friends and family, to chant to the picture of her guru. She invited me to join them but I refused. After all, being brought up as a practicing Catholic, going to church every Sunday, I felt like I would be betraying my faith. Meditation had not been something I had experienced back in Poland. Being in defensive mode, I placed a picture of an angel next to my computer screen which she noticed but said nothing.

'I can't get through to her, she is difficult to talk to,' I heard her saying a few days later, talking to someone in an office next door.

At first I wasn't sure who she was talking about, but my intuition was telling me that she was talking about me. A week later, the agency who had hired me informed me that it was too expensive for Emma to keep a contractor, and I got a week's notice and had to look for a new job. The stress, the fear and panic of what would happen to me again took over my life.

'What should I do now? What kind of job?'

I returned to my usual pilgrimage to the recruitment agencies in the high street.

A recruitment agent called me, a few days later. 'Monika, since you can speak both English and Polish, we have a job for you.'

And so I started a new job where I had the chance to challenge myself, doing new and exciting things, such as translations of the website content, liaising with both English and Polish businesses, and interviewing presidents.

'We would like you to interview the President of Poland,' my boss said, to my surprise, one day.

'The President of Poland? What do you mean?'

'Yes, Lech Wałęsa. He is coming to England to deliver a speech at one of the universities and he has agreed to an interview with us. Since you are the only one here who can speak Polish, we would like you to do the interview. What do you think?'

'Jesus Christ, what do I think? I would love that… but how? Where? I have never done an interview with anyone, not to mention the President of Poland!' I replied, feeling my heart rate going up in a sudden rush of excitement.

'Well, I'm sure you can do it!' my boss concluded and gave me the questions that I had to translate into Polish.

I called my mama with the news. 'I'm going to interview Lech Wałęsa! I'm so excited!'

'Are you kidding? Lech Wałęsa? That's unbelievable, such a privilege to meet him. I am so happy for you.'

'Yes, as long as I can speak without fear in front of the camera,' I sighed, already stressed at the very thought of meeting him.

Lech Wałęsa was the man who freed Poland and Europe from Communism, by demolishing it with his movement *Solidarność*, or Solidarity in English, the Soviet Bloc's first independent trade union. He won the Nobel Peace Prize in 1983 for his personal sacrifice and significant contribution to protect workers' rights. Communism fell in Poland in 1989, when I was only 11 years old, gifting me and the Polish nation with a democratic country. He became the President of Poland a year later.

When he entered the film studio, he was charming, funny and straightforward, just as I had imagined, which made me slightly less stressed about the interview in front of the camera.

'Oh, no, my dear, you are too tall, you need to bend your knees,' he said with a smile when I asked for a photo with him.

'Yes, Mr President, of course,' I replied and did just that, and grinned at the camera, all of which made me look like I was his height and, in the strange light, as if my front tooth was missing. Now that was a once in a lifetime picture and I looked toothless! Maybe next time!

Unfortunately, soon after, the company decided to change their strategy and I was made redundant. I had to find another job AGAIN!

I spoke to a lady with a Swedish accent and a fierce confidence, during an interview for a global company. 'It is a tough job. Are you up for a challenge, Monika?'

'I like challenges. I'll do whatever you tell me to do,' I replied without hesitation, desperate for a new job.

When I started it, I had to face new challenges and one of my biggest fears—talking to strangers. Part of the job was knocking on the doors of a hundred houses per day. When I knocked on the first door, my heart jumped into my throat and I thought I would pass out as if a dragon was about to come out and burn me alive with the wrath of fire.

'Thank you God!' I sighed, when nobody opened.

I knocked on another door and a lady came out. 'I'm not interested, darling, but why don't you try number ten?' she kindly suggested in such a nice way that I was less scared about doing it again.

My fear of talking to strangers slowly diminished. I was still a little bit scared, as I never knew what they might say. It was the fear of the unknown in its perfect form, but I had to conquer my fears. I had no choice. I had to work and I had to survive.

And survive I did. I soon started to work with big teams of people and became a very successful sales manager, achieving countless awards and incentives, being welcomed on red carpets with Champagne and strawberries in five star hotels in Algarve and Marbella. I loved my new job because it gave me the stability I needed so much in my life, being financially independent and in full control of my own destiny.

CHAPTER 19 - ADONIS

After my breakup with Adam, I was single and uninterested in dating for over two years, trying to understand myself better in solitude.

I read many books about mending the broken heart and how to live the life of my dreams. I was still far from it. I was still single. I thought that only the love of a man could fill the emptiness I was feeling. I tried many techniques to feel better but nothing was working as quickly as I would have wanted it. Concentrating on being successful in my sales job helped me deal with the sad reality of being single. I went for long walks with friends by the river in picturesque towns like Marlow and Henley-on-Thames. I also joined the local gym and yoga classes. I became stronger, but I still dreamt of love.

I spoke to my good friend Teresa one day. '*Cześć*, Monika, *jak się masz*? My friend's cousin, Darek, has just arrived from Poland and started to work as a cleaner. He's looking for a room and I know you have a spare bedroom. Are you looking for a lodger?'

'Oh, I don't know, I haven't thought about it, really. Why don't you come over so that I can meet him?' I replied.

After years of being alone, the thought of having company in the flat suddenly seemed like a good idea. When Darek, a Mediterranean-looking, 21-year-old man, with the most beautiful dark hair down to his waist and olive skin, walked in with Teresa the next day, I was speechless. A Greek God has just descended from Heaven! I thought. Darek was shy, staring at me with his mesmerising dark eyes, smiling with an innocent and childlike expression on his face.

'So, when are you moving in?' I asked, grinning continuously, as if my facial muscles had got stuck.

'Tomorrow, if that's ok with you?' he replied in a sweet voice.

'Great! I am sure you two will get on,' said Teresa with a smile.

'I'm sure we will, right, Darek?' I replied.

My spare bedroom turned into Darek's cave as soon as he had unpacked his two bags.

I was enchanted by his physical beauty, his shyness and very kind offers to fix a cupboard in the kitchen, or to help me carry heavy bags from the car. Having been alone for such a long time and suddenly having a nice man helping me, watching TV together and cooking in the kitchen soon warmed up my heart. Three months after Darek had moved in, realised I was falling in love with him. One night, I was watching a movie on the sofa and I missed him, waiting for him to come back from work.

'*Cześć, jak się masz?* Do you want to watch a movie with me?' I asked when he finally came back.

'*Oh, tak,*' he agreed eagerly and when he sat close to me, I felt electricity running through my body, which longed for only one thing in that moment—to be kissed. I rested my head on his shoulder, feeling as if it was the most natural thing to do, and my heart started to pound even faster.

When Darek kissed me, the whole world started to swirl around.

'I must tell you something,' he said when he stopped kissing me and gave me a chance to get my breath back.' I'm a virgin,' he continued.

'Oh, that's ok,' I replied and hugged him. 'We can take it slowly,' I added, resting my head on his chest where I could hear his strong heartbeat.

As our relationship grew, we started going out more, enjoying walks in the surrounding hills and playing tennis.

'Am I your girlfriend?' I asked him a month later.

'I don't know Misia, are you? I've never had a girlfriend before,' he replied.

'Well, I think I am. After all, we have a relationship, right?'

'Right, then you are Misia,' he said.

Darek's biggest passion, as it soon turned out, was playing computer games. He hid in his bedroom daily, playing, till the early hours in the morning. 'Can you please take the rubbish out?' I asked when I came back from work one day but he ignored me, as usual, and continued playing. 'Ok, I'll do it,' I said.

He stopped helping around the house, cleaning or cooking dinners. All he cared about was playing games. Our quality time together quickly diminished and mainly consisted of watching a movie now and again.

Darek complained about how he wanted to do more in life, rather than being a cleaner. I embarked on a mission to help him get a better job, motivating him, helping him with writing his CV. But as a result, tensions started to run high and we ended up arguing, mainly about his unwillingness to look for a better job and his addiction to computer games. Because that's how it seemed to me—he was addicted.

Every time he locked himself in his bedroom I watched TV in the living room but when I went to sleep, he came to visit me, but often left in the middle of the night. *Why doesn't he want to sleep in my bed?* I thought, but dismissed it as an unreasonable thought, trying to convince myself that it was normal.

Soon, tensions turned into arguments, sometimes daily. When I came back from work one day, I saw him playing games on TV in the living room. My blood reached maximum boiling point, like in a kettle. *Is this the life I am meant to live from now on? With a man addicted to computer games?* I thought, and told him to switch it off immediately, but he looked at me as if he was possessed by a devil and continued playing even more nervously, ignoring me.

'I said: switch it off!' I shouted again.

'Leave me alone!!'

'No, I won't leave you alone! All you do is play these stupid games!'

Possessed with fury, I tore out the cables from the TV set. He stood up and pushed me against the wall, before running to his bedroom and closing the door with a bang. I lay on my bed, knowing that I was living Hell on Earth, but didn't know how to stop it. I loved him. I wanted to be happy with him. I wanted him to love me back. And respect me. But deep down, I knew love was not supposed to hurt like this and just as he was addicted to his games. I felt hopelessly attached to him, desperate for his love and affection. The worst thing I could ever imagine was him leaving me.

A few hours after the arguments, I went to his room to make up. I was always the first one to reach out. An idea came to my mind. If we went away on a holiday together maybe it would help us? I knew Darek had never been on a proper holiday with a girlfriend before, so I decided to find a holiday offer to Ibiza.

'Shall we go? Please! Ibiza is a lovely island,' I said, showing him the offer on a computer screen whilst sitting on his lap.

'Ok, let's go,' he replied, but more with a resigned than a happy voice.

Just before our holiday, Darek found a better job in a restaurant, but as soon as he started to work there, he began telling me long stories about the nice girl from the Czech Republic he was now working with. Initially I didn't think too much of it but after a while I felt annoyed that he was constantly talking about her.

'I'm going to play tennis with Eliska, I'm talking your racket, *Pa!*' he said when I returned from shopping one Saturday, and then he left me alone in the flat.

This is not right, I can't let this happen. How? I will not sit here alone, going crazy and thinking about him playing tennis with her,

I thought as my blood started to boil again, so I decided to join them.

I saw them having fun as I was driving past the tennis court. I knew I had to do this. I had to let that girl know that I existed. That Darek was mine. I entered the court, smiling, but with a pounding heart in my chest, as if it was about to pop out. '*Cześć*, can I join you?' I asked, looking at the surprised expression on his face.

The girl immediately took her bag and left the court.

'I've come to join you, aren't you happy to see me?' I asked, but he didn't respond, and grabbed his bag and ran after her. I sat down on the court.

Is there something going between them? How could he run after her? He chose her! Why? I thought, sitting down on the court and looking at their silhouettes disappearing into the distance.

We avoided each other for days afterwards and I felt anxious about our upcoming holiday to Ibiza.

'Is there something between you and her?' I finally asked.

'No, of course not, stop it.'

'Do you swear?'

'I swear,' he replied and went back to his room.

I believed him.

Why wouldn't I?

He gave me his word.

Chapter 20 - We Are Not Going to Ibiza

'I'm not going! You go! I'm staying here!' Darek yelled a few hours before our flight to Ibiza.

'What do you mean? Stop being silly! We have a flight in a few hours. I've already ordered a taxi!' I exclaimed.

'*Dobrze*, I'll go,' he replied.

When the taxi arrived, Darek helped me put my suitcase in the boot and I followed him back to the flat to get his, but he stopped and turned around at the door. 'I'm not going! *Pa*!' he said, trying to close the door.

'What are you doing? You need to come with me. It's all paid for!' I shouted, trying to stop him close the door, but he was stronger than me, and he succeeded.

I went back to the taxi, wiping my tears, not wanting the driver to see me crying for going alone, even though he wouldn't have known that we had been meant to go together.

How embarrassing! This can't be happening, I'm sure it's just a cruel joke and he will follow me in another taxi, I thought, hiding my tearful eyes behind the sunglasses.

'Please come to the airport. We'll miss our flight. Why are you doing this? Please, come with me. Don't do this. I don't want to go without you,' I begged him on the phone, crying, as soon as I had reached the departure lounge, in the desperate hope that he would change his mind.

'I'm not going. I told you. I simply don't want to go. Have fun!' he replied in a cold voice and hung up.

How I survived the whole journey, arriving in the hotel late at night, would always stay a mystery to me. In the morning, I stepped onto the balcony with the stunning view of the blue sea at sunrise, feeling my stomach twisting and turning from the agony of being alone. *You should be seeing this with me,* I thought, staring at the yellow rays of the sun encompassing the turquoise sea surface, welcoming it for another sunny, warm day in paradise.

But I did not see its full beauty, as it was clouded by my darkest thoughts of pain and misery. I was stuck in the darkness of my own prison. I did not see the beauty of the new reality I was looking at, as the pain squashed any attempt to see the good in life. I was alone. Darek was at home. It was supposed to be our time, to be together, to spend relaxing quality time. To be happy.

Where is he now? Who is he with? Is he with Eliska? He told me it was over. He swore. What have I done to him to deserve this? Am I really such a horrible person? No, I'm not. Yes, I must be. My mind showered me with hundreds of thoughts as I tried to relax, lying on my blue towel by the sea, unable to hear the waves as the thoughts in my head were so loud and painful that nothing could calm them down.

The turquoise waves swished in and out, and so did my thoughts of pain. I called Darek. He didn't pick up, so I left a voicemail. I called again. No reply. I called and called but with no response. He was gone. How? Where? How could I have been left on my own? With such pain? All I wanted was to be loved. To be cared for. To feel complete. To feel happy. Was that such a crime? Did that make me such a bad person? I loved him. Why didn't he show me he love me? Why?

I stared at the vastness of the sea, bringing one wave after another, just like my tears, in perfect rhythm. When the sun started to turn red, the clouds on the horizon became the flames of fire. The sky was bleeding, just like my heart. How could Paradise for one person be seen as Hell by another? Paradise for happy couples hugging and kissing on the beach, and kids making sandcastles, was at the same time the saddest place on Earth for me. When the sun's performance was over and the curtain of darkness fell on my aching from too much sun and shivering from the change in temperature body, I stood up from the ground, which seemed to have held me melted into the millions of grains of sand, as if becoming one, and I went back to my room.

At breakfast, I sat close to a couple of Swedish girls. 'Are you here alone?' asked one, who introduced herself as Julia.

'Yes, I was supposed to come here with my boyfriend but he couldn't come,' I replied, hearing the reality of my situation in my own words for the first time.

'Do you fancy a boat trip tomorrow? There is a beautiful secluded beach on another island that we want to see. Do you want to come with us?' she continued.

'Yes, I would love that. I will,' I replied, glad to have met a good soul in my misery.

The beach was stunning, cocooned by rocks covered by trees and the crystal clear turquoise water made it possible to see the underwater world of rocks and seaweed, standing out on the white sand. I tried to enjoy its beauty but it was hard, and just as my dark thoughts tormented me, so did the dark clouds that came so close that we soon realised we had to go back to catch the boat. The heavy raindrops hit my naked body, only covered in a bikini and my blue towel, which became my only shelter. When we got on the boat, I could feel it moving backwards and forwards and started to pray for a safe way back to our hotel. The storm was getting bigger and bigger and to ease the stress we were feeling, the captain's helper organised a drinking session for us, walking around and letting us all drink local liquor from the bottle, cheering and laughing as soon as each person drank from it. The boat was rocking like a baby's cradle ,making me feel a bit seasick, but as soon as I had tried the drink of gods, I forgot I was on a boat in the middle of a thunderstorm.

'Monika, do you want to go to a famous Ibiza club with us tonight?' Julia asked as we got off the boat, happy to be standing on land again.

'Sure, why not!' I replied, as anything to distract me from being alone that night would have been appreciated.

When we entered the hot like a sauna club, I saw hundreds of people, stacked next to each other like sardines in a can, making up-and-down hand moves to very loud techno music, as if in some kind of trance. We stood, squashed in the crowd, and I also raised my hands up and down, something others would call dancing. Everyone was looking at the DJ, playing on a large balcony in front of us, as if he was some God that we should worship. I stared at the huge number of colourful lamps on the ceiling, with giant speakers on the sides, so loud that I couldn't hear my own thoughts anymore. A great distraction for sure! I soon got tired from the noise and the suffocating air, and when I saw a girl inhaling the air from a red balloon and instantly vomiting afterwards, I thought: *Jesus, what am I doing here?*

Chapter 21 - Painkiller

I rushed into Darek's bedroom as soon as I'd come back early in the morning. He was still sleeping, so I sneaked under the duvet. '*Cześć*, I've missed you,' I whispered, hugging him as he woke up, but he didn't say anything.

I looked around the room which now seemed to be empty and I noticed his suitcase in the corner. 'I'm going back to Poland today,' he said, staring at the wall, avoiding looking into my eyes.

'Why? Like, forever? Are you serious? Why are you going back?'

'I've had enough of England. I'm leaving today.'

'Please, don't do it, please don't leave me,' I begged.

'I've already bought the ticket. It's done. I'm going.'

I went to my bedroom and cried, trying to unpack my bag, thinking that it was some kind of nightmare I would wake up from, hoping he would change his mind. But he didn't. When he shut the door, leaving me alone in the flat, I opened my laptop and noticed that the keyboard had been changed to the Czech language.

She was here. He brought her to my flat whilst I was crying and missing him in Ibiza, I thought to my horror.

Deep down, I knew it was all for the best that he was gone but the pain in my chest was unbearable, and I soon realised that the only thing that would stop it was getting him back. The thought of not seeing him again was tormenting me as if my limbs were being slowly cut off, one by one. Going to work each day was a struggle. I felt as if I'd taken a painkiller each time he emailed me, responding to my desperate messages, pleading for his return. He also missed me and wasn't very happy to be back with his family.

'Please come back. I will buy you a ticket and you won't have to pay anything for rent until you find a job,' I said on the phone one day, hoping that if he did come back, he would be a better man, more mature and responsible and show me the love and care I had so desperately hoped for.

Three months later, I picked him up from the airport. It will all be fine, we will be happy now, I thought, driving him home.

My mama and friends kept repeating that it was not a good idea, because men did not change overnight. But I didn't listen. I wanted to be with him and that was it. I needed him. I loved him. Deep down, I knew that I was probably doing too much for him, but I just couldn't live without him.

The first few days after his return felt amazing. We cooked together and spent nice time together watching movies and going for walks, and Darek quickly found a new job. But after a couple of weeks, the same arguments began and he started playing computer games again, ignoring me for hours and not spending any time with me. He stopped helping around the house, cleaning and cooking, and he dived into his cave of complete and utter computer-playing madness. I knew he was addicted to it and it was his way of dealing with emotions, so I tolerated it and came up with another solution to get closer again. A holiday together, with sandy beaches, crystalline waters, charming little villages and tasty Mediterranean food.

'Darek, how about we go to Crete?' I asked.

'Ok, let's go,' he agreed.

After the disaster with Ibiza, all we needed was to finally spend amazing quality time together, sunbathing, holding hands whilst walking barefoot on the hot sandy beach at sunset, and enjoying romantic moments to keep our relationship happy. And Crete, the largest Greek island, seemed like the perfect choice for just that.

CHAPTER 22 - BARMAID

Cockroaches were everywhere, as if an Egyptian plague had descended upon us.

They were in the paths leading to the room, the room itself and the bathroom. After only two days on the outskirts of sunny Chania, I couldn't take it anymore.

'We will not stay in those apartments at the bottom of the hill any longer. There are cockroaches hitting against the walls at night and I'm scared to even go to the bathroom!' I exclaimed to the hotel receptionist, who didn't seem surprised at all.

To my relief, we were moved to a beautiful sunny room, in the main hotel building, overlooking the main pool area and the sea front. I was really happy but Darek didn't seem to care.

'Shall we meet by the pool later?' I asked, before he went out for a walk.

'Ok! See you there!'

I lay my pink towel on a white sun bed half an hour later.

'Would you like a mojito?' Darek asked, sitting down next to me.

'*Tak, prosze,*' I agreed with a deep sigh, happy to stretch my body in the white bikini, ready to get some colour from the hot sun rays.

' Ohh, *dziękuje,*' I thanked him, seeing my favourite cocktail in his hand.

'I'm going to sit at the bar, and you just relax here, ok?' he asked.

'Ok, sure,' I replied.

He went back to sit on a bar stool where two barmaids were chatting and laughing with him.

I tried to relax, reading my book, but after an hour, I went up to Darek. As soon as I did, they all stopped talking.

'This is Iza, she is from Poland,' he said, introducing me to a short, blond-haired girl.

'*Cześć*,' she greeted me and without waiting for my reply, she walked to the other side of the bar.

'Why did you come here? Go back to relax by the pool. I'll bring you more drinks,' he said.

'Ok,' I replied unwillingly, but I wanted to continue stretching my body in the hot sun, even though I had a feeling that something was wrong. After all, Darek seemed most content sitting at the bar, chatting to those girls.

In the evening, I put on my short pink dress and we went for dinner and drinks on a rooftop bar with breathtaking views of the sea, where we sat on a white sofa, enjoying the most amazing sunset over the sea horizon. Darek was holding my hand and I felt that we might finally make it work now, spending amazing, romantic quality time together, giving full unwavering attention to each other, without distractions of computer games or watching TV, which had seemed merely like existing under one roof, rather than a loving relationship between two human beings. We then went for a relaxing stroll along the rugged coast, gazing at the twinkling lights popping up as if little light bulbs were being switched on by God one by one. I wanted to hug him and kiss him, but he pushed me away.

'I want to get back to the hotel. I'm tired,' he said with boredom in his voice.

'Why? It's really nice in here,' I replied, disappointed.

'I'm just tired, I'll go back but you can stay here if you want,' he said and walked away, leaving me alone on the beach.

After watching the harbour lights for a while, I went back to the hotel room but Darek wasn't there. He didn't have a mobile phone with him, so I couldn't call him and not knowing what else to do, I decided to go to sleep. When I woke up in the morning, he was sleeping on a separate bed behind the stone wall, separating the room in half.

'Where did you go last night?' I muttered.

'I went for a walk!! That's all!'

'Don't do that, please, it's not nice to leave me like this,' I scolded him but he only got up and went to have a shower.

'Shall we go to the beach today rather than just sitting by the pool?' I asked when he came out wearing just a white towel on his hips.

'Sure,' he replied, without much enthusiasm in his voice.

The beach was glorious, with tall rocks surrounding it, as if it was a precious pearl in a shell. I tried to relax, lying down on the towel next to Darek, but somehow I could feel that something was wrong. It just did not feel right. He wasn't very affectionate towards me, unwilling to hug or touch or kiss me, something I really needed to feel that he cared for me. Without such small gestures, we might as well have been two colleagues on a weekend away.

'I'm going to get a drink at a bar. I'm thirsty,' he said after an hour.

'Well, I want to stay. I like it here, listening to the relaxing sound of the waves.'

'Well you stay then, I'm going,' he replied, and picked up his towel and left me alone again.

As much as I had tried to enjoy the sun gently caressing my skin with pleasant warmth and the sound of the waves swishing in and out, I couldn't stop thinking about him and what he was doing now. I took my towel and went back to the hotel half an hour later. Walking past the pool area, I saw him sitting and laughing with the barmaid, Iza, at the bar again.

'Bye! I need to go!' he said to her, as soon as he had noticed me.

'Where are you going?' I exclaimed, surprised to see him leaving so abruptly.

'To the room!' he yelled, without looking back and walked away.

I ordered a pina colada but somehow it didn't taste as good as it normally did. Maybe because of the unwavering feeling that something was wrong and that it shouldn't be like this. When I went back to the room, Darek wasn't there. I looked out from the balcony and I saw him at the bar again. Feeling my blood boiling in the Cretan heat and from seeing him playing with me in such a cruel way, I ran downstairs.

'We need to talk!' I said, walking up to him at the bar, pulling him away, towards the main road. 'Why are you constantly at the bar, talking to her? You should be with me now!'

'Because I like her. She comes from the same town in Poland as me and she is funny!' he replied with a silly grin on his face.

'How can you behave like this? I hate you! It's over! Do you understand me? It's over between us! I can't live like this anymore!' I yelled, having lost it completely now.

'Ok!' he replied and ran back to the hotel.

He is just being silly; he will soon get back to his senses, I thought, walking along the coastal road, looking at the rocks below and the restless sea, angry at his behaviour, even though it hadn't been the first time he'd treated me badly. When I got back to the room, he wasn't there and I couldn't see him at the bar. I walked around the pool and talked to people sitting there. Suddenly, I saw him walking in front of us with Iza and eating an ice cream with a grin on his face. He looked at me but kept on walking and disappeared behind the hotel building.

Where are they going? I thought, and went to sit on the balcony, watching the night falling the darkness onto my soul. He didn't come back that night and when I woke up in the morning, he wasn't in the room.

Where is he? I thought, dreading the answer.

CHAPTER 23 - GREEK TRAGEDY

The overwhelming, torturing pain in my heart started to blur my days with nights.

I chased after Darek, desperate to talk to him, but I couldn't find him anywhere. After a week of living in a horror movie, I finally managed to talk to him when he walked into the room.

'I want to go back home,' I said, with calm voice, even though I was boiling inside.

'I don't want to go back. Go, I'm not going,' he replied, shrugging his shoulders as if I had asked him an unreasonable request like wanting him to go to the moon with me.

'Are you sleeping with her? I saw a condom in your bag when you went to take a shower!!' I asked, but he didn't reply, got changed into new clothes, and shutting the door with a loud bang, he left the room.

I walked into the bathroom to take a shower and as the water was flowing all over my body, tears flooded my face, merging with the waterfall. I cried out loud as if I had experienced the end of the world, losing everything and everyone in one moment.

'Why? Why? Why?' I screamed, crying out loud, pulling my hair and squeezing my head as if it was about to shatter into a million pieces from the overload of nails, pushed into it simultaneously. I had never felt more hurt and lonely in my life, with my heart, ripped out of my chest whilst still being alive.

I don't want to lose you! I love you! Why don't you love me? My mind showered me with thoughts of despair, just as the water from the shower drenched my body.

How can I live without you? How? I thought, looking for him around the hotel corridors, looking like a zombie, with red puffy eyes. I walked around the pool area, on the beach and back to the hotel corridors but he was nowhere to be found.

'What are you doing later? Let's go for a coffee tonight. I know a lovely place in the harbour. Would you like that?' asked Alesandro, the hotel manager in his thirties, seeing me walking aimlessly around the reception area.

'No, thank you,' I replied, as it was the last thing I wanted to do but a second later, I thought that maybe it would help me forget about the pain for a while, so I agreed.

We drove though the winding roads of spectacular Cretan hills, along the coastline bathed in the sunset. It seemed like nothing special to me in that moment, as my misery in my heart was so deep, that nothing would make me see the true beauty of the surroundings.

Alesandro knew about Darek. The whole hotel knew about it. I had become a laughing stock for everyone. 'Many men that come here lose their mind and go after barmaids, no matter if they come with wives or girlfriends,' he said calmly, driving on the windy roads.

'What do you mean?' I asked, confused by his explanation of this being a normal state of affairs here.

'It's the hot weather in Crete! That's how men react to it!' he replied with a grin which I didn't like.

True, I had heard Hippocrates' claim that the Cretan air and sun had healing powers and could cure the sick, but I didn't know that it also made men go crazy, boiling their testosterone, so that they wanted sex with anything that moved and didn't run off to the trees! When we got the restaurant in the marina, we sat by the open window, having a coffee and ice cream, looking at the sunset. I tried to stop myself from crying, but my tears just kept piling up, as if they were summoned for a morning army report. Alesandro listened to my sad story and seemed to sympathise with me.

'Let's go to my place! I'll show you where I live,' he said, driving me back.

Walking into his apartment, located in a separate complex, I was silently praying that he wouldn't expect anything from me for the coffee and ice cream, but as soon as he had shut the door, he came close to me and kissed me.

'Stop, please, I can't do this,' I said, annoyed that he had tried to impose himself on me just like that. 'I need to go,' I continued, and ran out like a criminal who had just been released from prison, back to the main hotel building, looking for Darek.

I saw him sitting at another bar, talking to people.

'Go back to the room. I'll come later,' he said when I'd approached him, breathless from running.

I waited for him till midnight but since he didn't come back, I got dressed and went to the pool area.

'I don't know where he is,' I said to the couple that I had spoken to before, unable to hide my utter despair.

'He is with her, the barmaid,' the girl replied.

'No, he can't be, he wouldn't sleep with her!' I exclaimed.

'Do you know where he is? Please, help me find him,' I begged the girl and her boyfriend.

'He may be in her room,' he replied.

'Do you know where that is?'

'Yes, let's go,' he said, and when we were silently creeping along the corridor, we heard some voices.

'It's this one. Can you hear them?' he asked.

I put my ear against the door and heard Darek, talking and laughing with her. 'Open the door, right now! I know you are there!' I yelled, banging on the door as if Hell was about to break loose.

They went quiet.

'We will get the manager if you don't open the door immediately!' I shouted with even more fury, banging faster than the heart beat in my chest.

Darek opened the door. I rushed inside, wanting to catch the barmaid, without thinking what I would do to her once I succeeded but she was not about to get a cuddle from me, for sure! 'Get away from my guy! He is my boyfriend!!' I screamed in a voice that would wake the dead but Darek stopped me, pushing me against the wall and squeezed my arm.

I was possessed by unearthly rage, so he could hardly stop my moves, and I set myself free, but Iza quickly ran away. 'How could you do this to me! It's over! I'm leaving! I hate you! I hate you! I hate you!'

'Come on, just leave him, he is an asshole,' the girl's boyfriend said, trying to calm me down, dragging me out.

They escorted me back to my room but I didn't remember it the next day, probably from the shock I had experienced. Looking at the rising sun, I knew I had to do something. I had to stop this pain! And the only thing I could think of was to go back home, pack his stuff and throw it outside, for the wolves to eat. He didn't have a key so he couldn't get in. I also felt that I couldn't stay alone in the flat for another week's holiday, knowing he would stay here with her. I could have lost my mind completely and only God knew what I would have done to myself, so I emailed my good friends, asking if I could visit them in Portugal. They agreed. I bought a new flight home and then a return ticket to Lisbon. Having packed my bag, I reached into the safe to get my passport and I noticed that Darek's wasn't there. *Umm that's a shame, he was quicker than me, I would have taken it with me*, I thought in complete and utter fury.

'I'm leaving tomorrow and I will throw your stuff outside!' I announced to Darek when he had walked into the room, seeing me close my bag.

He looked at me, speechless, as if working out if I was serious or not.

'You didn't think I would treat you any different after what you have just done? I'm forced to leave my holiday a week earlier because you want to sleep with a barmaid!! I've suffered enough! You've hurt me enough! Can you hear me?' I yelled.

On the last evening on this Paradise island, Darek put on a white shirt and jeans, and tried to have a normal conversation with me. He suddenly decided to be nice, clearly because of not knowing whether I was bluffing or not. I knew it was the only reason. We walked to the beach and watched the moonlight, reflected in the ripples of the sea waves. I still hoped he would ask me to stay, apologise and want to be with me. I was desperate for any scraps of his love and affection. But he didn't. After a short chat, he left me on the beach. Alone.

'Why? Why me? Why do you want me to suffer so much?' I asked God, looking at the sky, covered with millions of stars.

But I also felt something new. A small sense of relief. As if a light of hope had shined in the brightest star in the sky. After all, it was the moment I had made the decision to stop suffering, that I found a way. A way to remove myself from this painful situation and walk away with dignity, which I had lost being with him, from seeing him hurt me over and over again, and allowing him to treat me with disrespect for so long.

'Enjoy the room for yourself. You can be with her now! On our bed!' I said with strange calmness in my voice, looking at him sitting on the bed before I left to catch my flight in the morning.

'Thanks, I will,' he replied, grinning, with no visible sign of remorse or guilt.

The taxi journey from the airport in the dark, cold rainy weather in England, put me into the darkest place on Earth. *He is with her now, in sunny Crete and I'm going back home alone. Why?* I thought, shedding tears down my cheeks, just as the rain drops shed upon the windows.

When I walked into the flat, I left my bag in the corridor, went into his room and packed all of his belongings in any bags I could find, as if I had received a pain-numbing injection in my heart that would allow me to do it. I stopped crying. I was giving myself freedom. Freedom from the unhealthy attachment to his lack of love for me. Love was not supposed to be about clinging to someone at any cost. Love was supposed to be about the courage to leave and not be afraid of being alone, but allowing myself to make space to find a soulmate. Love was letting Adonis be happy with his barmaid and the same time, giving myself the freedom to find true love.

'*Cześć,* Marcin, Darek's things are outside my flat. Pick it up or leave it. I don't care. He'll be back in a week's time because right now he is in bed with a barmaid in Crete,' I said when I called his best friend. After all, I still had feelings for him.

After all, despite hating him right now, I had cared for him for two years. After all, I had been part of his life and he was part of mine. But from now on, Darek was no longer my Adonis, the God of beauty and desire. He was dead to me. He died where he belonged. On his Greek island. And then, without even repacking my suitcase, I jumped in the taxi and flew to Lisbon.

CHAPTER 24 - ORANGES

'He, who returns from a journey, is not the same as he who left.'
-Chinese Proverb

Thank you, God, for my Portuguese *amigas*! I thought on the plane to Lisbon.

Maria and Jorge used to be my English students when I was working as an English teacher in the evenings, my part time job for a while in a local college. When they had first come to my class, they couldn't speak a word in English, not even able to fill out forms but since they were very quick learners, we could soon have first conversations. They had always been cheerful and happy, despite being tired after having worked all day. I'd visited them with Darek in their cottage. They were adorable and I was devastated when they had decided to go back to Portugal, preferring to live a more modest life but full of tasty, fresh Portuguese seafood and wine, rather than staying in rainy England.

Maria used to hate the English weather and she couldn't get used to it. I didn't blame her. Every time anyone asked me why I had decided to live in England, I had always replied with my newly learnt English sarcasm: 'Oh, because of the weather!!' Initially, I couldn't get used to days when it 'rained cats and dogs,' one of my favourite metaphors which, supposedly, came from old times when cats and dogs used to hide on the thatched roofs and slide off them when it rained heavily. I could understand cats might do that—but dogs? Umm, not an entirely believable story.

Maria and Jorge had stayed in touch with me so when I had emailed them from Crete, that devil's island which apparently turned every man into a wild animal possessed by the desire to seduce any barmaid they meet, they understood my difficult situation straight away. My email said:

'*Ola, como estas*? (Hi, how are you?)

Can I please visit you for a week? I'm in Crete right now but I'm going back to England tomorrow. Darek has met a barmaid and he is staying here with her. I have a week off left for my holidays and I don't want to be alone.

Beijos (Kisses)

Monika'

Their reply was simple:

'Of course *amiga*, come!'

I was ecstatic to hug them at Lisbon Airport. We couldn't spend too much time in Lisbon but it was enough to drive through old streets with colourful houses covered in beautiful tiles in pink, yellow, indigo and stop by the River Tagus, overlooking the red 25th de Abril Bridge, the largest suspension bridge in Europe, which made me feel as if I was looking at the Golden Gate Bridge in San Francisco. A truly magnificent view over the glittering river.

We then drove to where Maria and Jorge lived, a charming historic town in the southern Alentejo region, called Avis. It was very different to towns in England, seemingly sprinkled with enchanting white houses, decorated with flowers, yellow rims and red terracotta roof tiles, an old church and spectacular views of the never-ending olive groves, vineyards and cork oak forests, lakes and rivers. Rows of orange trees grew along the narrow cobblestone streets, abundant in the juiciest, most delicious oranges, hot from the sunrays!

'Monika, what are you doing, *amiga*?' Maria asked, laughing, seeing me fill up my T-shirt with ten oranges as we strolled through town.

'Well, we don't have free oranges growing on trees in England!!' I replied, grinning. 'Oh look *amiga*, two Portuguese dogs having sex! So typical!' I exclaimed.

'*Sim*, they are true Portuguese!' she replied, laughing at an unexpected view in the afternoon sun.

The doorways in their townhouse were very low, as if designed for dwarves, and since I was a tall girl, I had to bend my neck walking through them, as if I had arrived from the land of giants. When I forgot to bend my neck, I smacked my forehead right in the middle with a big bang. My tiny bedroom, painted in bright blue and with a traditional wooden bed with a tall headboard, had no windows so when the door was closed at night, it was pitch dark and a bit scary. Luckily, Maria didn't mention any Portuguese ghost stories before bedtime or I could have freaked out! The tiny balcony overlooked other rooftop balconies, with lots of flower pots in clay vases and wooden tables and chairs. I loved having my morning coffee there, slowly waking up to the warm sunrays gently caressing my face, a welcome relief from the stresses I had gone through.

Maria listened to my sad story whist drinking the delicious Portuguese coffee.

'That's awful, what a horrible man! This is unbelievable! Why, Monika? Why?' she replied with a strong Portuguese accent, making my misery sound a bit less tragic.

I tried not to cry, stopping my tears right before they were about to dive into the swimming pool of my sorrow. 'Well, he obviously had his reasons,' I replied, not knowing what else to say.

I knew I wasn't perfect myself, very emotional and sometimes overactive. But what woman, in my shoes, wouldn't have been? I still didn't deserve it. On our holiday in Crete. Or maybe I had been asking for it? God gave me many signs that I should have finished that unhealthy relationship, which was more of an emotional masochism than love, two years before. But I was stubborn and didn't want to listen to my internal guidance voice saying it wasn't good for me, ignoring it and letting my ego control my actions. After all, it had been me who begged him to come back to England, in spite of him cheating on me with the Czech girl and tricking me into going alone to Ibiza. What more should he have done for me to finally open my eyes? Oh, yes, how about running off with a barmaid, right in front of my eyes on a sunny island?! Every woman's dream holiday! The full Cretan package.

Unconscious of my destructive patterns, desperate to be loved, no matter what, and not standing up for myself when he had hurt me the first and second time, I had finally got a painful wake-up call. Shame it had taken me so long to realise I deserved more in life and I deserved to find true love, rather than keeping an unfulfilled and immature relationship, just because I was afraid to be alone. I had finally said 'It's over' for which I had paid a high price with his vengeance, but I was proud to have faced my fears and moved on with life, no matter how painful it would be, fully respecting myself and trusting that one day I would find the right man to feel complete. Finding my other half and be happy. Yes, I was afraid that it could never happen, but I was now ready to face my fears of abandonment and go forward, single and alone, but independent and in charge of my destiny.

Fortunately, being with my dear friends, sightseeing and visiting one of the oldest megalithic stone monuments in Europe, 2000 years older than Stonehenge, near the town of Evora, and eating delicious local food, helped me feel less unhappy. I loved Maria's platters, with piles of fresh, succulent prawns or her speciality dish, *cozido à portuguesa, a* tasty stew made with potatoes, carrots, beans and meat. I enjoyed drinking smooth, Portuguese wine with tantalizing aromas, followed by the insanely tasty, sweet dessert wine, 'Porto' from the Douro valley, which had originally been created for the British sailors in the 1600s to help kill bacteria in contaminated water and, obviously, to taste heavenly. Amazing food, with healing properties for body and soul, and the company of their

Portuguese family, made our dinners even more special. What more could I have wanted after my heartbreak?

Chapter 25 - Portuguese Tete-A-Tete

'Let the lover be disgraceful, crazy, absent-minded.
Someone sober will worry about events going badly.
Let the lover be.'

-Rumi

'Monika, this is Pedro!' Jorge introduced me to a dark-haired medicine student with a gleaming smile in the bar, which was very hot and full of locals talking loudly in Portuguese.

Pedro was a very intelligent man, gazing at me with his dark piercing eyes from behind the glasses and making me laugh. It was better than crying. He held my hand under the wooden table with affection, something I really needed after months of not feeling loved by Darek and eventually leading to a Greek tragedy.

'Would you like to go for a walk? I will show you the town at night!' Pedro screamed right in my ear when the music got loud.

'Maria, is it ok with you? Can I go for a walk with Pedro?' I asked my friend politely.

Maria said something to Pedro in Portuguese, with a serious expression on her face, as if making sure he would not do anything silly. At least, that was my guess, since my Portuguese language skills were limited to only five words.

The narrow streets of this magical town at night were dangerously romantic and the views from the terrace, which overlooked the twinkling lights of the nearby villages, were breathtaking. It was past midnight but the air was still pleasantly warm. I couldn't get enough of its exhilarating freshness, breathing it in deeply, as if smelling the most beautiful perfume.

I told Pedro about Darek and he was very sympathetic, trying to cheer me up by telling me Portuguese jokes which I didn't understand, but at least I could laugh. Something I hadn't done for a long time. He suddenly drew me towards him and kissed me passionately.

I loved it.

After I got my breath back, he kissed me again and I wrapped my hands around his neck, caressing his thick dark hair. I drowned in the sweet physical sensation of being kissed by someone who was actually nice to me. He then led me to his cute old car with a missing part of the windscreen which was covered with cardboard.

'Very creative,' I said, smiling at him when I got in.

'Oh, yes, Portuguese way, the best way!' he replied, giggling.

We drove out of the town and turned into a country road which slowly disappeared, as if we were in the middle of a field.

'Where are we going? I don't think you are supposed to drive here?' I asked, worried by the deep holes in the dry, sandy soil, making us rattle in the car as if we were on a funfair ride.

'You'll see,' he replied, grinning mysteriously.

After a while, it became so dark that all I could see were a few meters ahead, illuminated by the front lights.

'Come with me!' he said flirtatiously when we finally stopped next to tall bushes.

When I got out of the car, I saw a spectacular reflection of town lights in the calm, glass-like surface of the lake.

Pedro stood behind me, hugging my body tightly, shielding me from all the evil out there in the world.

'*Linda!*' He whispered that I was beautiful right in my ear, running his fingers up my thighs.

I surrendered to his gentle touch. Leaning against the car, gazing at the reflection of the moonlight in the lake, I felt one with the universe. My life suddenly didn't seem that bad now.

***

The following morning, I woke up in my bedroom, thinking about Pedro. What a night! He is amazing. Will I see him again today? I hope so. Please God, let me see him again, I prayed silently having my morning coffee on the sunny balcony.

Hearing the bell ring around midday, I rushed downstairs as fast as if running away from a burning blaze, just to see who it was. It was Pedro, wearing a slightly open white shirt and sunglasses, making him look like a model from a Portuguese magazine.

'*Bom Dia* Monika, do you want to see Marvao? A medieval village on top of the hills of Sapoio?' he said with a sexy smile and a cute Portuguese accent, moving his alluring lips.

It was a silly question to ask. 'Oh, *sim*, I would love that!' I replied, trying to play it cool but then I threw myself into his arms, giving him a big hug and a kiss, showing him how excited I was to spend more time with him.

Maria had things to do, so she didn't object to my little adventure with Pedro, and Jorge was going on a sports bike ride in the countryside—his true passion. A man with his toy, what could you do?

'It was an amazing night!' Pedro finally said, reaching out for my hand whilst driving down a narrow winding road up the massive hill.

'*Sim*, yes, it was,' I replied, blushing and squeezing his hand from the excitement and admiring the amazing scenery below.

Strolling, hand in hand, through the narrow maze-like alleys, passing white houses with decorative doors and windows, with only a few locals walking past, I went back in time, to the thirteenth-century Portugal. Pedro pressed me against the walls in empty streets, kissing me in a true, passionate, Portuguese way, making me dizzy from this sweet chemistry. When we walked up to the castle, up what seemed like a thousand steps, I saw the most spectacular view which took my breath away.

'Wow, it's beautiful!' I gasped.

'That's Valencia de Alcantara, can you see?' he asked, pointing at the distant Spanish town.

'Yes, we are so close to Spain! Amazing!' I replied.

We were so high up, I could almost touch the tiny, white, fluffy clouds in the blue sky. I didn't want to think about Darek anymore, praying I would never experience such a nightmare ever again.

In the evening, we drove to our favourite spot by the lake, watching the full moon and listening to the sweetest silence of the countryside before setting off for a *Galão*, an espresso with foamed milk. Drinking coffee at midnight was not something I would normally do in England but... when in Portugal, do as the Portuguese do!

I spent an amazing week with Pedro, full of adventures and the most romantic experiences of my life. Up till then, at least. We loved our company and we couldn't stay away from each other but I had to go back to England and face the sad reality of being alone again. A chance holiday romance like this, no matter how wonderful, unfortunately, couldn't last forever. That's why it was so precious when the universe made it happen, making rare moments like this stay in memory.

On the day of my departure, Pedro stood by the car when Jorge was loading my bags into the boot. I didn't want to say goodbye to him but I knew we couldn't be together. He would never move to England and I couldn't move to Portugal, as much as I would have loved to.

'Thank you for everything, I will miss you,' I said, hugging him with tears flooding my eyes.

I waved at him from the back window, before we turned, disappearing round the corner. I had loved Pedro's company, especially after one of the biggest emotional heartbreaks of my life. I was grateful that he had opened my eyes to this beautiful world, once I had finally stopped crying over a man who had hurt me. It was a once-in-a-lifetime experience sent to me by God to comfort me, after having gone through so much pain. A true blessing, which helped me forget about Adonis and his barmaid, at least for a week. A little bit of magic and romance was exactly what I needed then. Since I could not have what I had wanted (which was destructive for me, without even realising it), I had to like what I had. Whoever had said that when one door closes, God opens another, couldn't have been more right. I left Portugal grateful for my most genuine and caring friends, hot sun, romance, Alentejo wine, *caracois*, small snails cooked in broth with garlic that had to be sucked out of the shell in the hope they tasted like mushrooms, and warm, puffy *churros* with cinnamon!

CHAPTER 26 - SOLACE

'Dancing is not just getting up painlessly, like a leaf blown on the wind;
dancing is when you tear your heart out
and rise out of your body to hang suspended between the worlds.'
-Rumi

Upon my return from Portugal, I locked Darek's room and I didn't enter it for months as it was too painful and irksome.

I found it hard to understand for a long time how Darek could have been with another woman, right there, in front of my eyes, in such a cruel and heartless way. Over the coming years, I did my best to heal, reading books, spending time with friends and throwing myself into work and achieving successes which were essential for my sanity and self-esteem, whatever success meant: being the best sales manager, growing as a person or learning new skills which would help me go up the career ladder. Meeting with my single girlfriends and chatting about life and men did an awful lot of soul healing, the kind of therapy that could never be underestimated. It was just a shame I spent a lot of time feeling sorry for myself and re-living the pain of the past, rather than enjoying the beauty of each day and night, something that came much later as part of my realisation of how much time could be spent on enjoying the present moment, living in the now, rather than in the past or future.

Two years after the Greek tragedy, I was finally ready to try online dating. I created a short profile on one of the dating sites and when I opened my inbox the next morning, I saw 110 messages. I went out on a few dates, but I didn't feel much of the famously talked-about chemistry with them, which was necessary to fall in love. I often couldn't even have meaningful or intelligent conversations with the men I was meeting, bored with shallow topics such as the car they owned, or how fast they could go on their motorcycle. They often suggested going back to my flat only after the first or a second date.

'Shall we go to your place? Have you got some wine?' they often asked, not only inviting themselves to my place but also expecting me to serve them drinks, free sex and a wine bar all in one!

'Umm, I'm a bit tired, maybe next time,' I replied, frustrated that it was all they had ever wanted, without even taking me out on a few proper dates to get to know them.

I was hoping to find a life partner, just like many other single women out there, someone who I could be with for the rest of my life and not just for a mediocre five minutes. If lucky! Where was the courtship gone? Where were the hand-written romantic love letters I used to get as a teenager from boys at school, professing their love in the most endearing way, attaching dried flowers to them and hoping I would look at them in the corridor. Text messages didn't have the same romantic touch for some reason. As a result of unlucky dates, I was single for a long time, spending time in solitude, taking walks in nature, but still yearning for a miracle to happen.

When I'd declined the cheeky and ridiculous offers of men interested in one thing only, I had never heard from them again. What was that supposed to mean? But I only learnt about the three date rule later on. I guess that should have been also included in my 'Welcome to England' guide. Not that I'm blaming England for the way men were—generally afraid of commitment and mostly interested in having fun, of course—but the culture seemed to be an important factor in how dating was done, even though LOVE, the most powerful and universal emotion in the world, should surely have felt the same, regardless of the country one was in. My morals and values of what was right or wrong were deeply instilled in the core of my being and shaped the way I perceived the world and people. It didn't make me a saint, oh no, but I knew that lying was wrong, cheating was wrong and I knew that commitment was a matter of honour and the respect a man would show to a woman in how he related to her. I never put up with men who were not respectful. After Adonis, at least!

One man, after a first date, asked to meet me for a coffee. I agreed. 'Just so you know, it's your turn now to buy me a drink,' he texted me half an hour before, so I took my coat off and went back to my lounging, as I decided that I wouldn't waste time on someone who couldn't even buy a coffee.

'I knew you were only going to use me for money, just like all other women out there,' he texted me an hour later, having finally realised that I wasn't coming.

'Well, I didn't know that if a man buys me a coffee for £2, it means that I am using him for money! Good luck with your search for love!' I replied.

Another time, having been insulted by a man who told me he knew a girl prettier than me only because I didn't want to take him home, I came out of the pub as soon as he had gone to the toilet, and ran through the High Street as if I were being chased by a horde of zombies, laughing at what I had to do as a woman.

My search for love continued. I believed that I would be finally happy once I found it, once I became 'whole' with my soulmate.

'You should try dancing, Monika. I think you will like it,' Joanne, one of my colleagues, suggested one day.

'Oh... you have my attention! What kind of dancing?'

'Well, it's great fun, a bit like modern jive and salsa. And you can meet lots of people there!' she replied.

As scary as it seemed, I decided to test my bravery and give it a go. And why not? I joined Joanne on a Friday night, at one of the local evening classes.

Wow, I want to dance like this too! This is unbelievable! Why has nobody told me about this before? I thought, watching her dancing gracefully to the music.

When the beginners lesson had finished, the freestyle began so that we could mix and mingle to dance with each other. It usually meant dancing each song with a different partner, unless the partner was amazingly compatible and they would ask for one more dance. Initially, I felt very nervous every time a man asked me to dance with him but since it was up to them to lead and all I had to do was to follow their moves, I soon started to go with the flow and enjoy myself. Joanne was watching me from the distance with a big smile on her face.

'You are really good Monika! You have got talent!' she said when I walked up to her, out of breath from being swirled around the dance floor for an hour.

After that, I danced every week. The classes were full of different people, younger men with professional-looking moves, but also older men with equally impressive dancing skills who made me laugh a lot, making funny faces and joking. When I danced I was in a different world. A different dimension. Dancing became my passion. One I wanted to cherish forever. It became my new love. I stopped worrying I was single. I stopped worrying I lived alone. I stopped worrying about the future. When I danced, I forgot about all my worries and laughed till my belly hurt, even till the day after. My feet often hurt at the end of the night, even though I was wearing black dancing shoes with leather soles which made me feel like a ballroom dancer. The moment I put them on, I transformed into one. Or I wished I was one, with one wave of a magic wand. I felt anything was possible when I was wearing those shoes. I could do flips in the air, glide on the dance floor as if I was skating like a Russian Olympic medallist and do drops as if I was fearless and not care if the man holding me could let me go any time, hitting my head on the wooden floor. That's where the trust came in handy. A good exercise to learn trusting men again.

A tough thing to do for an independent woman who had been hurt many times! The best compliment at the end of the dance was hearing, 'This was the best dance of the night. I hope we can dance again soon,' which men said in a very English gentleman way. My belief in men with good manners was restored. But paradoxically, I was now also happy in my singleton life!

CHAPTER 27 - PIDDLES

'Hello!!' shouted a man in his forties, with a head full of brown hair, grinning from ear to ear, standing on another flight of stairs to the block of flats when I was unloading work materials from my car.

'Hello!' I replied, surprised and not entirely sure whether he was addressing me. But since there was nobody behind, it must have been me!

'How are you? Lovely day, isn't it?' he asked with a gummy smile which didn't leave his face.

'Yes, it is lovely indeed!' I replied politely, smiling back.

'I actually live on the south coast but I often visit my father who lives here. I've seen you passing a few times and I thought it would be nice to meet up for a coffee one day!'

'Oh, yes, ummm, sure!' I replied, and after this slightly awkward conversation, I quickly entered my flat and closed the door.

A few minutes later, I heard a knock on my door.

'Would you like to give me your telephone number so that we can arrange to meet up one day?' he asked, with a face of a puppy about to get a treat.

'Oh, ok, sure,' I replied, being put on the spot and unable to say no.

I became friends with Alexander, as that was his name, and we often went for walks when he was in the area. I visited him for a weekend in his cottage by the sea, in a small coastal village near Weymouth. We enjoyed our conversations about life and relationships whilst hiking along the tall cliffs, admiring the stunning blue sea and the English coastline.

'Tell me, Monika, what kind of man you are looking for?' he enquired, as if he was a policeman investigating a suspect with a lamp shining bright at my face.

'Umm, when I meet him, I will know!' I replied with a big sigh, hoping he would understand what I had truly meant.

In the evening, he cooked a delicious dinner, a fresh crab from the local fishmonger's and a potato salad accompanied with chilled Sauvignon blanc which we enjoyed on the patio, watching the sun going into hiding beneath the sea horizon. I liked Alexander's company and appreciated the efforts but nevertheless, I still saw him only as a friend. I didn't feel anything more. No matter how much I would have liked to. He was a nice, caring man with a great sense of humour, and a lot of English sarcasm, which I sometimes didn't understand. Being with him would have probably given me the stability I needed so much. But I hadn't fallen in love with him. I wished I could have forced myself to fall in love with him. My life would have been much simpler.

'Would you like a foot massage?' Alexander asked, as soon as we had finished watching a comedy.

'Oh, no thank you, I'm going to sleep now,' I replied, and to avoid looking at his disappointed face, I quickly said goodnight and went back to my bedroom.

'Hey, Piddles, fancy lunch and a walk?' Alexander called a few weeks later, teasing me with my nickname ever since I'd had to take an emergency wee in the bush when we were on top of the cliff with no toilets around.

'Sure, why not? Pick me up in five!' I replied.

'You know I only see you as a friend,' I said when we were walking by a river after a traditional English roast in an old country pub.

'Ok, I understand, but I still like spending time with you and you never know, maybe once you get to know me more, things will change,' he replied, with disappointment in his voice.

'Sure,' I replied, knowing that friendship between men and women was possible and some women would swear by it—or maybe they meant gay men only?

When we got back to my flat, we started watching a movie as I didn't want to tell him to just leave, but halfway through, I suddenly remembered that a freestyle dance session in Berkhamsted was on.

Should I go or should I let him stay a bit longer? Maybe this is what love looks like. Companionship and spending nice time together. Maybe I should just give him a chance and hope the feelings will come one day? Maybe I will fall in love with him as he says? He is such a nice man! I thought, hearing my logic fight for superiority with my emotions, or more specifically, lack of them.

Go! Go! an internal voice kept pestering me, no matter how much I tried to make it go away.

But it has already started at eight, and will be finishing soon. What's the point? continued my internal dialogue, but I felt I could not ignore THAT voice, which was really trying to tell me something.

'I'm really sorry, but I'm a bit sleepy,' I said finally.

He left after giving me a quick kiss on the cheek, as always. I ran to my bedroom, put my black chiffon dancing dress on, stood in the corridor thinking that it was crazy, hesitating for the last time, but then I jumped in the car.

I then drove to the only place where I should be that night.

CHAPTER 28 - DANCING WITH DESTINY

'Lovers don't finally meet somewhere.
They are in each other all along.

-Rumi

I was like Cinderella, trying to get to the ball and back before midnight strikes.

I stopped in front of the striking Berkhampsted Town Hall with the old clock showing half past eleven. Walking up the old stairs, I heard the dance music playing and shivers went down my spine from excitement, as if I was truly going to a gala ball organised by the local prince. When I entered the dimly-lit Victorian hall with wood-panelled ceiling, I looked around the dance floor full of joyful couples swirling around, men doing artistic drops on women and lifting them up in the air.

Walking towards the chairs to the left, I noticed *him*, sitting on a chair, wearing a slightly open blue shirt, with a head full of chestnut brown hair and a warm smile on his face, showing off his gleaming white teeth watching others dancing. Over the years of dancing, I'd seen lots of men, but *he* was DIFFERENT. I couldn't take my eyes off him, as if they were glued to him by invisible threads. I was struck by the cupid's arrow which had brought me here tonight. I sat down on a chair and stared at him, putting my dancing shoes on. He didn't see me and I wanted to get his attention. I knew he was The One, right there and then. For the first time in my life, I felt something that others would refer to as love at first sight. I had finally experienced it.

'Would you like to dance?' a man in his forties asked, reaching out for my hand.

I nodded and a few seconds later, I was showing off my best and most gracious moves, swirling around the dance floor, and gazing at My Man dancing with other women.

Maybe he is a professional? I thought, looking at the way he was dancing, and his very unusual moves.

When I finished dancing, I stood by the wall, as if paralysed and unable to move around as confidently as I normally would have.

'My friend would like to dance with you. Would you like that?' an old man asked, pointing at My Man and putting our hands and two souls together, as if two magnets had stuck to each other—the strongest pulling force of the universe.

With my left arm on his shoulder and right hand clasped in his, we began dancing to the rhythm, our eyes connected by the invisible thread as if we had seen more than just the physical, as if we had already known each other, from a previous life, from different dimension. I grinned, admiring that gorgeous face of an angel. His moves were shaky and I could sense the vibration of his body, as if he was nervous, so I helped him smooth the twists and turns, and breaking the rules of dancing by leading him.

'What's your name?' he asked, after what had seemed like an eternity of dancing with fire, two flames dancing in the wind.

'Monika! With a K,' I whispered to his ear, and immediately thinking, *Why have I just said that?*

'I'm John!'

'Nice to meet you, John!' I replied, just as our song had finished.

'Would you like another dance? You are a very good dancer,' he said.

'Oh, thank you, I have danced for years. And you?'

'It's my first time. I've only had one lesson. My friend showed me a couple of moves before we got here!'

'Oh, that explains your unique moves! And I thought you were a professional!' I replied, giggling.

After that dance, John asked me for another one, and then another one. He didn't want to let me go. I didn't want him to let me go, either. I noticed people smiling and talking into each other's ears whilst gazing at us.

When he finally thanked me, I went to the Blues Room, where slower music was played. But John had soon found me and to my delight, he asked for another dance. Holding me close to his chest, I touched the hot, wet shirt on his back and the whiff of his woody aftershave behind his ear made me dizzy from the sweet sensation of passion I was feeling for him. The world around us disappeared and there was just the two of us in the centre of the universe, united in the perfect embrace, with no beginning and no end. When the music stopped for good, I thanked him and sat down on a chair to take my dancing shoes off.

Is he going to ask me for my number? Please ask me! Please, I thought, gazing at him.

After a quick chat with his friend he came up. 'Do you want to give me your telephone number? Maybe we can meet again,' he asked.

Has he just heard my thoughts? I wondered. 'Of, course,' I replied and went home as if I had just been lifted to the clouds and back.

When I got back home around two in the morning, I snuggled up under the duvet, thinking about him, when I heard a ping on my phone.

'Hi Monika,

It was lovely to meet you tonight.

Please let me know if you got home ok.

John.'

I had never received such messages from other men. They never cared if I got home after a date. *This man will change my life,* I thought, ecstatic at the idea of having met someone I had been searching for all my life.

I knew John would change my life. But I did not know how much.

***

'Are you coming to the same venue on Sunday night?' he texted me a few days later.

'Yes, I am. See you there!' I replied, happy that he had asked.

When the lesson started and John wasn't there, I started to worry he wasn't going to come but after an hour, I noticed him walking in, making such presence with his height and a crisp white shirt that everyone noticed him. Especially women, who couldn't stop staring at him.

'Hi, nice to see you Monika,' he said reaching out for my hand to dance, and not letting me go for the rest of the night. We became inseparable.

'I'm a director for a global company and I spend a lot of time working in the Middle East,' he explained, when we sat down to catch a breath and have a sip of water. 'And what do you do?'

'I'm a pole dancer!' I replied, wondering if he would believe me and he must have, as he suddenly stopped smiling.

'I'm joking! I'm a sales manager!' I quickly clarified my silly joke.

But then, what if I were a pole dancer? Some women did that for a living. And I was a dancing Pole anyway. That was the beauty of English language, when the same word described two totally different things!

'Would you like to go for a coffee?' John asked when the lights switched on to indicate the end of the class.

'Now? Half past ten? It's bit late but… ok!' I replied.

Walking along the cobblestone streets, shivering from the sudden change in temperature on the frosty autumn night, we were looking for an open pub.

'He really did give it his all, tonight,' I thought when I sat down next to him and had a small glass of wine, not coffee, feeling his soaking wet sleeve touching my arm.

'I'm staying in the nearby hotel where I often play golf. I've been separated from my wife for four years,' he confessed, holding my hand tight under the large wooden table.

'Oh, I see,' I gasped, saddened that he was not truly a single man, and that it seemed to have been bad timing for us to have met then. But the desire get to know him more was stronger than any worries I had.

'Bye, Monika,' John said and placed a tender, warm kiss on my lips, holding my waist, just before I got into my car.

Wow, when will he kiss me again? I thought, waving at him as I drove off, feeling my heart jumping from joy to have met him, My Man, the man of my dreams.

CHAPTER 29 - STOPOVER

'A thousand half-loves must be forsaken
to take one whole heart home.'
-Rumi

'Hey Piddles, you can stay in my house for a few days, if you like. You are more than welcome!' said Alexander on the phone a few days later, when I had told him that I had no plans for my week off.

'Really? That would be nice.'

'Sure, just pick up the keys from my dad's. The weather is supposed to be nice so you can enjoy some time by the sea. I know how much you like it, I'm away working but will be back on Saturday, so I will see you then,' he continued.

'Great, I will do that, thank you, see you on Saturday,' I replied, grateful for his offer but a little bit worried that he might think it would mean something more, even though I had already set clear boundaries.

'Hey, Monika, how are you? Would you like to meet up again?' John texted me as soon as I had accepted Alexander's offer.

'Oh, I would have loved to, but I'm going to stay at my friend's house by the sea for a few days,' I replied, disappointed that he was late with his request.

'I can meet you in Weymouth, on the way, if you like?'

'Ok, that would be great!' I replied, happy he wanted to meet me in such distant location.

I got in the car, wearing my favourite beige shorts, nude heels and a nude silk blouse and drove to the centre of Weymouth, full of Georgian houses.

'Where are you?' I called him, walking along the sunny promenade by the blue sea.

'Look up the window!' he replied and when I looked up, I saw him waving at me in his turquoise T-shirt, smiling from ear to ear. 'Wait there, I'll come and get you.'

'You look gorgeous!' he exclaimed, walking up to me, lifting his sunglasses and grabbing my hands firmly to giving me a passionate kiss.

'Thank you, so do you!' I replied when he released me from his embrace.

He then helped me put my little travel bag in the hotel room, even though I wasn't planning to stay there, as I had a place to go to. Alexander's house. We sat on the beach half an hour later and John wrapped his arms around me whilst I was gazing at the never-ending vastness of the sea, feeling like the happiest woman in the world. I had never experienced a feeling like this before. I felt I had found my place on Earth. I never wanted to let him go, hoping to stay in his strong arms forever. I stood up and ran into the sea for a paddle, but he ran after me. We were splashing each other, excited to be running in the cold water, as if we were small children allowed to play in a puddle of mud after heavy rain. Every time I ran away from him, he followed me.

'John, I can't be with you,' I said, trying to be serious for a moment.

'Why?' he asked, frowning from surprise.

'Because you are still married!' I replied.

But he only embraced me tighter and kissed me tenderly. 'I love you!' he whispered softly in my ear, giving me shivers down my spine, through my legs and into my cold feet, sunk in the wet sand.

'I love you too!' I whispered back, blushing, hiding my face in his chest and inhaling the musky and woody smell of his perfume, making me dizzy from the unexpected feeling and confession from both him and me.

I hadn't said those words to anyone for years and I hadn't heard them from anyone either, including Adam or Adonis. Maybe because our relationships had not been love after all, but rather some kind of attachment. The only man who had ever said it to me was my first school sweetheart. After two years, however, he said he loved God more than me and became a priest, leaving me heartbroken for years and knowing I couldn't compete with… God. I actually started to worry I wouldn't be able to fall in love after being single for years, especially since the Greek tragedy, so this sudden passionate feeling for John was unstoppable and un-explainable.

In the evening, I changed into a black silk corset and a black skirt before we went out for dinner in an Italian restaurant, over-looking the marina at sunset. We sat face to face by the window in a secluded area, holding hands all the time as if they were glued together, kissing over the table, smiling and enjoying a delicious meal consisting of fresh lobster and Chardonnay.

'Why don't you stay with me tonight? Nothing will happen, I promise, I just want to fall asleep in your arms,' he said, taking an-other sip of wine, giving me a lascivious but at the same time, in-nocent gaze.

'Ok, let me think about it,' I replied, but having started another glass of wine, I knew I had already decided to stay as I couldn't drive now.

When we got back to the room, I jumped on the bed like a small child, excited to have so much space. John followed me, gently kissing and caressing my body. With every stroke of his fin-gertips, as if loaded with magnetism, he created the most passion-ate intimacy I had felt, as if our two souls had already known each other, making it such a familiar and comforting feeling that I wanted it to last till the morning. But I soon fell asleep in his arms and dozed off into sweet dreams.

***

'Would you like to stay another day?' John asked at breakfast, in an open air cafe on the sunny promenade, whilst I was enjoying the freshly baked croissant with strawberry *confiture*, a cappuccino and freshly squeezed orange juice.

'Yes, I would love that!!' I replied, pleased that he had asked.

'Great, let me see if I can prolong our stay,' he said.

I suddenly received a text from Alexander. 'Did you make it to the house last night?'

'Oh, no, John, what should I say to him?' I asked, confused about the whole unexpected and complicated situation.

'Well, just say the truth, that you have changed your mind. I'd like you to stay here with me, if you want that too?' he replied.

'Ok, I will.'

I replied to Alexander's message, 'Hi Alexander, I am really sorry but I will not be able to make it to the house. I'll return the key to your dad.' I felt guilty that I didn't go with the original plan, but how often does one find true love on the way to a friend's house, if ever?

'Let's go to Portland Island, shall we?' John asked when we finished our breakfast.

I nodded with a smile.

Driving towards Portland Bill, the most southern point on the island, I felt as if I had found myself in the Mediterranean, with quaint stone cottages in quiet villages, some of them made of the stone quarried here, appreciated for its whiteness and used to build some famous buildings around the world, including St. Paul's Cathedral and the UN Headquarters in Manhattan. Seeing the majestic rocks of this gigantic four-mile island, overlooking the immense vastness of the sea, glistening in the afternoon sun, I felt I'd found the place where the world ended. Kissing every time we looked at each other, walking along the tall cliffs, we met tourists who, upon seeing how much in love we were, offered to take pictures of us. We then had the delicious succulent fresh crab sandwich, sitting

MONIKA WIŚNIEWSKA

on a wooden bench close to the impressive red and white lighthouse which had been warning ships, passing through the English
Channel, for almost 300 years.

'This restaurant has the best view in England,' I concluded, in
awe of the scenic location.

Later, walking through the coastal moor, I noticed a secluded
spot, perfect for us to lie down in. John rested his head on my
chest and I could comb his thick hair with my fingers, gazing at
the clear blue sky, with not even one small fluffy white cloud in
sight. I couldn't feel happier in the moment. I was in love. I had
finally experienced what I had read in books and had watched in
romantic movies for all my younger years. This feeling seemed like
another 'face of love,' one which I had never experienced before
during any of my previous attempts to have relationships. It
seemed that they had only been an *entre* to what I was about to experience on the deepest spiritual level. They had simply been re-
hearsals before the finale of the Italian opera, with the Maestro of
life making it all finally happen for me.

At night, our traditional hotel room was full of twinkling reflections of the moonlight in the gentle sea ripples, as if playing a
midnight sonata by smoothly touching the keys of a piano. We
both stood by the window, slowly removing each other's clothes,
unwrapping each other's most precious gifts. John put his warm
and muscular arms around me, squeezing me tight, taking my
breath away. We marvelled at each other's naked silhouettes, staring at each other's eyes, feeling grateful to God that we had finally
met. Our bodies were entwined in the physical dance of two souls,
as if we were two Roman sculptures, brought together to create
one unified masterpiece of art. Every gentle stoke of the tips of his
fingers on my smooth skin and every tender kiss on my face and
neck felt like an electrifying current and a surreal experience of the
most magical physical connection between a man and a woman.
But it wasn't just physical. It was a sublime, erotic experience,
without the need for more. It wasn't needed and it wasn't neces-

sary. The warm presence of our bodies, wrapped in each other's arms, was more than what most people would call satisfying. It was more than I had ever experienced before. I knew, that this was the LOVE I'd been searching for all my life, making it the most magical and sensual experience that only Adam and Eve could have felt in Paradise.

We marvelled at the exquisite beauty of each other's physical bodies but saw each other's souls in the vortex of our eyes, taking us deeper than this physical dimension on Earth. The realisation that we were together for a reason made me want to explore it more and more. What was the reason, since we had met in not-so-perfect life circumstances, but feeling it was perfect regardless? As if life could ever be perfect, with the right place and the right time! In that moment, nothing else mattered, because for us, it was the perfect time and the perfect place, in our own centre of the universe. We became that centre for each other.

CHAPTER 30 - REALITY MIX

'Fancy lunch in Cookham, by a river?' John asked on the phone a few days later.

'I'd love to,' I replied and when he arrived in his black car, I waved at him from the balcony like Juliet happy to see her Romeo.

John seemed a bit distant in the car, but when we sat at a round wooden table in the restaurant patio by the river bank, overlooking the old bridge with green metal finishes, he finally put my hand into his, intertwining our fingers, and I knew we would be fine.

'I want to file for divorce, but I'm scared,' he said, looking at me with sad, teary eyes which showed how hard this decision was.

'Are you sure you want to get divorced?'

'Yessss,' he replied. 'I can't live in hotels anymore, just to avoid bad atmosphere in the house. But we've been married for so long and we have two lovely sons whom I don't want to hurt,' he added, confirming his internal battle with a decision that would change the rest of his life.

Gathering from his sad stories of how miserable his past few years had been, I could understand why he would finally want to do it. Nobody would want to live in such circumstances. His confession that his wife hadn't been working for years and was spending all their money, getting them into debt with credit cards from overspending and living over the top, despite his more-than-average, substantial salary, made me feel angry that such an amazing, loving man, had been treated so badly.

'I'm really sorry to hear how unhappy your life has been, feeling unloved and unwanted in your own home,' I said.

'Yes, I've really had enough. I need to change my life. I can't live like this any longer,' he replied with more confidence.

The reality we found ourselves in was not perfect but it didn't stop us from wanting to be together. I knew it might get tough, but it was nothing compared to the feelings we had for each other, and that was all that mattered.

***

'Hey, Moni, how are you?' John texted me, putting a smiley face at the end, when I was doing my weekly shopping a few days later.

'I'm great, thanks, and you? Where are you?' I replied, also with a smiley face.

'I'm in the house, just cooked some dinner for my wife and the son.'

'Oh, that's nice. So where are you going to sleep tonight?'

'I'll sleep in my bed. But don't worry, she'll be back late and we've slept like strangers next to each other for years. Nothing ever happens,' he replied, as if it was normal to sleep in the same bed with someone he wanted to divorce so desperately.

'I can't believe that you are going to sleep in the same bed with your wife and are telling me about it. It's not right, John,' I replied, feeling the blood rushing through my body, letting me know that I was in a situation I would have never wished to find myself in.

I then switched my phone off to avoid making a hasty decision that I might later regret. The next day, John called me and apologised, explaining that now he had moved to the spare bedroom, which sounded much better and it also meant I could continue seeing him. I knew I could trust his word and that he was honest with me. I knew once he had made his decision, he would stick to it, and that he had fallen in love with me as much as I had fallen in love with him.

A few days later, we went to Windsor. With only a few yellow leaves sprinkled on stripes of grass along both sides of the Windsor Great Park, we walked like tourists, taking hundreds of pictures of the largest and oldest castle still in continuous use for 900 years, supposedly the favourite residence of Queen Elizabeth II. The Royal Standard flag proudly swayed in the gentle breeze over the Round Tower, indicating the Queen's presence in the castle which was built by William the Conqueror in 1066, following his invasion of England. It was one of the many places I had learnt about during my studies in Poland and now I could admire it with my own eyes, touching the thick grey stone walls as if I was part of them, feeling a unique connection with every molecule of my body.

Walking hand in hand through the park, I watched hundreds of the Queen's deer at a distance, laying down in big herds. Stags with huge antlers looked majestically, as if to protect their territory, where hundreds of females were slowly chewing grass and relaxing in the afternoon sun.

'Are we watching them, or are they watching us?' I wondered, looking at their surprised look.

It was so quiet and peaceful that all I could hear were big metal birds flying above my head (the planes) and sweet, loving words whispered by John. 'I love you so much. You are so beautiful. I adore you!' he repeated softly in my ear, giving me shivers.

'And you are so handsome, I love your eyes, I love your smile, I love everything about you,' I replied, not really knowing where all these sudden words of admiration were coming from, directed at a man that I had only met a few weeks before, who had turned my whole world upside down, to what it had previously seemed, a happy single life.

'Let's have something to eat,' he said.

A divine lunch, fit for Greek Gods, whilst sitting opposite each other at a cute, square table outside a Greek tavern on one of the quaint cobblestone streets and close to the shortest street in England, Charlotte Street, was exactly what we needed on that warm autumn afternoon. Charlotte Street was just under 52 feet long and right by the Crooked House of Windsor, a visibly slanted seventeenth-century building which reminded me of the Leaning Tower of Pisa. John fed me delicious portions of the Greek mezze platter, of grilled halloumi, falafel, tzatziki, organic hummus and rice wrapped in vine leaves. I enjoyed it all, together with Greek white wine. We looked like cute puppy dogs from a cartoon, gazing at each other from underneath lashes, blushing, smiling and feeding each other. How could I have eaten all previous years without such a perfect little ritual? All those years suddenly seemed wasted, when eating food was just a simple way to survive and not to experience one of the most wonderful physical pleasures. Why did it taste so divine whilst being in love? Was this what love tasted like? Like a culinary heaven?

***

'Love is composed of a single soul inhabiting two bodies,'
-Aristotle

A month later, we flew to Scotland for a weekend away. John had received an invite to one of his friend's birthday parties, which meant we could stay in a romantic country hotel, just outside of Edinburgh, with glorious views of the city at night and the surrounding countryside.

When we came back from dinner, I wrapped his naked body on top of mine. 'How can I be sure that you will only be with me from now on?' I asked for assurance, before surrendering to him completely.

'Because, I'm committed to you. My wife knows I want a divorce. My marriage has been over for years. I only want you,' he replied with a calm voice, looking at me with his dreamy eyes, and I knew it was safe for me to surrender.

It was time for us.

Our two souls finally united.
From now on, we became One.
We became inseparable.

CHAPTER 31 - MILLIONS OF MILES APART

'At the touch of love, everyone becomes a poet.'
-Plato

'I miss you, baby!' John said on the phone each day when working abroad.

I felt connected to him on the deepest possible level. His love filled my whole being and this blissful feeling of love was with me day and night, no matter what distance he was and no matter how long he was away. His heart became part of my heart. I now had two hearts in my chest, beating together in perfect harmony. Every minute without him was both a pain and a blessing. I wished there were no times when we were apart, but I knew he was always there for me. It was the most intensive loving feeling I had ever felt in my life.

'Mama, he cares for me so much. He calls and emails me all day long and showers me with gifts to show how much he cares for me. He is wonderful,' I said on the phone.

'That's amazing, darling, I'm so happy for you. I can tell that he's really fallen in love with you, it's like he's gone crazy about you.'

'I know. He has gone crazy, and I love it!'

'A delivery for Miss Monika!' a young man announced when I opened the door to the most gorgeous bouquet of red roses with a note:

'Miss you so much!

You are the most beautiful and wonderful woman in the world.

Love, John.'

'Oh, John, thank you so much, what an amazing surprise!' I called him straight away to thank him for this most romantic gesture anybody had done for me.

A few days later, I received another bouquet with three red heart-shaped balloons and a box of 12 cupcakes which were all individually signed: 'I love you Monika x!'

I had never seen a more romantic confession in my life. What kind of man would order cupcakes with 'I love you' on all of them? I had never heard of any men capable of such romantic gestures. Until now. It obviously meant something. Maybe that he loved me so much that he didn't care if I put on weight?!

Another day, a wine case was delivered to my doorsteps, with my own designed label on them: 'The Wiśniewska House Red,' together with a box of red roses packed meticulously into a heart-shaped box. My own wine. From the Wiśniewska vineyards! Wow, now that was something else! Another day, a card attached to a flowers bouquet said:

'To Monika,

Your lips speak soft sweetness, your touch a soft caress,

I am lost in your magic, my heart beats within your chest.

All my love,

John.'

Gifts and notes and surprises like this made my heart sing from happiness, feeling cherished and adored by the most wonderful man in the world every single day. A month after we had met, John sent pictures from our trips to Weymouth and Windsor to a photographer and ordered a custom book with us on the cover. He then posted it to me. It was a delightful surprise. He put a lot of effort into showing how much he loved me. After all, gifts were one of the love languages and the element of surprise made our relationship alive and exciting.

One delivery, however, containing a small white box with a silver heart chain with a diamond, was most unexpected. I put it on immediately and I knew I would wear it for the rest of my life. John's heart was truly beating together with mine. I could always carry him with me and never feel lonely again. I had finally found the love I had been so desperately looking for all those years, dreaming about it, watching romantic movies and fairytales, giving me hope for the happily ever after for all women who wait for it out there. I hadn't been truly happy until I found true love. Until I found it in John.

***

'I can pick you up from the airport from now on!' I said to John who was to land at Heathrow Airport and take a taxi home.

I wanted to see him the moment he arrived, despite it being at five in the morning on Friday. I had no problem getting up at 4 am and drive to see My Most Loving Man, coming out of the arrivals, rushing to hug and kiss me. I would have never done it for any other man before. Until now.

'I've missed you so much, baby,' John said with tears in his eyes, pulling me to his body tightly and kissing me passionately, not caring if other people could see us.

'Welcome back! Come on, let's go home,' I replied, ecstatic to see him, tired after a long flight with sleepy but still-sparkling eyes.

'I don't want you to be living in a hotel. It costs a lot of money and you can stay here with me. My home is your home,' I said.

'Ok, thanks baby,' he replied and moved out of his house a few days later.

'Welcome home! I'm so happy we can be together now,' I greeted him at the door when he arrived with only a couple of bags with clothes and personal belongings, having left everything else in the house for his soon-to-be ex-wife.

I knew that this decision was very hard for him but sooner or later he would have done it anyway. I was glad I could help him get out of that miserable life he was living between working abroad and hotels and not having a loving happy home anymore. From now on, we were inseparable. We did EVERYTHING together and we could not stay even an hour without calling and texting.

'I miss you, baby!'

'I miss you too, my love!'

During his time in England, I went to work in the morning and John stayed at home, cooking and preparing the most romantic lavish dinners, always opening the door with the biggest smile, kissing and hugging me, gifting me with big bouquets of flowers and romantic cards expressing his deep affection, making me feel his love from the moment I entered the house.

I loved his surprise platters, filled with wild Scottish smoked salmon with capers, caviar, prawns with Marie Rose sauce, freshly prepared baby leaf salad with cherry tomatoes, grapes, strawberries, sprinkled with extra virgin olive oil and balsamic glaze, accompanied by a bottle of Sauvignon Blanc or Champagne, followed by a delicious dessert, such as chocolate mousse with raspberries and whipped cream. John prepared truly divine feasts which I appreciated at the end of a hard working day. He was the Dream Man, the sexiest, loving man on Earth who could cook and prepare the most delicious meals as if he was a Michelin star chef! He showed his appreciation with compliments and words of gratitude, he spent quality time with me giving me his unwavering attention, listened to me, to my feelings, dreams, stresses. He was the man every woman would have wanted in her life. And an amazing lover on top of that! I was the luckiest woman on Earth to have John in my life.

After dinner, we danced to our favourite blues music, in the living room, filled with warm flickering candlelight, love signs on the walls and pictures of us in silver frames. We were so full of passion for each other we often ended on the floor, not making it to the bedroom. Our sensual rituals of massaging our bodies with the most sensual strokes and heavenly smelling essential oils of black pepper, ylang ylang and rose, created an intimacy and a feeling that we couldn't live without each other. Our days and nights were filled with the most amazing loving moments I could have ever imagined. At the weekends, John surprised me with delicious crêpes Suzette, pancakes in a sauce made of orange juice, caramelised sugar, butter and orange liqueur, presented in a grand flambé performance. I loved adding whipped cream, not worrying about calories. They were so divine that I could eat them every morning for the rest of my life. John, looking suave, dressed in his best shirt, a casual navy jacket and brown suede trousers, invited me to the best restaurants.

'Are you ready for a night of a lifetime?' he asked in a husky voice.

I nodded, styling my hair into silky waves, putting on the most flattering make-up, a sexy dress and heels. When I sprayed my tuberose and jasmine perfume, feeling like a true princess taken out on a date by my Prince Charming, the most suave man I had ever met, he couldn't stay away. He grabbed my waist tight, inhaled the intoxicating, sensual fragrance and made a loud cry: 'Oh my God! You smell like heaven! I could eat you now!' to which I laughed and kissed him tenderly on his forehead, 'Ok, later. Now let me get ready!'

'I want to join the gym you go to and attend the same classes,' John said one day.

'Really? You would like that? That would be amazing!' I exclaimed.

Now we could work out, do yoga and swim in the pool together. After all, why do anything separately when we could not bear a minute being apart without missing each other so greatly. Getting into the Jacuzzi, after a cold shower to cool the hot body from the sauna session, I hoped we could be alone to have a moment for a nice chat. I loved the closeness of his body in the hot bubbly water, touching his wet hair, giving him a sneaky kiss on his wet neck when nobody was looking. I adored him, as much as he adored me.

'I heard that someone isn't feeling well and needs help,' I said to John with a cheeky smile opening the flat door when he returned from playing golf. It would not have been an unusual statement, if it wasn't for the fact that I was dressed in black heels, white suspenders and a white nurse mini-dress with a matching hat on my head. It was an outfit that John had sent me when working away, and I had finally found the right moment to surprise him.

'Oh, my dear God!' he replied, still standing outside the door, with eyes, sparkling as if they were fireworks on New Year's Eve.

'Come in, let me help you!' I replied with a husky voice, moving to the side of the open door, giggling at his reaction.

'Do you like it? I'm your nurse for the day!' I said, kissing him gently on his lips whilst he wrapped his arms around me and ran his fingers from my thighs up to the top of my neck as if checking if I was real and not just his fantasy.

'I love it! And I'm very unwell, I actually have a massive headache and a back pain,' he replied, pulling me by the hand towards the bedroom.

Fun days like this only made our relationship more multidimensional. It gave extra layers to it, as if there was nothing that we couldn't do to surprise each other. We were excited at the possibilities of exploring new things together, as if going into the unknown to see what else was waiting out there for us to discover.

We also continued dancing every week at local venues. After all, that was how we had met, how God had wanted us to meet. We loved dancing to both slow and fast music. When my favourite songs came on, I went mental. I had so much energy in me that I was unstoppable. We were swirling around as if we were the only ones on the dance floor.

'Baby, I thought you would rip my arms off! You were on fire!' he gasped, seeming completely out of breath.

'You look great together! Lovely couple!' one lady said, after having watched us dancing, something that happened quite often. Our connection was unreal, an inseparable bond of two human beings dancing to the melody of life.

'I can't wait to snuggle up in our bed with you, Mr!' I whispered in his ear, deeply inhaling the scent of his perfume on his hot skin, the biggest aphrodisiac to my senses.

'Ok, let's go now!'

'No, one more song and maybe then you can take your lady from the dance floor and drive her home safely!' I replied, with a smirk.

'Yes, Ma'am.'

Flirting with the man I loved always made things more exciting, and showing that we cared about each other, adored each other's company and expressed it in a genuine and open manner, all created a bond that nobody would be able to destroy. Every couple's dream. To be happy, indestructible and last forever.

' There are two ways to a woman's heart.
One is easy and one is difficult.
You can either show her genuine admiration for her beauty of body and soul
or
you can be horrible and sarcastic, hoping she won't hit you with a frying
pan.
The choice is yours,'
- Monika Wiśniewska

Chapter 32 - Two Sides to Every Coin

'No man is free, who cannot control himself.'
-Pythagoras

'I don't think she'll be nice to you once she realises that her "luxurious lifestyle" and living off your salary is going to finish, especially now that you've told her you have someone,' I said to John, after he had tried to convince me that the divorce was going to go smoothly.

Unfortunately, my words turned out to be a prophecy. John's soon-to-be ex-wife turned vicious when he slowly cut off the unlimited tap of money supply, leaving her with a fixed allowance which was still three times bigger than my salary as a manager. But she moaned that it wasn't enough to cover all her costs, including the hairdresser's, manicure, pedicure and holidays. John finally got the courage to tell her to find a job and even helped improve her CV. She had stopped working years before because John had been earning a lot of money and she hadn't felt the need to work.

John was naive enough to think that now she would suddenly get a job and become independent of him, so that they could go separate ways in peace and start a new life. But he couldn't be more wrong in his assumption. He thought she would be kind to him and mature enough to take the pressure off him, after all those years of marriage, but my intuition was telling me that it would never happen. He wouldn't listen to my warnings, though, repeating that he knew her better. Soon, he became acrimonious with sudden outbursts of anger, especially after visits to his solicitor. He also had to pay for his wife's solicitor in order to get divorced, so essentially paying for two, fighting against each other.

One night, I was sitting with John on the sofa, not knowing what to do, crying together with him, till it got completely dark, as neither of us put the lights on. Days like this became more and more frequent. I didn't know how to help him, other than being next to him.

'It will all be fine. I'm sure, it will be. Don't worry. No matter what happens, remember I will always love you,' I said, resting his head on my chest.

I could feel his enormous pain and I suffered as much as he did, but sometimes, I didn't have enough energy to cheer him up. I tried my best, but our arguments became more and more exhausting.

'Just stop giving her money and she will have to get a job. Simple!!!' I exclaimed from the kitchen, trying to cook dinner.

'I can't do it! By law I need to give her everything!' he shouted back and closed the bedroom door with a loud bang.

His sons were another reason for arguments. One evening, during our romantic dinner, he was just staring at his plate as if he was in a different world, drowning in thoughts.

'What's wrong?' I asked repeatedly, but he didn't reply, so I walked up to him to hug him, holding his head close to my belly, gently stroking his hair.

'I love you. It will all be fine. Don't worry.'

'My younger son doesn't want to work either, living together in the house with his mother who doesn't work. Now he also doesn't want to talk to me!' he finally mumbled.

'Well maybe if you stop giving him such a huge monthly allowance he will also have to find a job then!' I suggested, feeling helpless and frustrated by the situation I could do nothing about.

'I don't want to talk about him!!' he shouted.

Without finishing my meal, I took my car keys and left the house. I had to get away or I would have suffocated. I couldn't look at the man I loved so much in such a miserable state, staring aimlessly, stuck in his own scary world, unable to communicate calmly. I drove to the nearby supermarket car park and wept in the car. It was a dark winter evening and pouring with rain. I felt he blamed me for his miseries. I hated when he turned against me like this, with violent outbursts of anger directed at me. It took me an hour to calm down before I could get back home and sneak into bed, which was empty. I got up and looked in the spare bedroom. He was sleeping there. For the first time.

The next day, we made up. Arguing was heartbreaking for me. I stood so close to him in the kitchen that my nose was touching his cheek, but he avoided my eyesight. I closed my eyes and rapidly opened them, staring straight into his, as if I had seen something unexpected, making his lips slightly move, showing a tiny smile. When I did it again, he finally burst out laughing.

'Stop it, baby' he muttered, trying to be a serious tough guy but when I repeated my funny eye move one more time, his cold demeanour melted and he gave me a warm kiss. We were fine again.

'I'm sorry. Please let's not argue anymore. I'll always be here for you, no matter what happens. Remember that,' I whispered, wrapping my arms around him.

The pain of arguing was unbearable because I felt it with every molecule of my body and soul. My biggest despair, though, was my lack of knowledge on how to help John ease his suffering. I'd never gone through a divorce myself and seeing how it had affected him, I prayed that I never would. I didn't realise that it could be so painful. I swore to myself I would never get divorced once I got married, and that I would do anything to keep the love and commitment alive and never, ever give up. Obviously, that kind of commitment would only be possible from myself, as there would be no way I could control another person's behaviour. I could only do my own best and commit to being the best I could, hoping that my man would do to the same.

Another cold autumn night, I left the flat in the middle of a full-blown argument. It was pouring with rain which joined my flood of tears while I was walking aimlessly along the dark streets. I needed to calm down, trying to make sense of our intensive arguments. I suddenly noticed John on the other side of the street, walking in the opposite direction. He stopped, looked at me with teary eyes and continued walking. How could he look at me from the other side of the street as if I was a complete stranger and walk away in the opposite direction? I thought to my horror. When I'd returned home, I went straight into my cold and empty bed. How can we be so close to each other in one moment and act like enemies and complete strangers the next? Our arguments are only because of his issues with divorce. Not ours as a couple. Why do we need to deal with it? I thought with desperation.

When he came back from his night walk, I heard him standing in the hallway, so I got up and dragged him, holding his hand, to the bedroom, tucking him into bed, like a good mother would with a small child. We hugged and fell asleep, as if nothing had happened. Nothing had happened after all. It was just another day. No relationships were ever perfect and things like that could happen, right?

CHAPTER 33 - BIG EARS

'I would love to go to Poland with you in December to meet your family,' John said one day, knowing he had to work during Christmas but still wanting to experience delicious food and Polish hospitality.

'Are you serious?' I would love that! I'll be so happy if you come with me! How splendid!' I exclaimed.

My mama was thrilled about having earlier Christmas together with John, whom she was really looking forward to meet. Within days, she had already made a list of all the traditional dishes she wanted to prepare.

John, ever since I had met him, had always made the effort to look his best and I loved the way he looked and dressed but one day he surprised me, though. 'Look, baby, I bought this hair dye for men,' he said, showing me a box with a picture of a man with dark hair, whilst standing in the kitchen.

'You don't need it! You look handsome as you are!' I replied, smiling, trying to give him more confidence in his model looks.

'I want to cover my grey hair! For you!' he insisted, so I did it for him and the colour turned out to be very natural and all his grey hair was gone. We were now ready to meet the parents the next day.

Our flight to Bydgoszcz turned out to be a bit scary. Just before we were about to land, the plane started to circle around the airport due to very heavy snow and strong wind, making us rattle inside. The pilot announced that the visibility was very bad and that we would need to fly to another airport, in Gdansk. John wasn't happy about it because he didn't feel very well during the whole flight, suffering from a headache and holding his head with hands. I didn't know what was wrong with him. I worried he wouldn't want to go to Poland again because of our re-route. When we had finally landed, we got on the bus which was to transport us back to Bydgoszcz, where my mama was patiently waiting with our neighbour, Jarek, who had kindly offered to pick us up from the airport.

'We are on the bus from Gdansk now and we should be there in about three hours. Can you please wait?' I asked her on the phone, and she agreed but the journey on a bus in the dark, freezing cold and snowy weather, with John holding his head, suffering from some weird pain, was the last thing I would have wanted for him as his first experience to meet my family. When we got to Bydgoszcz, I was relieved.

'Hello, John!' Mama said in perfectly practised-with-me English, giving him a warm hug.

'Hello, Mama,' he replied in such a sweet way that it melted my heart.

'What's wrong with him?' she asked in the car, driving through the countryside which was completely covered by a few inches of snow.

'I don't know. He has got a strange headache,' I replied, having noticed that his ears had become swollen.

Oh no, it's not looking good, I thought, without saying anything as I didn't want to worry him.

When we finally got home, she gave us *barszcz*, the beetroot soup and *pierogi*, the dumplings with mushrooms. We then went to sleep in the spare bedroom upstairs, but John woke up in the middle of the night, making me terrified about his health.

'What's happening, *kochanie*? Tell me,' I asked, touching his back, which seemed very hot under his T-shirt.

'I'm not well,' he replied, holding his head in both hands.

'Ok, that's it, we are going to the hospital. Get dressed! I'll wake up mama and stepdad,' I replied, scared that it was getting serious.

'It looks like *alergia*,' the duty doctor suggested an allergy.

'He dyed his hair yesterday,' I confessed, wondering if it could be a clue.

'Ah *tak*, so that's what it is! He wants to look younger?' the doctor replied with a grin.

'Umm *tak*, he does!' I replied, laughing, but gazing at John's not-so-amused face, I quickly stopped. Thank God he doesn't understand Polish, I thought.

A nurse gave him a massive injection in his backside whilst I was holding his hand tight, as if he was undergoing a life-threatening operation.

'Ok, done. The allergic reaction should disappear in a day,' she said, with calm confidence, making John smile as soon as I'd translated it into Polish.

'*Dziękuję bardzo*,' he thanked her, making her smile at his cute Polish accent.

When we got back home, we all sat in the kitchen to have a cup of tea. John's big ears made him look like a cute fennec fox. I tried not to laugh, but every time Mama looked at me, with a well-known expression of trying to hold it together although she was about to burst out laughing, I almost lost it. I knew she thought the same. But it wouldn't be nice to laugh at someone because of his swollen ears. Not a noble act at all!

John's big ears went back to their normal size the next day and he could enjoy his stay for the next few days. Trying to look younger had come at a cost. I explained to John that I accepted him for who he was, regardless of grey hair but what he needed to do first, was to accept himself in his own eyes. Not always a simple thing to do!

CHAPTER 34 - INTERVIEW

'We need to come back here!' John exclaimed, looking with astonishment at Waddesdon Manor, the most spectacular country house he had ever seen in England.

This magnificent residence was built in style of a French chateau from the Loire Valley for Baron Ferdinand de Rothschild in the 1870s, mainly to serve as an entertainment for the rich and famous, including Queen Victoria, who was supposedly very impressed by the electric lights which looked like candles in massive crystal chandeliers. The Wine Cellars, containing a private collection of over 15,000 bottles of wine, many with specially designed labels by great artists, made us want to come back there for a wine tasting experience, which couldn't be in a more perfect setting.

It was January but it still wasn't as cold as the weather we had experienced in snowy Poland. We walked around the gardens, where statues were now covered by white cloths, protecting them from any possible damage from low temperatures. In the house itself, we admired priceless collections of furniture, textiles, books, paintings and porcelain, gasping in amazement every time we'd entered another room. The ostentatious East Gallery displayed the incredible automation of an elephant statue, ridden by an Emperor, playing music when the key to the side was turned. It was a marvellous artefact made of bronze and mother of pearl, a true masterpiece from centuries before.

'Look at that clock! Look at that painting! Wow!' I exclaimed with childlike excitement, pointing at more and more magnificent pieces of art.

'It's beautiful!' John said, standing next to a marble sculpture of a lady with a hat on. 'But not as beautiful as you!' he added, gently kissing my neck, giving me shivers as if an electric shock ran through my body.

I loved when he complimented me. In moments like this, we lived in a world with no worries or problems. We were in a different world. Stunning, opulent and full of possibilities. In moments like this, we were happy and nothing else mattered. Waddesdon Manor often had special exhibitions, which sometimes meant walking down a path where a meters-tall chair, split in half by a giant box of cigarettes would suddenly appear in front of our eyes. Or where millions of tiny colour-changing lights were planted along the woodland paths, transporting us into the fairytale setting of an enchanted forest.

'I want to apply for a job based in Holland. What do you think?' John asked.

'Oh, that would be amazing! But does it mean you would have to live there?'

'Yes, but I want you to move there with me. Would you like that? Do you want to live in Holland?'

'I would love that. Yes, let's do it. Let's leave this country and just move there,' I replied, having had enough of living in England.

Being close to John in Holland, once we had dealt with the divorce, sounded like a perfect solution. I was getting more and more tired with his daily calls when he complained about his job whilst working abroad for months. Moving away to another country seemed like the best thing to do. We could start over fresh. All he needed to do, was get the job.

***

'How did the interview go?' I asked John after a day of walking on the beach in the Hague whilst he was interviewed by the vice president of the company in the head office.

Walking along the sea front, we found an open air cafe with glass walls, protecting us from the freezing winter wind. The wooden tables with built-in gas fires kept us warm, so that we could sip fresh mint tea and eat traditional Dutch apple strudels with whipped cream.

'I was put forward for the next stage, so it looks very promising,' John said, rubbing my hand to make it warm.

'I'm so excited for you. It will be a great promotion. And you won't have to suffer in that horrible place in the Middle East anymore,' I said, happy it had gone well.

Being close to Amsterdam, we decided to visit it for a day, but once we got there on the train, it was so cold that all we wanted to do was to hide in warm places, such as the Sex Museum, full of the most bizarre sex objects collected over the years one could imagine. Seeing the tall statue of Venus at the very entrance and huge plastic phalluses, we knew it would be a fun place to see and it was indeed full of interesting art collections about human sexuality. After a boat cruise along the seventeenth century canals, admiring the cute narrow houses with gabled facades, watching locals riding bikes like pros, we felt completely frozen and dreamt of sitting in a warm restaurant, drinking hot chocolate. Afterwards, we walked past half naked girls in large shop windows with adjacent rooms which resembled cubicles. Not the nicest view to see and not entirely what I'd expected from the famous Red Light District.

'They all look so young,' I whispered into John's ear when we were walking through it.

'Yes, you're right. They shouldn't be here,' he agreed.

'What's with those mushrooms for sale in shops?' I asked.

'They are happy mushrooms! Drugs. Do you want to try them?' he asked with a smile.

'No thanks. The last thing I need is drugs,' I replied, even though I regretted not trying them since they were perfectly legal in Holland.

On the train back to the hotel, John became stressed again.

'What is it?' I asked, worried.

'It's the solicitors. I hate them!' he shouted loudly and I looked around, hoping that nobody could hear him.

The divorce was a never-ending story. I was desperate for it to finish, especially before we moved to Holland. It was a burden which no couple would've wanted to carry on their shoulders, but seemed an intrinsic part of ours. Trying to build the future, with baggage from an unfinished past, was not the best way for love to grow. And it certainly didn't help.

CHAPTER 35 - GYPSY

'I'm going on a professional golf training course in Spain! Do you want to come with me?' John asked, to my delight, one day.

'Yes, sounds great! I've never been to Alicante!' I replied, as it was a great opportunity for us to get away for a few days.

I packed all my best summer dresses and a new pink bikini. It was only springtime but I was hoping the weather would be hot. We checked into the hotel by a golf course where John would spend his days, getting trained. All I could do was relax by the pool or get a taxi into town. We did manage to spend the first day together though, walking along the marina and getting on board an old pirate ship, a replica of an eighteenth century Spanish galleon, with tall masts. John took a picture of me pretending to be a royal, sitting on Neptune's throne.

'Take a picture of me on a cannon!' John exclaimed.

'Look, there are swings on the beach. Shall we try them before we see the castle?' he asked, wrapping me with his big arms when we were looking at the spectacular views of white yachts in the port.

I nodded, grinning. Having a laugh on the swings and feeling like a small child sounded like the perfect idea. The day was hot and all I was wearing was my bikini under a see-through turquoise beach dress, longer at the back and shorter at the front, freely flowing in the wind and perfectly matching the colour of the sea. The castle of Santa Barbara, on top of Mount Benacantil, had the most breathtaking views of the town, the harbour and the turquoise sea on the horizon. It used to be a medieval fortress but now it served as a background to my photo session with John. I tried posing like a professional model, showing off my long, tanned legs with my dress flowing in the wind as if it was singing to a gentle melody of Spanish heat, summer and romance.

'Look at me! Here, yes, very good!' John encouraged me to pose for the camera in this magnificent setting.

'You look like a goddess! You are my goddess!' he said, grabbing my waist and kissing me passionately, in between photo shots.

We finished the day drinking our favourite martini and mojito cocktails, relaxing on white leather sofas by the beach bar, overlooking the harbour, bathed in the reddish sunset. Afterwards, we had dinner in one of the local seafront restaurants serving a seafood platter packed with fresh oysters with lemon juice, crispy calamari, prawns in garlic, lobster and crab meat. We were eating this divine feast, gazing into the evening darkness of the marina, which was now full of twinkling lights.

'*Salut!*' John raised his wine glass.

'To an amazing time in Spain! And to your golf coach certification!' I clinked his glass, smiling.

Having gone for a walk on the beach afterwards, John suddenly picked me up in a piggy back style. 'What are you doing' I exclaimed, laughing, but he had already started running, with me jumping up and down on his broad shoulders along the beach.

Laughing and gazing upon the luminous stars above, I thanked God for this craziest, strongest and most wonderful man on Earth. Walking back through the old town, we stumbled across the water which shot up from various places on the square floor, and we bet who would avoid getting wet. I won. John got his trousers soaked at the last attempt, looking sweetly embarrassed that he had lost. He never liked losing.

The next morning, I was browsing the Internet on John's tablet when a new email popped up. It was from his soon-to-be ex-wife, complaining how unhappy she was, asking for more money and trying to make him feel guilty for leaving her and his sons who were also missing him. I got very upset. He had told me that their communication was only through solicitors now, but from the way he was replying to her, made me wonder if he still had feelings for her.

Does he still love her? Maybe he would go back to her? I thought, horrified.

When I sat on the beach later, I texted him that I wanted to go back home.

'Why, baby? I'll go with you, I don't care about the course,' he said after called me immediately.

'Don't be silly, it's important to you, I want you to be a golf coach.' I tried to calm him down, unsure of what to think of my own contradicting emotions.

***

Playing golf was John's biggest passion. Apart from me, of course. He sometimes took me to the golf club so that I could practice with him, showing me how it was done, but I wasn't that great. I might have looked like a professional golfer after he had dressed me head to toe in the right golf clothes, white trousers, pink shoes, a T-shirt and a white leather glove. But the sad reality was that I could hardly hit the ball. I did hit it in the end, but I had missed it many times, before I finally did it, making it fly a few meters forward. Most balls ended in the next door player's space, as if they could magically make a turn in the air. Strange how that happened!

How can anyone hit that tiny little ball on the ground with such a long metal stick, right from above their head and do it perfectly, at the right angle? I thought with frustration, appreciating John's skills even more.

It was one of the toughest sports I had ever tried in my life. But it didn't stop me from enjoying the Scottish Open with John a month before we went to Alicante and one hilarious moment when were walking along the wet surface next to the marquee.

'Be careful, baby! It's very slippery here!' he warned me but before I'd even had a chance to reply, I saw him slide down to the mud, covering his white golf trousers in black streaks, but lifting himself by holding my hand within seconds and continuing to walk next to me, as if nothing had happened.

'John, what was that? Your whole back and trousers are dirty. We need to get it cleaned,' I said, shocked by his suave demeanour as if I wouldn't have noticed anything.

I tried to stay serious and not laugh when he walked into the men's toilet. 'Not the best weather for white trousers, mate!' some man said, walking past and laughing, making John's cheeks red.

'Don't worry, it will wash off,' I comforted him, once he came out, but he didn't have a good mood for the rest of the day.

The next day we went for a boat trip on a lake, drinking the strongest Scottish whiskey, making me cringe and John laughing at me every time I had sipped it. I kept looking for the Loch Ness Monster—and I found it! It was huge, purple with a long neck and standing close to a boat house.

'I always knew Nessie existed!' I exclaimed, hugging my 'purple Scottish monster'.

***

The moment John had told me that since I was upset, he would go back to England with me, I stopped imagining that he would go back to his wife and I spent the rest of my day on the beach. On my way to the taxi rank in the evening, along the seaside promenade, an older lady, with long black hair and wearing a long, red dress, holding a bunch of red roses, walked up right in front of me, making me stop.

'One euro only! One euro! Please!' she begged, putting a red rose in my hand, without giving me a chance to say 'No.'

When I opened my wallet, she dived into it to look for the euro coin, making a loud noise from touching the coins, and being so quick that I couldn't even object. 'You see? One euro!' she said with a smile, showing me the coin.

I took the rose and walked away. When I reached the taxi, I looked into my purse to check if I had enough money but the folded €300 that John had given me were gone.

I called John immediately, 'Some woman stole all my money!'

'What woman? Don't worry, it's only money. Are you ok, baby?' he said with worry in his voice.

'Yes, I am, don't worry,' I replied, glad to hear how much he cared about my safety.

'Get a taxi and come to the hotel. I'll pay the taxi driver when you get here, just call me and I'll come out of the classroom, ok?'

I was relieved to see him, walking up to the taxi. I hugged him, feeling guilty I had lost the money out of stupidity.

'Don't worry, it happens. I love you,' he hugged me tight, making me instantly feel better.

My worries that he could go back to his wife seemed silly in that moment. After all, he did care about me and my wellbeing and he expressed his love in the most wonderful way, bailing me out of a taxi ride after having been robbed. He was the real knight in shining armour that any woman would loved to have in her life. For me, that was a sign of true love.

CHAPTER 36 - CITY ON FIRE

'How about we go to Vienna?' John asked, making me happy at the very thought.

When we arrived at the five star hotel on Kahlemberg mountain three weeks later, we walked onto our presidential suite balcony, covered with dark wooden decking, wrapped by a glass balustrade, and we marvelled at the spectacular views. The opulent bathroom, tiled with luxury cream marble tiles, containing a large bath with golden taps, was big enough for us to bathe together.

'Shall we explore the city?' John asked, shielding my body from behind whilst I was looking at the most beautiful view of Vienna, split in half by the river Danube.

'I can't wait!' I replied, kissing him tenderly on his warm neck, deeply inhaling whiffs of his favourite perfume with vivacious notes of pepper and fresh spices of cedar and patchouli, making me dizzy from love again.

It was a hot summer day so I put on my short blue lace dress and red sandals, and after a quick coffee on the hotel panorama terrace, we walked outside to wait for the taxi. Kahlemberg mountain had been made famous by the Polish king Jan III Sobieski who had rushed to Austria with his army and had quickly won the Battle of Kahlemberg in 1683, liberating Vienna from Turkish occupiers who had besieged the city for over two months. If it hadn't been for our courageous Polish king and his army of 20,000 heavy riders, including 3,000 elite winged hussars, the Ottoman Empire could have ruled Western Europe and the Turkish language would have been widely spoken in many more countries! Jan III Sobieski entered the city of Vienna in full glory, paraphrasing the famous Julius Caesar quotation by saying: 'Venimus, vidimus, Deus vicit.' ('We came, we saw, God conquered.') I had always been amazed by the bravery of the Winged Hussars who, in my opinion, were the most beautiful cavalry in the world, with their shining armour, brightly-coloured heraldry and long wings made of ostrich or eagle feathers attached to their backs, making a loud whistling noise to unsettle and terrify the enemy. They had never lost one battle in 125 years, even against enemies five times larger. Unfortunately, just under a century later, the only token of gratitude Poland had received was being invaded and having our land stolen. But that was a different story, altogether. Sobieski's name was clearly visible on the commemorative sign of the Baroque church, close to the hotel, now run by the Polish priests. I felt proud to be Polish and a nation of true, brave fighters. What a wonderful king we had! The sign next to it commemorated the visit to the church of Pope John Paul II in 1983.

The taxi ride down the mountain gave us amazing views of the city.

'What is this wonderful smell?' I asked John, holding his hand, breathing in the fresh hot air, saturated with the most unusual aroma, knowing that it definitely was not his perfume.

'It smells like garlic,' he replied, but with little certainty in his voice.

'Umm, garlic flowers? That's new to me!'

When we arrived in the city centre, I was astounded by the tall buildings accompanied by magnificent, white, Roman-looking sculptures with fierce face expressions, some of them, as if crying out, begging to be taken away from the flames of hell.

This is what Rome must feel like! I thought, looking at marvellous pieces of art everywhere.

Our first stop had to be in a sunny cafe, in the middle of a large square, where we had two large ice coffees with whipped cream on top and giant waffle cones, overflowing with the most delicious Italian ice cream.

'Shall we go for a ride in a horse-drawn carriage?' John asked, winking.

'Oh, I would love that. Let's go!' I replied and when we walked up to the first carriage with a white horse, the lady 'driver', with blond hair and a bowler hat, invited us to sit on luxury black leather seats.

Our tour around the city landmarks allowed us to admire the most impressive architecture, statues and countless fountains, gushing with water high up in the air, providing a gentle refreshment to the Viennese people in the summer heat. Our lady tour guide kept turning her head around to tell us stories about the historic buildings we were passing but since she spoke with a strong Viennese accent, we looked at each other with confusion.

'Did you get it?' I asked John, unsure if it was just me not being able to understand a word she was saying.

'No, I didn't. Did you?' he replied, making us both burst out laughing simultaneously, but it didn't stop us from enjoying the most magnificent and romantic ride any couple could experience on a perfect summer day, with the sun and wind caressing our skin, making us feel as if we were royalty on a regular carriage ride in nineteenth century Vienna, on our route to visit the Emperor in the palace.

'*Kocham Cię*,' John whispered to my ear with his sunglasses on, reflecting shining window displays in the sunshine.

'I love you more!' I replied, kissing him on his warm lips and inhaling his perfume, mixed with the pheromones of his skin.

Our camera was on fire as we took over 300 pictures—even our carriage reflection in shopping windows.

The sun started to sink behind the tall buildings when we later wandered along the streets, not caring where our feet would take us. We found a perfect spot, a riverside bar, where we rested on white rattan chairs with velour cushions, drinking Champagne and having local snacks, looking at the sunset reflected in the calm surface of the river and enjoying a cooling evening breeze, a pure delight after a hot day.

'*Na zdrowie!* Cheers! I love you so much!' John said a thousandth time.

I knew John loved me. I could feel it. He said it ten, twenty times a day and I was never bored with it. I had never experienced love like this before. So intense, and so true.

'You are my soulmate! I can't live without you!' he added.

'And you are mine!' I replied, knowing in the core of my being it was the one and only truth that he was the man I was supposed to be with for the rest of my life.

I kept gazing at the Celtic symbol of love he had sent me a month into our relationship and turning it around my finger, as if I were casting a magic spell to make this moment last forever. The silver ring was engraved with 'I WILL ALWAYS LOVE YOU,' and when it had been delivered a few weeks before, I was ecstatic, as I had never met a man showing his feelings in such an open and honest way before.

'Shall we get the taxi to the hotel?' John asked at twilight.

'Can we first go for a walk, please? I want to see the city at night' I begged, knowing it would be amazing to see the city lit up with millions of lights.

He agreed but he wasn't too happy, dragging his feet, tired from walking around the city all day. When we got back to the apartment, I walked out to the balcony and tears flooded my eyes. John switched the lights on in the living room.

'Please, don't! Come and see this,' I asked.

He switched them off and stood behind me, hugging me tight, nuzzling his nose against my hair to inhale my tuberose and jasmine perfume.

'Look at this view! It's magnificent!' I gasped.

'Oh yes, it is splendid, indeed!' he replied in husky voice, kissing my neck tenderly, giving me electrifying shivers, as always.

The view of Vienna at night was breathtaking. It was spectacular during the day but this was something special now. I was thrilled to be there with the best man on Earth, watching the flickering lights in the distance and the gentle warm evening breeze, caressing my face, making it feel surreal. The city, lit up with a million lights, made it look as if it was glaring with fire. John went back inside to take a shower but I stayed and stared at the sky, sprinkled with stars, feeling like just a small dot in the vastness of the universe.

'Thank you, God! Thank you for this amazing life I have and this most wonderful man!' I said, silently.

'I want to sleep outside!' I whispered to snoring John, unable to fall asleep.

'What? Are you sure?' he asked with a sleepy and surprised voice.

'Yes, please,' I replied, so we took our pillows, two duvets and lay them on the balcony, using one of them as a mattress and the other one as a cover.

John was spooning me with his warm body when I was gazing through the clear glass, touched by the unbelievable beauty of the view to the core of my being, making me tearful. Crickets played an exclusive, goodnight serenade on top of the world, right up in the clouds for just the two of us, as we snuggled under the warm cover.

'I want you!' I whispered in his ear and he looked at me with disbelief, lifting his head, speechless. 'Yes, now. Nobody will know!' I whispered, nodding with a smirk.

It was such an idyllic setting that we couldn't let that chance get away. What if we never had it again? Not many people could say they made love on the balcony, overlooking Vienna at night. John made my wish come true but kept gazing at other balconies in case he heard any suspicious sounds. I was running my fingers through his thick hair, gently touching his face and kissing him tenderly, wrapping myself around him, hoping he would never let me go from this embrace.

'You always take me to heaven and back' I whispered, gazing at the vastness of the sky and luminous stars, thanking God for this moment of unreal body and soul connection.

CHAPTER 37 - FAIRYTALE

'Music and rhythm find their way into the secret places of the soul.'
-Plato

'I can't wait to see the palace!' I said to John at breakfast on the restaurant terrace, overlooking the perfectly visible city in the morning, including the grounds of the palace, nestled in it.

'And the live Strauss concert!' John added, pouring more coffee into my white china cup.

'Oh, especially that,' I replied, hearing the birds chirping in the pine trees on the hills, putting another slice of smoked salmon and brie on the crispy freshly-baked roll, before sipping the delicious Viennese coffee and, of course, a glass of Champagne.

Visiting Vienna gave us an amazing opportunity to see a live concert in the city where Johann Strauss II himself had been born. We couldn't have chosen a better place. Thinking about Strauss made me reflect, as he had never given up on his passion to compose and play music, despite the fact that when he was a child, his father punished him for it, wanting to force him choose a different career. In spite of his father's discouragement, Strauss became one of the most famous composers of all time, knowing it was his one and only passion which he pursued, no matter what obstacles. If he had given up and worked as a bank clerk, the world would have missed out on the magical melodies of the 'King of Waltz'.

But many years before Strauss, Schönbrunn Palace had witnessed a six-year-old Mozart giving his first concert for Maria Theresa, the only female head of the Habsburg Dynasty. She was a beautiful and powerful woman who played an important role in the era of enlightened absolutism. She supported human rights, compulsory schooling and transformed Schönbrunn, a wedding gift from her father and originally a hunting lodge, into a magnificent palace where she brought up Marie Antoinette, the future wife of King Louis XVI and 15 other children. A truly impressive woman of her time! Especially because of that number of children! But she wasn't perfect. Oh, no. Nobody ever was. As a strict Catholic, she was very intolerant towards other religions and introduced a chastity court where they charged prostitutes, homosexuals and adulterers who were punished severely for immorality. She did not charge her own husband though, even though he was guilty of unfaithfulness. Maybe she gave a blind eye to his immoral conduct because she loved him? The things women could forgive in the name of love!

When the taxi drove us down the mountain, with all the windows open, I could smell the unusual smell of garlic flowers saturating the air again. John checked his phone and turned his face to the window, crying.

'What's happened?' I asked.

'It's my son. He sent me a message that I'm not a good father,' he muttered, wiping his tears.

'You're not a bad father. You know it's not true. He is obviously upset,' I replied, but he only released my hand and I felt I was drowning in his misery again, suffering as much as he was.

When we got out of the taxi, we slowly walked up the front gate of the palace.

'Do you need tickets, sir?' the man asked cheerfully, a huge contrast to John's tone of voice in the taxi.

'No, thanks, we've already got them,' John replied, in an official way, as if upset that the man had even dared to ask him the question.

'You look so beautiful together! Beautiful couple!' the man continued, with a strong Viennese accent, staring at us grinning.

'Thank you' I replied, gazing at John, amused, as we had always made an impression on people, especially when we were dressed up. We were both tall, and today I was wearing heels, but even then, John was still taller. My pink mini dress matched the pink necklace, and a beaded hair band on my auburn hair shimmered in the sun—at least, that's what John had always said.

When we entered the grounds, I gasped. A magnificent Baroque palace, 1,441 rooms, in pale yellow, with hundreds of large windows and dressed in black shutters, unveiled in front of my eyes. The crystal clear blue sky reflected its beauty in full glory and I knew I had arrived home. This was the life I was meant to be living. Maybe I had lived there in my previous life? It all seemed very familiar. The name 'Schönbrunn' meant 'beautiful spring'—referring to the artesian well from which the water for the palace used to be drawn. It was a summer residence of the Habsburgs where Emperor Franz Joseph, the longest-serving Emperor of Austria, and Empress Elisabeth, or 'Sisi', lived happily, until she was assassinated during one of her travels in 1898, by an Italian anarchist in Geneva.

Inside the palace, I marvelled at one stunning room after another, full of Rococo style furniture of master craftsmanship and walls covered in mammoth paintings. We walked through the Vieux Laque Room, where Napoleon held his conferences, and the stunning Millions Room, panelled with intricate rosewood from India, smiling at each other, kissing tenderly when nobody was looking. I really tried to ease the tense atmosphere and see a smile on John's serious face.

'We will be here tonight, listening to the concert!' I said, walking into the Great Gallery, a perfect setting for a grand ball, with the right amount of dance floor.

The white-and-gold stucco decorations and crystal mirrors were designed to reflect candlelight, now replaced by over a thousand bulbs in guild chandeliers and sconces, creating the illusion of larger space. The ceiling frescos were so vivid and clear that I could swear the artists had just finished them a few days before. It looked like the most magnificent Rococo 'party room' in the world!

'Do you want to call your son and just talk to him?' I asked as soon as we had walked outside, strolling through the gardens, immersed in the hot afternoon sun.

John nodded with a face full of melancholy so I walked away, allowing him to make the call in private. After a few minutes, I turned around and saw him staring at his phone.

'And?' I asked, walking up to him.

'He isn't picking up,' he replied with disappointment in his voice.

'Ok, well, maybe try later,' I replied and continuing to walk through the centre of the Great Parterre, the beautifully designed gardens with symmetrical beds of flowers, shaped meticulously, as if embroidered onto the grass.

When we stopped by the Neptune Fountain, made up from stunning white sculptures of the God of Sea himself and his entourage, a tourist offered to take a picture of us. We both smiled to the camera but it wasn't the smile of... us.

Once we had reached the Summer House on the hill, looking back at the palace, I was determined to finally cheer us up. 'Let's enjoy this day, ok? You are a good father, remember that,' I said, hugging my body closely to his, holding his head and kissing his forehead.

It worked. His face lit up and I saw a small movement of his lips, as if he was trying to smile.

'Finally!' I said. 'Come, let's see the rest of the gardens,' I said, and I pulled his hand, but after stopping at every sculpture and waterfall, it was finally time for me to put my evening outfit on and get ready for the concert—after all, that's what we had been waiting for, the Strauss concert in Schönbrunn Palace.

Having collected my bag from storage, I rushed to the bathroom where I changed into a knee-length white dress, layered with black lace underneath, brushed my glossy hair and refreshed my make-up. My nude heels, with a fastening around my ankle, finished my look. I had never felt more beautiful.

'Wow you look sensational!! John exclaimed, walking up to me with sparkles in his eyes.

'Have you just got married?' a passer-by asked, when we were posing for a perfect photo with the palace behind us at sunset.

'Not yet!' John replied, smiling at the man.

Would he want to marry me? a thrilling thought came to my mind. If he did, he would make me the happiest woman alive! I knew he was The One for me. I had known it from the moment I had seen him for the first time in Berkhamsted Town Hall.

'We have a reservation for two,' John said to the waiter in confident manner when we walked into the restaurant, before he even had a chance to ask.

The waiter walked us to a small table in a secluded area where we enjoyed drinking local aperitifs, fresh salmon with salad and a famous Viennese cake, the *Sachentorte*, the tastiest chocolate cake with jam and lustrous chocolate glaze. Absolute heaven! When we walked back to the palace, the dusk was already creeping into the gardens, but the fresh air still felt pleasantly warm.

'Look, the lights are on! The concert is about to start!' I exclaimed, with childlike enthusiasm, looking at the windows of the Great Gallery.

'Would you like to join me for an evening concert, my princess?' John asked, reaching out for my hand and bending forward.

'I would love to!' I replied, curtsied him, lifting my chin up with a Mona Lisa smile and placing my hand in his.

John kissed it gently, a true chivalrous gesture which I had seen many times back in Poland, where it was still common way to show courtesy and extreme politeness.

We walked into the Great Gallery holding hands and felt everyone's eyes on us, giving me shivers over my body as if an electrical current ran through it. Maybe they think we're celebrities? I thought.

'There you go, sir! These are your VIP seats,' said a young man dressed in a navy blue uniform who pointed John to the middle of the front row.

We were the only ones sitting there. Could we have received more prominent seats? So that's how the Queen must feel, I thought.

I was squeezing John's hand from excitement and sheer disbelief that this was really happening. The whole room was lit up by tiny bulbs in crystal chandeliers, sparkling as if they had a party of light and shadows, illuminating the shimmering gold on the white walls and mirrors. All the tall windows were wide open, and the dusk falling over the hustle and bustle of the city was telling it to sleep. The fresh warm breeze felt like a gentle veil touching my skin, hot from excitement.

Hearing the first tones of 'The Blue Danube', I became tearful. I gazed at John. He looked back at me shyly, with glossy eyes, letting me know he felt the same. The vibrations of beautifully sounding flutes, clarinets, timpani, violins and trumpets playing in perfect harmony saturated my whole being. The music and I became ONE. John suddenly stood up.

'Would you like to dance, my lady?' he asked, reaching out for my hand.

'Yes,' I replied, blushing.

He stretched his arms and I placed one hand onto his palm, holding his back with the other, and we started dancing the waltz. I was wearing a long white dress, underpinned by hundreds of the thinnest silk layers, swishing every time we turned, and John a tuxedo, with a crisp white shirt and a bow tie. The whole world was swirling around, making me dizzy, and after a few dozen turns, I left his embrace to rest by the window, for the gentle breeze cool me down. John followed me and reached out for my hand, sheathed in a long white silk glove.

'Madam? Shall we continue?'

I nodded and we were now turning faster and faster to the rhythm, my back was straight and I was looking away from John's face so as not to get dizzy again. All the lights reflecting in the mirrors and chandeliers turned into one continuous stream of light, as if we found ourselves in the middle of the sun. We were surrounded by others dancing around but we were in the centre of the room. All women were wearing long white dresses and men, black tuxedos. When the orchestra finished the last and fastest piece of the waltz, we stopped and John lifted me by the waist and turned me around in the air.

'I love you so much!' I said, hugging him tightly in this most romantic and touching fairytale moment in my life.

'Shush!' I suddenly heard John, trying to get the petulant family with children sitting behind us to stop talking. My dreamy vision instantly disappeared.

Halfway through the concert, we were invited downstairs for a glass of Champagne.

'*Cześć*, Mama, the concert is just unbelievable, I'm so happy, and so is John!' I exclaimed on the phone, excited about this sublime concert experience.

'Oh, marvellous! Enjoy yourselves! Can I say hello to John?' she replied, in a happy voice.

'*Cześć*, Mama, *jak się masz?*' John asked her how she was.

'Ahhh, *dobrze, dzięki!*' ('Good, thanks'), he replied smiling, finishing the conversation and giving me the phone back, as that was all they could say to each other in Polish, making it their small ritual, every time he was around.

The second half of the concert ran smoothly and without the disturbances of the annoying family behind us, who had now gone after probably realising that it was not the disco music they had hoped for! When the concert had finished, we went outside and the glorious evening wrapped us in a warm embrace of cool, sweet air.

'Thank you for the most romantic evening of my life,' I whispered, kissing John's ear and holding his hand tight.

Before we left, we had asked one of the leaving guests to take the last picture of us, standing right in the middle of the white staircase, smiling, cheek to cheek and holding hands. I lifted my right leg in a Hollywood movie style and the 'Perfect Love Picture' was taken, the kind of spontaneous picture that could happen once in a lifetime. The kind of picture that later would end up printed on a canvas and hang in the most prominent place in our living room. We couldn't look more stunning, more in love, more happy and in a more perfect setting. When I later examined the print canvas that John had ordered, I noticed that the black lace on my dress had the same design as the black brass balustrade wrapping the palace staircase.

This dress was meant to be there. I was meant to be there. We were meant to be there, I thought, feeling shivers running through my body from the sudden realisation that it had happened for a reason, that God had wanted us to be there. We had been at the right place, at the right time. It had been our destiny. I knew this experience would stay with me forever. It couldn't have been more perfect. Fairy-tales did exist, after all. Well, ours did!

CHAPTER 38 - VIENNESE CHARM

'Oh, look at that beautiful giraffe!' I exclaimed the next day in the zoo on a hot, sunny morning.

I had never been to a zoo before, so what better place as my first experience of a huge variety of exotic animals than the oldest zoo in history? Set up in the 1700s as the private royal menagerie, it was located in the grounds of Schönbrunn Palace. My heart warmed, watching giant pandas munching on bamboo, something they could do for over 14 hours a day! We then saw zebras, flamingos, monkeys, tigers, lions, meerkats and huge hippos, sunbathing by a pond, not far from koalas, falling sleeping on trees, making me wonder how come they didn't fall down. A herd of adult and baby elephants were having a mud bath, splashing muddy water at one another, having a daily shower.

Thank God for this zoo! I thought as the enclosures where the animals were kept looked quite spacious, created probably the closest to their natural environment.

I had never been a fan of keeping animals in cages, but this zoo was impressively designed, allowing me to marvel at hundreds of different animal species which I would never see in my lifetime, unless of course, all I could do would be to travel around the world as a job. We enjoyed hanging down from giant nets and making funny faces and cross eyes whilst eating delicious ice cream and drinking iced coffee, topped up with a mountain of cream.

Moving into the Arctic area, we cheered at the cutest Peruvian penguins, huge polar bears and serious-looking sea lions. In the giant aquarium, I kept touching the glass tunnels above my head, trying to get attention from flat and colourful fish. We took pictures of everything, even a fake elephant with a smiley face situated right in the entrance hall. All our problems stopped in moments like this. Nothing else existed. There was no divorce and no horrible ex. As it should be for any couple.

'Fancy going up there?' John asked, pointing at the 252-metre-high Danube Tower, the tallest tower in Austria.

'Oh my God! That is really high!' I replied, excited about the spectacular views we could see there.

Having a choice of taking the high-speed elevator which would reach the viewing platform on the 150th floor in just 35 seconds, or walking up 779 steps, we chose the lift. For obvious reasons. After a quick cocktail in the restaurant and enjoying the 360 view of the city at twilight, we went for dinner sitting on the cobblestone street, drinking perfectly chilled Austrian wine, eating tiramisu, laughing and joking about the exciting day we had just had.

'It was an amazing day. Thank you sweetheart!' I said with gratitude to my amazing man, raising the glass of Austrian cocktail.

'Yes it was! It's because it was with you! You make me so happy!' John replied with a smile and flirtatious wink, clinking my glass.

We spent the last day of our trip closer to our hotel, on the Kahlemberg mountain itself, strolling hand in hand through the never-ending vineyards, wrapping the slopes of the mountain. The hot and humid air was saturated with gentle drizzle, which created a fog, and the thick grey clouds covered the sky, making it impossible for us to see Vienna now.

'It would be great if we could come back here for a wine tasting tour,' I said, looking at the signs from the local vineyard producers advertising their local wine.

'Yes, we sure will!'

After our last Austrian meal at the hotel, watching a storm enfolding in front of our eyes with the darkest clouds covering the sky and rain gushing sideways, with massive bangs and noise on the restaurant windows, we took a taxi to the airport. It always felt depressing going back home, wondering what we would need to deal with now. Being away and enjoying moments like this felt better than facing routine and mundane reality. Why could holidays not last forever?!

CHAPTER 39 - ENGLISH BLISS

Weather in England continued to astonish us with gorgeous hot, sunny days, so we decided to go back to that special place where we had spent our first sensual moments and where we declared our love to each other for the first time, with our feet sunk in the sand, Weymouth, the picturesque town in on the Jurassic coast, called 'England's Bay of Naples' and where the first ships with Dorset emigrants set off for New England. Our traditional hotel room on the top floor, with colourful floral wallpaper, overlooked other rooftops and the sea. After unpacking our bags, we drove to the Isle of Portland to admire the same stunning sea views and experience the same feeling of standing on the world's end.

Driving through the Chesil Beach causeway, admiring the beautiful scenery of the sea on both sides of this only 160-meter-wide strip of land, I kept gazing at my most wonderful and sexy man, wearing designer sunglasses and with hair fuzzed up from the hot wind coming through open windows. I felt completely safe and looked after. I felt loved by my soulmate who I was meant to be with for the rest of my life. There could not have been a better feeling in the world. How could there be?

In the morning, I quietly climbed out of bed and sat on the window frame in my white nightie, watching a couple of sea gulls making a nest for their newly-hatched babies. I was fascinated by how they were building it together, bringing small sticks and feathers to make it comfortable.

'Look at the seagulls, sweetie, they are building a nest!' I whispered to John who had walked up to me.

'That's exactly like me! I'm also making sure we live in the nicest nest possible,' he replied, gently placing a kiss on my bare shoulder.

He then took an unexpected picture of me, gazing long at the happy seagull family. It was a spontaneous picture. The kind of picture that could end up on the cover of a book one day.

'Have you ever been to Brownsea Island?' he asked.

'No, I haven't, where is it?'

'It's in the Poole harbour, come on, we should spend a day there.'

I was very excited, sitting on top of the open deck of the ferry, wearing a red jumper and white trousers, gazing at John taking pictures of cute old pubs along the Poole harbour. The British Union Jack flags were dancing in the wind and when we got off on the island, the air was hot and fresh, as if we had landed on a different planet, unspoilt by civilisation. We kind of were on a different planet, as the island was a nature reservoir of outstanding beauty, with only 200 red squirrels, an unusual sight in England since most of the squirrels were grey, after having forced the red ones into Europe. It was funny to hear that, as squirrels in Poland were red and I didn't think of them as special. Until now. But then all squirrels were God's creations and unique in every sense, grey or red. And if some are more vicious than others, well, that's just like humans. Strolling with John, hand in hand through the woodland, breathing in fresh air filled with gentle whiffs of pine trees and sea salt, I noticed the most magnificent show of peacocks' feathers. They posed for my camera as if they were supermodels, obviously used to being the centre of attention for all tourists.

'I fancy a swim, do you?' John asked, having stopped on the stony beach where the soft waves of crystal clear water were touching the shore.

'I'm not sure.'

'Well, I'm sure,' he replied and after having taken his shorts and blue T-shirt off, showing off his six pack and muscular body, he dived in.

'Wait for me!' I said, bravely following him into the water, knowing John was a fantastic swimmer and I knew I could trust him and feel safe anywhere with him.

'It's so peaceful,' I whispered, hugging his wide wet shoulders, hearing nothing but the seagulls flying above our heads with a soft swooshy sound of their wings, birds chirping in the woodland and his breath.

I wrapped John's body with my arms and legs, kissing him tenderly in crystal clear water, with nobody around, as if on a desert island. Just the two of us. Far from the stresses and problems. Just me and him. We would be so happy living like this together forever.

I took a picture of him coming out of the water just as I was drying my body covered with goose bumps from the change in temperature.

'You look like an MI5 secret agent!' I shouted, taking pictures and admiring his muscular body emerging from the water, looking truly spectacular.

'*Kocham Cię,*' he whispered, laying down on the towel next to me.

I want to be his forever, I thought.

***

Our love flourished. When John was in England, we used every opportunity to see new places, beautiful scenery, nature and history. There were a few well-preserved historical places in our area where we could walk around the most spectacular, perfectly maintained gardens, woodlands and historic mansions where the English aristocracy used to live in. Being a great fan of English history, I loved visiting these mansions which were so well preserved that it created the impression that the people of the era still lived there. Such visits were always a sweet treat to my soul. It was easy for me to imagine what their life looked like, how they spent their time, leaving an open newspaper on the ornamentally-crafted, velour sofa or having a cigar by the fireplace. Walking through the corridors, I imagined servants bumping into me, rushing to serve the lady of the house who had rung the bell, carrying a tray richly decorated with blue and gold designs, a fine bone china English teapot, filled with freshly brewed Earl Grey tea and a matching jug with milk and a cute cup with a saucer. The long dining tables, covered with white linen tablecloths, tall silver candelabras, colourful flower arrangements and crystal glasses, looked as if they were freshly prepared to be seated by the guests, about to enjoy the most exquisite dinner. The enormous crystal chandeliers, lit up with hundreds of light bulbs, emanated a unique atmosphere and the smell of old wooden floor, furniture and fabrics truly transformed me into those times.

One of our favourite places was Cliveden, a stunning mansion located in Buckinghamshire, no more than 30 miles from London. Walking up the long gravel drive to the house, I felt like royalty or aristocracy, the celebrities of the past, who had visited there over the last 300 years to take part in exclusive parties and dinners, including people like Queen Victoria, Winston Churchill and Tom Ford. The estate of 160 acres was originally bought by the second Duke of Buckingham, George Villiers in 1666, who built the house there, according to the rumour, for his mistress, the Duchess of Shrewsbury. The things men of the past did for love! Cliveden had later been bought in 1893 by the American millionaire, William Waldorf Astor for over a million dollars. He liked England so much, he decided to buy it and create magnificent gardens, a giant maze for the water garden, install the Fountain of Love and 'French Dining Room' from the Chateau d' Asnieres which had been skilfully dismantled and put back together into one of the rooms here. It took impressive craftsmanship, stripping the gilded walls and ceilings of a French chateau and transporting them to England! Why go to France to admire such beauty when he could have had his own French room in England? Additionally, Nancy Astor, the first female member of the British Parliament, whose painting hung in prominent place in the house, had also entertained many dignitaries of the time.

The view from the terrace overlooking the long parterre with meticulously designed plant beds, filled with all possible colours of flowers in symmetrical patterns as if they were embroidered onto a lush carpet, was breathtaking. John hugged me tight from behind as I was leaning against the Borghese Balustrade and the gentle warm breeze turned my shoulder-length hair into swaying waves. We didn't speak, absorbing the beauty of one of the most magnificent gardens. The River Thames was visible in the distance and the vastness of the grounds, covered in woodlands, gave me a feeling of being free. Free to enjoy such stunning scenery. Having rested on the warm grass right at the very end of the parterre, we could gaze at the stunning architecture of the house. John took his shirt off and let the hot afternoon sun touch his skin, turning it slowly into a pink colour.

'Next time, we should come here with Champagne and strawberries, just like we did the other day by the river in Marlow,' he concluded, reminiscing about the most relaxing and romantic afternoon picnic he had surprised me with, after work once.

The air was pleasantly warm, and the sky was pure with only a pair of kites flying over our heads in some kind of a ritual, and the peacefulness that surrounded us was so relaxing that we snoozed into a short sleep. John lay his head on my thighs and I caressed his hair, shimmering in the sun. I felt connected to nature, the most interesting English history and John. It was a perfect moment for us as a couple to enjoy, just being together and not worrying about a thing. Except one—but it was not something I wanted to talk about in moments like this. It would only spoil the joy of experiencing such bliss.

One afternoon, when I returned from work, John surprised me with a gift outside my door, a pink mountain bike and a cute pink protective helmet and black gloves.

'For me?? I exclaimed.

'Yes, for you, baby. We can now go on biking trips in the countryside. I also got you these,' he replied with a grin, showing me special big padded white underpants to protect my precious backside during long bike rides.

'Oh you are so romantic!' I replied laughing, 'and caring!' I added.

Riding up and down the lush green countryside hills and valleys, where our only companions were sheep, staring at us and probably wondering why we were there, left us so exhausted that we collapsed on the warm grass, bathed in the afternoon sun and having a short nap. In such blissful moments, I forgot about the whole world—but my back pains had become worse as if my body was desperately trying to tell me that something was not right. I lay on the amethyst mat which I had ordered from America as a pain-relieving tool for my muscles by warming them up from within, thinking that one day it would get better. I just did not know when.

CHAPTER 40 - TWILIGHT

'What do you mean, she wants everything?' I exclaimed, after John had shouted that solicitors couldn't do anything to stop his wife from taking everything, hearing the deep, querulous sounds of his voice from behind the shut door to the bedroom, the night before our trip to Prague.

Divorce was a battle for money, contributing to endless fights and stress between us, putting a huge strain on our relationship. During our flight, I was sitting in the front seat of business class, holding my feet, frozen from air conditioning, and I didn't speak a word, exhausted from the argument the night before. We had even been silent during our Champagne breakfast at the business lounge at Heathrow Airport, only watching other passengers who seemed to have been more excited than we were about the trips they were about to go on. But luckily, another escape to a different world was about to rescue us from the misery we were living.

As soon as we unpacked our bags in the hotel room, we sat down in cafe, bathed in warm morning sunshine, situated in one of the streets. Delighting in the freshly baked local bread, croissants, strawberry jam and cheese, I kept gazing at John whose face still showed signs of stress.

'We need to relax. My back is really hurting now, let's enjoy this trip, ok?' I announced calmly.

'Ok, you are right. Sorry, baby,' he replied, kissing my hand tenderly.

'Shall we try a Thai massage?' John asked, pointing at a hand-written sign in the street when we started strolling hand in hand.

'Oh, yes, that would be amazing, I really need it,' I replied with enthusiasm at the very thought of someone touching my back to relieve my suffering.

A few minutes later, two Thai ladies led us upstairs to two adjacent rooms, separated only by a colourful material. My masseuse, a short but physically strong Thai woman in her twenties, bent my arms and legs in all possible directions as if trying to break them off. The sensation was not the most enjoyable one and rather painful, especially since my whole body was sore at the slightest touch and not as relaxing as the Thai massage we had once had in London. But at least this time, John wasn't asked if he wanted a 'happy ending' whilst I was in an adjacent room. I had never heard of THAT type of massage before and I was upset that she had offered it to him, knowing that he was there with me.

'My masseuse didn't ask me if I wanted one!' I replied to John after he had told me he hadn't taken up the offer.

This strange memory had stayed with me and every time we went for a massage I had to say to John, 'Just remember, say no to the happy ending!'

After the massage, walking towards Prague's oldest preserved bridge, the Charles Bridge, I felt much more uplifted. 'God, I really needed it. I feel much more relaxed now.'

'Me too,' John replied, giving me quick kiss showing that his spirit was lifted too.

The Charles Bridge was lively with passing tourists, artists playing instruments and displaying their paintings and sketches of the city. The Lesser Town Bridge Towers, connected by a gate, led to the historic part of the town and the route to the Prague Castle. Thirty majestic statues of saints on both sides of the bridge, including Saint John of Nepomuk, who had been drowned in the Vltava river as a punishment for not sharing the Queen of Bohemia's confessions with the King, served as unofficial bridge guardians and stunning decoration, giving it an indescribable charm that I had not seen before.

'It's like we have stepped into Prague a few hundred years ago,' I said, leaning forward against the bridge wall, looking into the depths of the river, John shielding me with his body from a strong but warm morning gale.

'Fancy an evening boat trip?' he asked, watching the boats passing by.

I nodded with a grin.

At twilight, we climbed onto the open-air top deck of a tourist boat, both dressed in white jumpers and trousers, taking a seat facing other, at a small square table, covered with a crisp white linen tablecloth. As the twilight deepened, turning the navy blue sky into deep shades of pink and red, with only thin white stripes from the planes high above, we were eating a creamy mushroom risotto and sipped Sauvignon blanc, marvelling at the charming sites of historic Prague. Upon the return from our trip on the river, it was already pitch dark. The views of the castle and the city and the postcard-perfect reflections on the river surface, glistening from millions of lights, were even more delightful now, as if blurred by a drizzle that left undistinguished marks on canvas. John, being a true gentleman, wrapped his navy blue jacket over my shivering shoulders and hugged me tight, moving his arms in strong movements up and down in order to warm my body up from the cool night breeze. I wanted him to hold me like this forever.

After a stroll across the bridge at night, gently lit up by tall brass lanterns, giving it a true medieval atmosphere, we touched the shiny picture of a dog underneath the statue of Saint John Nepomuk, which according to a belief was supposed to ensure we would come back to Prague, and returned to our top floor hotel room. We sat down in silence on wooden chairs on a balcony, staring at the castle on the hill which looked spectacular, covered with millions of lights.

'Tomorrow, if you like, we can go and see it,' John suggested, gazing into my eyes and taking my hand into his.

'Oh, that would be amazing. You know how much I love castles. Being in Prague and not seeing one would be a sin!' I replied, beaming.

'Of, course my lady, as you wish,' he replied in a serene and distinctive manner.

'Thank you for an amazing day,' I whispered, looking into his sleepy eyes.

'Let's go to bed,' he replied with a wink, reaching out for my hand and leading me back to the bedroom.

CHAPTER 41 - TIME TRAVEL

'What's an ice bar? I asked John, having noticed the street sign the next day.

'Well, let's go and have a look, shall we?'

Before we were allowed to get in, we had to put on two warm silver, puffy jackets and gloves.

'You can only be there for half an hour as the temperature is very low—minus seven degrees Celsius,' a young man informed us, leading us downstairs.

Everything in the bar was made of ice, including the glasses for vodka shots and the bar itself. There were frozen wine bottles and wine-filled glasses inside the walls. In the corner there was a sculpture of a naked man and a woman. John touched the ice boobs and I touched the ice willy. Totally indecent!

'Come on, drink from it!' John challenged me for the picture, as it was possible to pour the vodka from the top of the sculpture's head and drink it from... umm... his ice penis.

'No, I won't do it! Stop it!' I replied, embarrassed.

'Why don't you drink vodka from the lady's breast?!' I challenged him back, grinning and he did just that.

Having poured his vodka from the top of the sculpture's head, he drank it out of the ice boob!

'How could you? That's so bad!' I exclaimed, giggling, examining the picture I'd just taken as a proof.

'You know I only love you—don't be jealous!'

Later, after walking up hundreds of steps up the hill, we saw Prague Castle with a large courtyard in front of it and magnificent views of the city. According to the Guinness Book of World Records, the largest ancient castle complex in the world, covering an impressive area of almost 70,000 square meters. I was buzzing from joy. After all, I had arrived in just another one of my castles! A summer residence, perfect for a hot sunny day! We were so excited, we performed our signature dance in front of the tourists who had no idea why we were dancing, hugging, squeezing each other and kissing, but giving us a few bravos and claps once we had finished! I was jumping up and down like a small girl, leading John by the hand to the castle entrance.

'I want a picture with this handsome soldier in the booth!' I announced, looking at the guard in light blue military uniform, even before we had entered the grounds, with John being next, taller not only than the soldier but also the booth itself!

The castle, with breathtaking views from the windows, was stunning. We walked through the Vladislav Hall, where the coronations of Czech kings, lavish Bohemian banquets and even knights' tournaments used to take place, as it was large enough for the knights on caparisoned horses to fight there, thanks to the 'Knights' Stairway'. The castle dungeon was my least favourite place. Situated in a dark cellar with tiny windows, it was filled with horrible looking metal torture devices, including a hanging metal cage, shaped like a human body and containing a full-size skeleton. Metal boxes, used as a punishment and torture device, made it impossible for the prisoner to stretch his legs and would suffer in torment till he finally died. The air was heavy, making it difficult for me to breathe, making me dizzy, but I didn't think it was because of the heat outside.

'Oh it's so good to be out. It's as if I could feel the souls of the people that had suffered and died in there,' I said.

'Yes, it feels haunted and I didn't like it either,' John agreed, but seemed to feel much better once he had tried archery in one of the Golden Lane museums, wanting to show off his knightly skills, in case he would ever need to fight for me and any intruders invading the castle, but he missed.

'Oh don't worry sweetie, if I was in real danger I'm sure you would reach the right target,' I said to comfort him.

Golden Lane, the cobblestone street, was full of small houses in various shades of blue and pink and yellow, presented as if the people of the era, goldsmiths, guards and fortune-tellers were still living there. The sewing machine was prepared for the creation of a white linen pillow case and the brass scales had just been used by a servant to measure the right amount of gold for a chain. The house entrances were incredibly small, making John a head taller and looking like a giant in a tiny people's wonderland. On the way down the hundreds of steps from the castle, on the right hand side, we noticed an old-looking pub.

'The oldest medieval pub in Prague,' I read out loud from the sign above it.

'Shall we?' he asked, taking my hand, leading me into the darkness, broken down by only a few candles.

When the waiter, wearing medieval clothes, served us at the table, we felt as if we had truly gone back in time. The atmosphere was out of this world. We could hear the medieval music, drink dark beer from giant jugs and eat honey ribs, the same way Henry VIII would have eaten them, with his fingers. Human skulls were scattered all around the walls and the low Gothic-looking ceiling and the one on our table became our new photo partner when we pretended to kiss it, goofing around.

'Isn't it amazing that we are following the footsteps of Mozart? First we were in Schönbrunn Palace where he used to play, and now we are in a pub where he used to drink!' I said, in my eureka moment, squeezing John's knee under the table from excitement.

Strolling along the old streets later, we entered the square where crowds of people had gathered in front of the Astronomical Clock, waiting for it to strike midnight. We stopped and watched the spectacular show of Death ringing the bell to invert the hour-glass and move the 12 Apostles, appearing one by one in the window.

'Dinner on a rooftop restaurant?' John asked, pointing at the perfectly placed-in-front-of-us sign, outside a hotel.

We were lucky to get a table without reservation, especially one overlooking the square and the rooftops. The sky was covered in stars, the still air, despite such a late hour, was still warm and refreshing. The three-layer platter we had ordered had the most delicious selection of seafood I had ever tasted in my life. The royal crab legs, the most delicious, sweetest white crab meat were to die for, not mentioning fresh oysters with lemon and garlic, giant prawns and calamari. All this accompanied by rustic bread, dipped in extra virgin olive oil with balsamic glaze. I was in heaven. Well, very close to heaven, on top of the roof in the centre of Prague, almost touching the stars and hearing a violin in the square.

I want to be with you for the rest of my life, I thought, gazing at the man of my dreams, sipping another glass of Champagne.

CHAPTER 42 - LAKE HOUSE

'I want us to have a house here!' John announced, stretching his athletic body on a sun bed in the garden outside my family house in Poland, flicking through the stunning designs of houses in a magazine.

'Really? In Poland? Why?' I gasped, serving him a glass of apple juice with ice, wearing only my black bikini.

'I want us to have a house by a lake. Like this one,' he said, pointing at a modern design of a house with the front made of sliding glass doors and a spacious terrace on the first floor with glass railings.

'We could buy this design, a piece of local land and have it built the way we want it to. Would you like that?'

'It's a gorgeous house but it's over a million zlotys! A lot of money!' I replied, surprised at his sudden suggestion, aware of his upcoming financial divorce settlement.

'Yes, but it's much cheaper than buying a house in England!' he continued, as if trying to convince me into something I would love anyway.

'Would you like to live in Poland one day?' I asked shyly.

'Yes, I could stay here forever,' he replied with calm confidence, making me feel excited about our future together and vast opportunities once the divorce was over.

John loved Poland, my mama, family and Cezar, whom he had a lot of fun playing with. Mama was ecstatic to have us and we could truly enjoy the weather this time, unlike during that snowy and cold December a few months before. We cooked traditional Polish dinners with Mama: baby potatoes with fresh dill from our garden, cucumber and cream salad, steaks in breadcrumbs, white cheese dumplings, cherry and plum soups, perfect for hot summer weather, *gulasz* and *gołąbki* (which in my funny, literal translation meant ' little pigeons' and having said that I almost made John stop eating them, but he calmed down as soon as I explained they had been made of pork mincemeat and rice, wrapped in cabbage leaves and cooked in a tomato sauce). John loved going with us to the local cake shop to buy various creamy cakes with orange mousse, chocolate, rum or strawberries and obviously, lots of ice cream. My mama was a 'feeder'. She fed us five to six times a day whilst we were sunbathing in the garden, drinking cold juices in the 35-degree heat. I loved watching John doing push ups, showing off his muscles, covered in sun cream, making them look perfectly shaped in the sunshine.

'I love being here,' John said, sitting in the garden with a fly-swatter for hitting the flies daring to sit on his gorgeous sexy body that was slowly turning into a nice golden brown colour.

'*Aww, mama, dziękuje bardzo*! ('Oh, mama, thank you very much'),' he said when she had brought him another drink or a plate full of snacks.

His Polish was getting better and better each day. He always said with a smile, '*Tak, proszę*!' ('Yes, please') and '*Dzień doby'* ('Good morning'), coming downstairs for breakfast in the kitchen.

'Fancy a bike ride in the evening? It will be cooler after seven,' I suggested.

'Yes, I would love that, have you got a bike for me?' he replied, winking.

Yes, I've got two old bikes from my teenage years. You can have the one with bigger wheels because, well, you are bigger,' I replied laughing, hoping he would appreciate my old super bikes.

'Let's stop here,' I said, when we had reached the top of a hill nearby, overlooking the fields of barley, shimmering in the setting sun.

'It's so quiet and peaceful,' John said.

All we could hear was the sound of a tractor in the distance and the mooing of cows. We were deeply breathing in the fresh countryside air, filled with the smells of grass and fresh manure.

'I hope you like the smells of nature?' I said, glad that John had appreciated the full package of smells and sounds of a Polish countryside.

'Come, let me show you something,' I said, getting back on my bike and riding down the hill with cool wind flapping in my hair and under my white T-shirt.

'This is the chapel and I like coming to it when there is nobody around,' I said, leaving my bike on the grass outside the small red brick building with stained glass windows and a large wooden door, before walking down the steps to the lake.

'Oh, this is amazing,' John said, sitting on a small step right next to me.

We sat in silence, looking at the calm surface of the lake, reflecting the rays of the setting sun and watching a fisherman in a white boat on the other side. I silently prayed for our happiness. I knew that John did too. His face turned serious and he stared at the lake in a meditative state.

I wish I knew what he is thinking about? I wondered, reaching out for his hand.

'Come, it's time to go back for supper,' I said after a few minutes, hearing my belly rumbling, craving for some scrambled eggs with chives and crusty bread with butter.

***

The large lake on the other side of the town was our favourite place in the world. We rode there on bikes in the hot dry afternoon sun. Me, wearing just a short coral beach dress with a bikini underneath, and John, only his blue shorts, showing off his tanned and muscular bare chest. The hot breeze was tangling my shoulder-length hair when John pushed my bike from behind every time I got a bit tired from riding up the hill. He was a strong man. The strongest I had ever met. During one of our bike rides, I got a weird flashback of what had happened to me when I was only 17 on a similar hot sunny day when my mama sent me to the shop in town to get some butter. On my way back, halfway through the countryside, I noticed a boy, in the corner of my eye, riding on a bike beside me. He suddenly grabbed my steering frame, forcing me to stop on the side of the road between the trees. He was as tall as me, with the black eyes of a wild animal. He came closer and with one forceful move he tried to pull my shorts down. It didn't work because luckily, I was wearing a one-piece swimming costume underneath my T-shirt.

'Why are you doing this? Please don't do it,' I begged him, in complete shock but trying to stay calm, in this completely unexpected situation. I was dating my first sweetheart at that time and I was still a virgin, so all I could think of in that moment was to try to speak to his reasoning. He stared at me for what seemed an hour.

'Ok, just kiss me,' he said and I did kiss him, quickly on his lips.

He then let go of my bike and allowed me go away. My heart was pounding, letting me know that I had just been in serious danger but had somehow got away. I walked into the house and sat on the sofa in the living room, but I was shaking and my tears were flowing down my cheeks.

'What's happened, why are you crying?' my mama asked, but I didn't know how to explain what had happened and my stepdad was listening.

'Come on, say what's wrong?' he asked.

'A boy stopped me on my bike and wanted to pull my shorts down, but I asked him to let me go, so he just told me to kiss him,' I replied with a shaky voice from sobbing.

'Where is he?' my stepdad asked and stood up.

'I don't know. I think he was standing by the railway station when I was going back home and he followed me.'

'Ok, let's go!' he said.

'Where?' I asked, but my mama told me to follow my stepdad and we all got in the car, without saying a word.

When we had reached the train station, we saw the boy standing holding his bike, with what suddenly seemed like tiny wheels.

'Get in the car!' my stepdad shouted at him, walking up to him. He told him to sit next to me on the back seat. I was petrified.

'What's your name?' he asked the boy, while driving.

'Marek' the boy replied, staring at the window, avoiding my eyesight.

'What did you want from Monika?' My stepdad was investigating like a policeman, but the boy didn't reply.

We were driving further and further away from the town and I had no idea where we were going.

What is my stepdad planning to do? I thought, before we finally stopped in the middle of the countryside, with only fields around us.

'Get out!' My stepdad shouted at him, and when the boy stood behind the car, my stepdad told him to take his jeans off.

The boy did just that.

'What is he trying to do?' I asked Mama, who was confused as much as I was.

'Go and get the cows now!' my stepdad said, taking his trousers back to the car and driving off, leaving the boy wearing only his pants, walking a few kilometres back into town.

'That will teach him!' he said to us, giggling now with a small feeling of justice.

***

Swimming in the lake with John, in over 30-degree summer heat, and water feeling like a pleasant veil on the skin, couldn't be a more relaxing experience. I wrapped John's body with my arms and legs, and kissing his ear, I whispered how happy I was. I deeply inhaled the smell of his black pepper aftershave which, together with his natural pheromones, was the biggest aphrodisiac in the world, a drug that I couldn't get enough of.

'I love you, I love you, I love you!' John exclaimed.

'Please stop it, people can hear you!' I scolded him, looking around, seeing people on the beach, enjoying the show of affection.

'I love you, Monika Wiśniewska!' he screamed even louder, so all I could do to silence him was to kiss him, the best way to express my love back to him.

CHAPTER 43 - MOSQUITO

'Are you my Teutonic Knight?' I asked John in front of the largest castle in the world, Malbork.

'Yes, I am, and you are my Polish Princess,' he replied with a husky voice.

'I don't think I would like you as a Teutonic Knight, I wouldn't betray my country and sleep with the enemy,' I replied jokingly, knowing the history of the crusaders. After all, Malbork Castle had been founded in 1274 by the Teutonic Knights, who bore a black cross symbol, as their headquarters to fight Polish Christians in order to rule their own Baltic territories.

Strolling along the humongous red, brick walls, surrounded by an empty moat, I marvelled at the grandness of this 21-hectare castle, over twice the size of the castle we had visited in Prague. As we walked through the chambers, John sat on a wooden throne pretending to be the Grand Master of the Order. I then tried to make him jealous, kissing Nicolas Copernicus, or rather his handsome statue, and John avenged himself by kissing the very attractive ladies in the clothes of the era. The traditional steak in breadcrumbs, potatoes and a salad, accompanied by the local beer, was exactly what we had needed after the castle visit and having returned home on the train, we wanted to stay outside as the evening temperature was refreshingly pleasant.

'How about I help your mama cut the grass in the garden?' John asked, as our garden was pretty large, and it could take over two hours to do it, especially with a small mower like ours.

'Ok, *tak*,' Mama replied, and laughed with me, seeing John going around in circles with Cezar running in front of him.

'Can I have a go??' I asked ten minutes later, but John didn't want to stop as this simple task could get quite addictive.

I was proud to have come to my family home with the man who was my soulmate. To finally be happy and not being looked as a 'loser' who couldn't find a good man. I knew John was serious about me. Why else would he be like this with my family, treating me with outmost respect?

The following day, we visited our lovely neighbours and their five-year-old daughter. They were so excited about our visit that they organised a barbeque with lots of delicious food, which John absolutely loved. Everyone was so happy for me. Daria kept look-ing at John so he decided to play games with her, drawing with crayons on a blanket while stretched out on the grass and piggy-backing her around the garden. Daria's grandma, the sweetest lady, gave him a present. A red and white T-shirt with 'Polska' sign and our coat of arms, the Polish White Eagle on the sleeve. John put it on immediately and kissed the emblem, making everyone say, 'Awwwww'.

'Why is the white eagle a Polish emblem?' John asked.

I told him that according to the legend, Lech, Poland's mythical founder, noticed a huge nest, with a white eagle stretching its large wings over the red light of the setting sun, so he decided to settle the first town, Gniezno, meaning nest. The white eagle, spreading wings to protect all Poles, no matter where they lived, became the emblem. The red background symbolised the sunlit fatherland and spilled blood. Or at least, that was what I'd heard.

***

'Let's hire a rowing boat!' John suggested at breakfast in the garden the next day.

'Yes, let's do that!' I exclaimed, as I had always dreamt of a man who would do that with me.

Once we set off, I watched my handsome, sexy, topless man, rowing a boat in steady moves, showing off his six pack, smiling at me, making me feel like the most cherished woman in the world. When we got to the middle of the lake, we stopped and I leaned my back against his chest, listening to the silence and kissing gently in the warm afternoon sun. But then, I noticed a secluded beach where my first sweetheart, Jarek, had broken my heart when I was only 18.

'I'm so sorry Moni, but I decided to be a priest,' he'd announced with tears in his eyes after our two-year relationship, 'I love you, but I love God more than you,' he'd added.

His words: 'but I love God more than you,' had haunted me for years afterwards. The heartbreaking realisation that he'd loved someone more had a huge impact on my future love life, which had become non-existent for years and I hadn't let anyone close to me. And the fact that this someone he had loved more was not just a human being, but God, meant I couldn't do anything about it. After all, I couldn't compete with a love for God.

***

'I want you. Now!' I said to John, stopping my bike on a secluded beach on our way back from the boat trip.

'Now?' he looked at me with a coy look.

'Yes, now.'

'Follow me!' I grabbed his hand and pulled him towards the trees, running through the bushes and grass, far from the path.

'Here,' I said smiling and being a bit out of breath from running.

'Quick! Kiss me!' I said, pulling his head towards me in both hands, and he placed a tender, warm kiss on my lips.

I leaned against the tree, wrapped by his strong arms as if we were one with the universe. I inhaled the remains of patchouli and cardamom perfume on his neck and right behind his ear which drove me to a frenzy. I was gazing up into the dark, blue sky, peeking through the trees, when John was kissing my collarbone, making me feel ecstatic. Until, mosquitoes started to bite my arms and legs and we had to run away quicker than we had got there! Sometimes romance was not risk-free but, it was still worth it!

CHAPTER 44 - DENIAL

'To love is human. To feel pain is human.
Yet to still love despite the pain is pure angel.'
- Rumi

The pain all over my body was getting worse.

Despite us going away all the time and despite trying to relax, having massages and using the amethyst mat, when I heard they opened a massage centre in my hometown using some innovative mats which were used in physiotherapy, I had to go there to check it out. When me and John entered the room, we saw people sitting on chairs, covered by beige body-size mats, with a built-in massage function. We both sat next to each other to enjoy a free half-hour session.

'Jesus, this is so good, I need to get this massage mat. But how can I transport it to England? I asked John.

'Well, just send it as a parcel and by the time we get back to England, it will be there.'

The mat was quite expensive but my body was in constant pain and I would have paid any price to make it stop hurting. It cost me over £500 altogether with postage and once we had it in the flat I was using it every day, watching TV or listening to the music. My left leg started to feel so sore with my calf muscle turning rock hard, making it painful to walk, that I had to see a doctor who suggested physiotherapy. But the physiotherapist was not able to massage it out and I ended up unable to work. I spent most days lying down, without moving, and stopped going to the gym like I used to every day, and I also cried a lot.

John was very supportive and wanted me to get better. I wasn't. Our calls when he was away were both a blessing and a curse. I was sometimes so drained talking to him when he was sobbing on the phone, unhappy, stuck far away from me, desperate to get away and move to Holland. I prayed we could finally do it and stop this misery.

'I want to start a new nest with you. I hate England, I don't want to be in this country anymore, I want to get away,' John repeated over and over again.

'Don't worry, I'm sure you'll get that job you applied for. You're the best candidate. You will do it and we will start everything all over.'

'Yes baby, we will do it. We will get away from this horrible country,' he replied.

John booked a series of ten massages for me in the gym. I had knots and hard muscles everywhere, in my back, shoulders and legs, and I needed a professional to get rid of them, feeling my whole body had been taken over by an alien, which I needed to stop from spreading.

'Oh my God, your back feels as if all your muscles went into a spasm. I have never seen anything like it,' the young masseuse said during my first massage.

'Oh, it doesn't sound good, but I'm sure you can fix it,' I replied, but every stroke she made and every time she tried to press and get rid of the knot I wanted to scream as it was ridiculously painful.

I knew that something was not right. After the sessions, which seemed more like a torture hour, I was even more sore and the cycle was never-ending. I started looking for other healers. I even found a lady who massaged me in a special Asian way in her house which was filthy and smelly, with some dirty clothes on the bed.

What am I doing? This is crazy! I thought when I had left.

I felt lonely and missed John more and more. I loved him so much that every day of him being away was an emotional pain in its own right. I just wanted us to be together forever, every day, not being apart every other month. When I went back to see the doctor, I explained how much pain I was in and that nothing was helping me.

'I think it's because of depression. You should start taking medication,' he said and I was shocked.

After all: me, depressed, mentally ill, on psycho drugs... no way. Impossible.

'No, I don't want to take antidepressants. I'll continue with massages and natural ways of healing,' I replied and immediately called John, telling him how ridiculous that doctor's diagnosis was. 'I'm not a psycho,' I added. After all, I was living the happiest time of my life, having found true and everlasting love, regardless of the arguments and stress—but that was something that many couples had to deal with anyway.

CHAPTER 45 - CYPRIAN NEWS

'I was not born for one corner.
The whole world is my native land.'
- Seneca

Paphos in November felt incredibly hot, especially after flying out from a rainy and gloomy England.

Our five star hotel overlooked the turquoise sea and I couldn't wait to immerse my hot body into it, the moment I had seen it from our balcony. The first thing I did was to put my black bikini on and run to the beach. John pretended to be a shark whilst I was filming him with my camera from the shore. He came out of the sea in a true macho style. His body was perfect. The muscles, the physique and the way he showed off his biceps as if he was a professional body builder on a TV show who was about to get a winning prize.

After a typical Cypriot lunch, fresh sea bass, octopus and grilled halloumi with fresh salad, we found a secluded and rocky area by the sea where we could sit on wooden chairs and simply let go and admire the sound of the waves, hitting the rocks with huge power. The wind was quite strong but still pleasant and John, standing behind me, massaged my aching neck and shoulders which were full of hard bumps feeling on fire every time he pressed them. He did it in the hope of getting rid of them, but the pain was so excruciatingly bad that after a while, tears were falling down my cheeks and I was making strange screams to show that I couldn't take it anymore. I knew it was supposed to be good for me but I didn't understand why it was so painful. The couples massage later that day seemed like a better option. We giggled, undressing in one room, and lay down on two beds beside each other.

'How is it, baby?' John asked with a sleepy relaxed voice. 'Is it as good as my massage?'

'Oh, it's wonderful, but nothing compares to your touch,' I replied, full of appreciation of his efforts to ease my pain every day.

In the evening, we dressed up for a cocktail party for two on a terrace by the pool which was beautifully lit up. We then went to the beach and listened to the waves whilst gazing at the stars, and jumped on the swings with childlike exuberance.

'*Kocham Cię*,' John exclaimed, swinging backwards and forwards like a small boy.

'*Też Cię kocham*,' I replied and having stopped swinging, I wrapped my arms around him, looked at his face with eyes sparkling in the reflection of the stars and placed a gentle kiss on his forehead, hugging his head to my heart, hearing the crickets and gentle waves hitting the shore, as if we were on a desert island, living our life in love, peace and happiness.

If only life would be so simple, and moments like this could last forever. Why couldn't they?

***

'Yes!!!' John exclaimed, running to me while I was sunbathing on the beach, 'I got the job! We are moving to Holland!'

'Seriously? Is it for real? Oh my God, I'm so happy! I knew it! I believed in you! You are the best!'

'Yes, it is for real!' he replied, lifting and swirling me in the air, laughing and kissing.

The next day, we rented a car and drove around the island in search of the ancient ruins, filled with hope for our new life.

'Look, it's the Aphrodite rock! I exclaimed when we were driving past the sign on the road, 'Maybe we should stop here and swim around it three times to guarantee finding true love, as the legend has it?' I asked with a smile.

'We don't need it, baby. We've already found true love,' John replied, gazing at me and holding my hand with firm reassurance.

The Paphos mosaics took us back in time. The most marvellous discovery by a farmer in the 1960s had led to the uncovering of a whole Roman town and the most preserved mosaics of the Eastern Mediterranean. The Romans had decorated their floor with pieces of art created from the tiny little colourful tiles. An absolute masterpiece. And we were so lucky to see it. The Roman Odeon, a small amphitheatre nearby, became a perfect scenery for my poses right in the centre of it, and black and white pictures. The next stop for us was the underground Tombs of the Kings, carved out of rock, where the rich people of those times had been buried.

'They look like the houses of living people!' I said to John with amazement, gazing into the creepy spaces of this town of the dead, with magnificent sea views.

'If you were an aristocrat in those times, you would have been buried here,' I said, teasingly.

'Only if you were buried next to me,' he replied, making my heart melt like hot wax on a candle.

'So when are we moving to Holland, then?' I asked, changing the subject, as talking about our deaths was the last thing I had wanted.

'Probably in January, because it takes time to organise the transport for our furniture, rent a house there and do the handover in my current job,' he replied with full eloquence, letting me know that he had everything under control.

'It's a shame. I wish we could go tomorrow.'

'I know, baby. Soon. I promise,' he replied, hugging me tight, as I was looking at the red sun, wrapping the endless sea with flamelike ribbons, hoping his words would come true.

CHAPTER 46 - DIAGNOSIS

I will join you for Christmas in Poland on Christmas Eve,' John said, after I had decided to go there two weeks before, to spend more time with my family.

But my health got worse. I felt that the knots had spread everywhere now. Watching TV, I kept pressing them on my neck and throat with my fingers, as they seemed to be even there, even on my cheeks, trying to take the enormous pain, but it soon became unbearable. It was at its worst yet. Huge muscle spasms, radiating from my back and surrounding my chest, felt as if the Devil himself was trying to suffocate me and take me to hell with him. I lay down on my bed or sofa with a hot water bottle, taking pain killers, but they didn't seem to help much. My mama and stepdad were worried, feeling helpless, taking me from one doctor to another who couldn't diagnose what was causing such pains. I had various tests done and they all came out fine. According to them, I was perfectly healthy. One night, I woke up finding it hard to breathe.

'What is it, Moni?' Mama asked when I had run to wake her up.

'I don't know, I just find it hard to breathe,' I replied, sobbing, finding it hard to speak.

'We're going to the hospital! Get dressed!'

When we were driving on the cold, snowy night, I felt embarrassed that I was causing so much hassle and trouble, but I also felt I had reached my limits. I couldn't bear this pain anymore and needed help. From anyone. From anywhere. When the duty doctor saw me, I explained how I felt, adding, with sobs, 'Nobody knows what's happening to me.'

The doctor prescribed the strongest painkillers available and muscle relaxants to ease the spasms in a series of injections for the next ten days.

'The doctor in England suggested that it was most likely due to depression, but I didn't want to take antidepressants. I'm not a crazy person,' I finally admitted with embarrassment.

'Well, I think it's worth trying them out. Your symptoms could be a sign of depression caused by prolonged stress. It has got nothing to do with you being a crazy person,' he replied, gazing at me from under his thick eyebrows in a look which certainly meant he was serious.

I was in so much physical pain that I was willing to try anything and, indeed, after only a few days of taking antidepressants, my body started to release me from my own prison of the never-ending cramps, gradually melting the pains away, liberating me from the confinement of my own body. I felt hopeful again, seeing light at the end of the tunnel that implied I could be healthy and pain free. But the realisation that I had become ill from the intensity of the long-lasting emotional stress made me sad and worried about the future.

'Could it be because of the divorce? What if it finishes in a few years and my health is going to be affected forever?' I asked Mama, with sudden clarity about the whole situation now. 'I feel as if I'm getting divorced, even though it is not my divorce at all, and all I wish for John is to be free and happy again from this misery and sorrow,' I continued.

'I'm sure it will be over soon,' she replied trying to console me.

How can someone I love so much be both good and bad for me? Love is not supposed to contribute to loss of health, sorrow and suffering, I thought, feeling as if a heavy curtain had suddenly been lifted from my eyes, letting me see the light and the true paradox of our relationship.

CHAPTER 47 - GINGERBREAD

'To know that we know what we know,
and to know that we do not know
what we do not know,
that is true knowledge.'
- Nicolaus Copernicus

Waking up to the magical, winter wonderland of fields covered with a fluffy, white blanket of snow, couldn't be a more perfect scene for Christmas Eve in Poland.

The stillness of the cold air let the trees, wrapped in a layer of frost, sparkle in the morning sun. The mist was slowly dying down further at the distance, where the meadows bloomed in lush greenery in the summer and only a deer couple with a baby were walking in the freshly fallen snow, making first footsteps of the day. Christmas with John in my family home in Poland was the true celebration of our love. We decorated the table in the living room and put the English Christmas crackers, which John had insisted we bring with us, on each plate.

'What are they?' Mama asked.

'It's a surprise, you'll see. It's one of the English traditions,' I replied, hoping she would like it.

The whole house was filled with the mouth-watering smells of a cheese cake getting a light brown crust in the oven and Christmas carols, played on the radio and TV stations in each room. John and I were excitedly dressing for dinner, spraying lots of John's musky and amber perfume on each other, as if bathing in it. I had always loved the intensity of men's fragrances, especially warm and woody in the cold winter weather like today.

According to our Polish tradition, as soon as the first star had appeared in the sky, we could start our Christmas Eve dinner, but the avalanche of heavy snow at dusk made it impossible for us to see it as the sky was not clear. We started our dinner regardless, hoping that the first star was already there. Sharing the holy wafer with one other and expressing good wishes in a touching moment that had always made me tearful, was immediately followed by the English custom of pulling crackers and checking each other's tiny secret gifts hidden inside the paper tubes. It was a true combination of Polish and English traditions which put a smile on everyone's faces, especially when we all put silver paper crowns on our heads, something we had never done before.

To start our dinner of 12 traditional dishes, first came the hot beetroot soup with mini dumplings filled with mushrooms, then the herring salad and fried carp which I had never been a fan of—especially, when as a small child, after having befriended them, joyfully swimming in our bathtub, they ended up on my plate on Christmas Eve. Thankfully, my mama had finally objected to this so-called 'tradition' and decided to only buy ready-prepared fillets—a bit more of a humanitarian approach! The most exciting part, after dinner, was obviously opening the presents that had been placed under the Christmas tree in the morning. I got most, for some unknown reason. I must have been a very good girl that year. I gasped, having opened the box from Santa, or rather John, at a black and silver watch, dressed in sparkling diamonds.

'A watch with diamonds. To show your time with me,' he whispered to my ear, making me blush from such a generous and unexpected gift.

'Thank you, you are too kind,' I replied, placing a soft kiss on his lips.

My mama had also received a lovely golden watch, making her ecstatic because watches had always been her sweet indulgence and knowing it was from John, she jumped from her chair and rushed to him to give him a big kiss and a hug.

'You are welcome, Mama,' he replied, hugging her.

Even Cezar got a cute little present, a white tooth-cleaning bone but inexplicably, it first ended up between John's teeth so I took a picture of him, growling like a dog. Cezar was watching him, thinking, 'Who does he think he is? It is for me,' or at least that was what he could have thought. After dinner, we all rested on the sofa, watching Christmas movies—ones that John had already seen, so that there was no need for me to translate them. I lay my head on his warm chest, hearing the relaxing pounding of his heart, feeling blissful with the man I loved and who loved me so much, back in my family home.

John had brought a 'professional' Santa Claus outfit for my mama so that she could dress up as Santa before our visit to my neighbours' and surprise the sweet little girl, Daria, with gifts from us and her parents, packed into a big white potato sack. The whole house was laughing and screaming when we were entering it with an unrecognisable Mama, holding a long wooden stick, covered in silver foil. John, just like everyone else, had to fall on his knees in front of her before being given a present, trying to convince Santa that he had been a good boy—just another hilarious tradition. In my opinion, he had always been a good boy. At least till then!

Just before midnight, we went to the cathedral to take part in *pasterka*, the traditional midnight Christmas mass. My stepdad had to drive very slowly through the country roads covered by a layer of freshly-fallen snow. The windscreen wipers moved fast to help with the visibility when the thick snowflakes hit it with great speed. The cathedral, packed to the brim with worshippers, dressed in warm fur coats and hats, was filled with heavy scents of mixed fragrances and the lights on the high ceiling and brick red walls, reflected the shadows of statues of saints. Standing close to John, squeezed in the middle of the crowd, gathered in the church at midnight, I felt joyful.

'Thank you, God, for this amazing man and his love. Please bless our future,' I prayed, expressing my love to John by glancing at him, without the need to say a single word.

John didn't understand the priests' preaching, nor our singing, but I could see in his calm, composed face and sparkling eyes that he was touched by the atmosphere of this spiritual experience.

'I prayed for our happy new beginning in Holland,' I said to him, having left the church and headed into the freezing cold air.

'Me too,' he replied, kissing snowflakes falling onto my cold nose.

As soon as we had got back home, we jumped under the double covers of our bed and hugged.

'I am so happy that I experienced this special day with you. Thank you. It was the best Christmas Eve in my life,' I whispered, staring into John's sparkling from the bedside candle eyes and caressing his face with tips of my fingers.

'Thank you for having me here, baby,' he replied and wrapped me in his warm arms.

The next day, we walked around Toruń. This magnificent Gothic town, with many UNESCO-listed sights and where the Teutonic order in the thirteenth century had built a castle, was surrounded by majestic red-brick wall defences, overlooking the river *Wisla*. I strolled with John and Mama around the old town which was now covered with a thick layer of snow. John lifted me in his arms for a photo by the river and then again by an impressive Christmas tree next to the *Mikołaj Kopernik,* or in English, Nicolaus Copernicus statue, of the famous astronomer who had discovered that it was actually the Sun that had been in the centre of the universe and the Earth had revolved around it, not the other way round as had been thought before.

Having entered the sweetshop, every child's dream place, we were transported into a paradise of deliciously smelling *pierniki,* Toruń's most famous gingerbread, filled with fragrant pear, rose and strawberry jam in various shapes and sizes, including hearts, angels, Christmas trees, and Toruń town houses. I ended up with not less than two bags of them, a true feast for my soul and inner child! Afterwards, we were delighted to try the most delicious pancakes in one of the famous town's restaurants, filled with minced meat in tomato or garlic sauce, followed by sweet versions: white vanilla cheese with blueberries.

'We need to come back here next year. It's a feast that needs to be repeated!' John announced, having finished his second pancake.

'Ok, let's come back here next year,' I replied, excited about our future plans together.

CHAPTER 48 – MOONLIGHT WISH

New Years Eve, with a live band and a traditional Polish feast, in a local hotel was the night I had been looking forward to.

With John wearing his black tuxedo with a bow tie and me in a short nude lace dress with a fur throw on my shoulders, we had to have a quick kiss under the mistletoe before leaving for the party. When we arrived at the venue, having been dropped off by my stepdad, we entered the ballroom, decorated with hundreds of colourful balloons and ribbons, with tables bending under stacks of food, and men and women dressed in evening attire, talking and laughing loudly. The waitress showed us a secluded table for two on a balcony, overlooking the dance floor. We were presented with more and more amazing food, brought on big platters, one after another. There was herring in garlic oil, vegetable and mayonnaise salad, beetroot soup, croquettes with mushrooms, a steak in breadcrumbs with potatoes and a salad, and many more delicious dishes which filled our bellies to the brim, and the only thing that we were given to drink was Polish vodka.

'That's the only alcohol we have!' I said, worried that John might not enjoy it.

'Ok, let's do this,' he announced, opening a bottle and pouring a shot for both of us with a smile.

'*Na zdrowie*! Cheers,' I said, clinking my shot glass with his and drinking it in one go, making a funny face from the sudden burning sensation in my throat, as if it was on fire.

'Would you like to dance, madam?' he asked. in an English gentleman manner, reaching out for my hand across the table.

'Of course, let's make the dance floor ours!' I replied, grinning, and a few minutes later, we ended up showing off our signature moves that we had learnt in England, making people stare at us. We were on fire, with lots of energy and enthusiasm, hugging and kissing each time a song finished.

'I love having so much fun with you,' he whispered in my ear and kissing me right below it, giving me shivers, whilst gazing at the ceiling covered in colourful balloons, feeling ecstatic to be in his embrace.

Just before midnight, we put our coats on, and hugging each other, we stood in the small courtyard, watching a spectacular fireworks show right above our heads, making me scream every time they burst into millions of sparkles, lighting up the dark winter sky into a colour frenzy. John kissed my cold lips and I made a wish that this joy would never end.

'Happy New Year!' I exclaimed.

'For the best year of our lives! In our new home in Holland!'

At around two o'clock in the morning, after more food, drink and dancing, we felt it was time for us to go back home. It was too late for my stepdad to pick us up and a taxi would take ages to arrive at this time of night.

'Fancy a walk in the snow?' I asked, uncertain whether he would be happy to do it. After all, it was more than two miles in freezing cold temperatures through the countryside.

'Yes, sure, why not? Let's walk!' he replied to my delight.

Once I swapped my dancing shoes for warm boots, we walked through the town streets covered in a few centimetres of snow, skipping like small children seeing snow for the first time. Our teeth were chattering from the cold air as we were squeezing each other's hands in furry gloves. When we turned into the country road leading to my house, alongside the rail tracks, it got pitch dark as there were no street lights there. The freshly fallen snow was much deeper and squeaking under our feet from the minus seven temperature. The tall trees on both sides of the road, with the frost wrapping every branch, turned the alley into a magical tunnel from a winter wonderland, where I could touch the branches, making the sparkling white shower fall on our heads. The full moon, bigger than in England—or at least it always had seemed as if it was, for some inexplicable reason—was shining bright, leading us on the path, just as a lighthouse would show the way to two lost souls at sea. The way to our new life. New year. New country. New home. The life we had been dreaming about for so long. And nothing and nobody was going to stop us.

'I love this. It is so relaxing, being here with you in Poland, I love your mama, Cezar and the countryside,' John confessed, making me want to pinch myself.

Am I dreaming? Is this real? Am I really here in the middle of the night, in the freezing cold Polish countryside with the most amazing man by my side? This is unreal! I thought when John pulled me towards him firmly, squeezing me close to his chest and kissing me tenderly with raw passion.

His lips were cold but his breath was warm, making me dizzy from the perfect juxtaposition of the change in temperatures and the passion. Even his nose turned into an ice cube, pressed against my cheek. Once he released me from his strong embrace, I glanced at the moon, watching us carefully and I said a silent wish: 'Please God, let us be finally happy once we start our new life in Holland and help us forget about the nightmare of the divorce. Please bless our path. Thank you.' I said my silent wish, glancing at the moon, which was watching us carefully in this special moment, hoping that that the feeling of gratitude combined with the wish would make it work, like a magic spell for the Happily Ever After.

'I can't wait to slip under the cover of our bed and ravish you tonight,' he whispered before we had reached the house.

Cezar, on hearing the doorbell, started barking as if we were burglars trying to break into the house. It took a while for my mama to wake up and let us in, frozen from the night walk in the snow. I lit a candle on the bedside table and snuggled into bed, wrapping John's cold body around me.

'I'm so cold,' I whispered, my teeth chattering from the shivering.

'Let me warm you up, then,' he replied in husky voice and covered our heads with a duvet.

'I love you so much. I will never leave you,' he added in this romantic and delightful moment, making me feel that our happy life was only about to start.

CHAPTER 49 - DUTCH DREAM

'Goodbye England! It is time for me to say goodbye to my home for the last few years! I am starting a new life with my soulmate in Holland, in my new home where I will relax in a Jacuzzi and sauna, sipping wine by a marble fireplace! I can't wait!' I announced in one of my social media posts a month later. And: 'I am going to miss you all as I move to Holland next week with my Knight!' And: 'I have never been so happy. It's soo wonderful to start our new life and John is just amazing.'

I knew I had made the right decision. To leave everything. For John. For us. Despite my internal voice, whispering now and again that it was a shame that John hadn't proposed to me before the move. I tried to silence that sneaky worrying voice because, after all, he had given me a promise ring when we had got back from our trip to Cyprus a month before.

'Come on, baby! Let's choose something nice for you,' he'd suggested, pointing at my favourite jewellery shop at the airport.

Unsure what to choose, my eyes kept stopping at the gorgeous, sparkling rings in the long display cabinet. They all looked divine.

'Do you want to try this one?' an older blond lady at the counter asked, watching me staring at one of them, as if my eyes had been glued to it.

I looked at John and he smiled nodding. The ring looked stunning on my finger and it was the kind of design I would have dreamed of as an engagement ring.

'It's a promise ring. For you,' John whispered when we had walked out of the shop.

I looked at him and blushed. My heart was pounding from excitement, unsure what a promise ring had meant, but after checking on the Internet later, I learnt that it was a kind of pre-engagement ring, normally something teenagers would have given to each other. We were far from being teenagers but it was fine with me, still happy to have received it, knowing deep in my heart that as soon as the divorce nightmare was over, John would give me a proper engagement ring. I didn't want to pressure him with anything.

***

On the day of our move to Holland, we were fully prepared, with all my furniture and our belongings neatly packed in boxes. The removals team of four men entered the flat early in the morning and within a couple of hours, everything ended up in a big white lorry. Walking around the rooms, I couldn't believe how quickly they'd got empty. For some reason, I had mixed feelings. I even felt... sorrow. After all, my time in England was definitely over now, and I knew I would never come back here. I had started from zero, years ago, and I had worked really hard to get a good job and be able to live comfortably here. I was proud of what I had achieved. My mama was proud of what I had achieved. I'd started at the bottom of the career ladder, cleaning tables at Stansted Airport, and worked my way up to become a successful professional. Without connections, without help from anyone. Just thanks to my hard work and commitment, never giving up and always seeing the light at the end of the tunnel. Now I had finally reached that light, moving with John to start a happy new life in Holland. My final Together-Forever I had been dreaming of since I was a little girl. Despite my worrying thoughts popping up, I had to trust that we were a strong couple, an indestructible loving union. I knew that he would look after me from now on, living in another country where I wouldn't have a job and had to rely on him. At least for a while, as he had promised to help me find a job, as soon as we had settled properly.

Silently saying goodbye to our nest where so many good and also not-so-good things had happened, I was happy to leave all the arguments, crying and despair behind us. It was over now and we could finally move on, to the life we had been dreaming of for so long. I hoped that John would finally be happy in his new job as vice president of a global company, a big promotion for him, but most of all, allow us spend more quality time together, with no distractions from his soon-to-be ex-wife or stresses from work.

'How much will you have to travel in this new job?' I asked, shortly before we had moved.

'Only about 20 per cent of the time. I will need to travel, but I will be at home more often, which means that we can spend more time together,' he replied and I trusted his word. Why wouldn't I?

CHAPTER 50 - MILLION-EURO VILLA

A stunning villa, in a quiescent village neighbourhood, not far from Amsterdam, seemed like the perfect choice as our new house.

Shortly before our Christmas in Poland, John had called and emailed me a lot to discuss different options and eventually we had decided on the most beautiful house we had ever seen, in a small village, surrounded by open fields and greenhouses but not too far from big cities. The landlady, a lovely Dutch woman in her seventies, had had it for sale for over a million euros for two years, so she had eventually decided to rent it out. The best part was that it was free, as John's company was paying for it with a generous allowance! I loved John's company! Who wouldn't?

'We are here, baby! Look at this!' John exclaimed with childlike enthusiasm, having stopped the car after a drive from the airport, and when I got out of the car on that cold winter afternoon, I was in awe of the majestic white mansion covered by a thick brown thatched roof surrounded by narrow water canals, as if floating on an island.

Our personal castle with a moat, I thought.

'Do you like it?' John asked, cupping my face in his hands and kissing me tenderly.

'I love it! What a mansion! 'It's gorgeous!' I exclaimed, staring at it as if I had just seen Paradise.

I knew I had arrived. At our Dream Home. When John opened the big white door to the large hallway entrance, I saw three opulent white leather sofas in the middle of the living room with a matching marble table and a TV stand, perfectly blended with the luxury cream marble floor covering the whole of downstairs. Red velvet curtains, framed tall glass double doors leading to the patios around the ground floor, and crystal chandeliers gave the space an ostentatious Roman look.

'Imagine opening that door in the summertime to enjoy this huge open space!' I exclaimed, running around our new house as if I were a butterfly that had got trapped, as it was a huge difference to the modest space of my two-bedroom flat in England.

The open plan kitchen, together with the dining area, consisted of sparkling white finish cupboards with silver handles and black marble tops. A large curved wooden staircase with brass railings, led to an even more stunning upstairs space consisting of three large bedrooms.

'This would be a perfect room for our relaxation area, with a massage table in the middle!' I said with a cheeky wink, having entered the first bedroom painted red.

'Oh, the landlady said she had a spare professional massage table which we can use. If you want it, of course?' John asked a rhetorical question with a grin.

'We are so lucky!' I replied with a deep sigh of disbelief that this was our new reality, deciding that the second bedroom, with black and white striped wallpaper, would contain my old furniture from the flat, and the third one, the master bedroom, the biggest and the brightest one, would contain our new furniture.

The long corridor, leading to our new master bedroom, was essentially a huge built-in wardrobe on both sides, with the left side to be mine and the right one John's. When we entered the luxurious en suite bathroom with a large Jacuzzi, a sauna for two, a spacious walk-in shower and his and hers sinks, I jumped from excitement.

'This is exactly what we need. You have no idea know how many cosmetics Monika has got! I can finally have my own space in the cupboard!' John said, smiling at the landlady who had just joined us on the house tour.

Once the removals van parked outside our new house, all our belongings ended up inside and we could slowly unpack, choosing the best new place for each item around the house.

'We need more furniture!' we exclaimed simultaneously, laughing at the sudden realisation of the new reality we found ourselves in, with the space was so huge, that nothing we had brought from our nest could give it a homely feel.

The next day, we ordered a new white leather bed for the master bedroom and went to a local furniture store to get more cupboards and a white dining table with chairs for the kitchen. I was thrilled that we could decorate our new home the way we wanted to and put own mark on it.

'You are the lady of the house now,' John said, kissing me on my neck when I was preparing the bed with our new white and yellow damask-design bedding covers.

'I love seeing you making it so beautiful and homely. I'm so happy we are here. Are you?' he continued, holding my waist tight.

'I'm very happy, let me finish making the bed and I'll cook some dinner, ok?'

What could have been more thrilling and exciting than moving into a new house to start a new life? Every couple's dream come true. Leaving the old. Moving onto the new. A new and brighter future. Especially since a past like ours had not always been paved with roses.

CHAPTER 51 - HAPPILY EVER AFTER

What a wonderful place I am living in! Is this real or am I dreaming? Umm, what am I going to do today? I thought, having woken up alone in the morning.

As a lady of leisure—as that was my new title given to me by John—I spent all my time making sure the house was cosy and beautiful but because it was so huge, unlike my flat back in England, I often spent the whole morning tidying up downstairs and had no energy to clean upstairs. The landlady recommended a local cleaner who could come in once a week and help me clean it, but I replied that I could do it myself, as what else would I be doing all day if I didn't have to clean? And there was no rush for me to do anything. I had all the time in the world so in the first few days, I started my mornings relaxing in the hot bubbles of our Jacuzzi, filled with muscle-soothing lavender sea salts, caressing my still-aching muscles.

I deserve this life. I really do. After all, I had only got ill from the stressful life in England, I thought. And then: But other people are at work right now. I should be working too, shouldn't I? Why am I in a Jacuzzi at ten in the morning, relaxing, when John is out there travelling, working hard. Am I like his ex-wife now, not working and not contributing to anything? And then: I do deserve it. I should just enjoy it.

The annoying feeling of guilt began to pester me as if it was a naughty child constantly striving for attention and not letting go until it got what he wanted. I attempted to convince myself that I did deserve to live in this ostentatious villa while not working, but I was slowly losing my internal battle to the voice of my conscience, which constantly knocked at my heart's door, saying:

'Maybe you don't deserve it! Maybe you are a bad woman now!' Why couldn't I just accept the abundance from the universe? Why was my ego trying to associate me with whom I had been before? These and other questions, eventually found their answers. But it took a while.

My main chore was… cleaning windows. I had to do it almost every day because by the time I had finished cleaning them downstairs, the ones upstairs were dirty again. The thatched roof didn't help as all the water from it splashed all over the crystal clean windows as soon as it had started to rain again. And it did rain a lot! I had always thought it rained a lot in England. I was wrong! I was happy when I bought a special window vacuum device to make cleaning windows more efficient and quicker, but it still took a lot of time. But then again, what was the rush?! I soon became obsessed with clean windows. Was it my way to feel less guilty? I wanted to be grateful for my new life now, but I had always worked, from the moment I had arrived in England. And I was proud to have achieved a lot in my career. But the question of 'Who am I now?' started to arise in my head, as if I had suddenly lost my identity and the feeling of who I truly was. I wasn't a wife. I wasn't a successful professional. I was the girlfriend of a successful businessman and now a full-time housewife, or lady of leisure, in a million-euro villa in Holland. Was this what I had wanted? I guessed so, since I had agreed to it. Was I always going to be only this?

What now? What next? We had achieved our goal. John had achieved his goal of a promotion and moving to Holland. What about me? I am a different person to John. I need to work. I need to have my own money. What about my retirement? What about my financial future? These questions popped into my head more and more often but soon silenced by: Oh. It's fine, just enjoy it.

The house always seemed empty, no matter how many beautiful pieces of furniture we had bought or how many flower vases I had placed in the rooms. The smell of fresh flowers was always redolent of spring and I loved the look of them, even though I was buying them myself now. John stopped doing it, ever since we had moved to Holland. But despite the beautiful surroundings, I was still alone, looking at the perfectly decorated rooms. John was away 80 per cent of the time and the emptiness seemed ten times more now, including the emptiness creeping into my heart. John wasn't as attentive to me as he had been back in England, calling me less frequently, both when working in Holland and travelling around the world.

'I need to go, I have a meeting in five. Bye, baby!' he said, finishing his short calls more and more often.

'Oh, ok!' Let me know how you are later,' I replied, hoping to hear from him again but when I didn't, I assumed he was just busy with new colleagues, dinners and drinks.

My main highlight of each day was visiting Zeus, the landlady's little black pony, with a bag of carrots I had bought in the supermarket for €1. Zeus always seemed happy to see me and enjoyed crunching juicy carrots in his strong white teeth when I brushed his velvet smooth hair and talked to him softly.

'I love you, Zeus, you are so beautiful' I whispered in his ear, happy I could be useful and needed as Zeus had become my best friend in Holland—or rather, my only friend.

We had brought a highest-quality TV set from England with music albums from classic tenors and the newest movies. Playing music loud when walking around the house helped me feel less empty, both in the house and in my heart. The divorce was still on. It had followed us here. There was no end to it and it seemed to be getting worse. John had outbursts of uncontrolled anger and despair which were even worse than in England. I stopped asking about the details of what was happening. I didn't want to know anymore, especially after driving back from a supermarket in a rented car one afternoon, when John started shaking and crying at the wheel, hitting the curb and damaging the wheel. His eyes were red and swollen from tears and my heart started pounding from the stress and adrenaline.

'Please, stop the car. I'll be driving from now on,' I said with shaky voice before swapping seats.

Another day, we were driving back from the city after another argument. I felt sick from a massive pain in my stomach, as if the nerves from the back of my spine wrapped around my belly and chest and squeezed me mercilessly. I sobbed from pain, but John was still shouting and screaming.

'Please, stop, I'm really not well!' I begged, but he continued driving nervously and speeding unnecessarily, as if he had lost his mind.

An enormous cramp gave me a sudden convulsion and I vomited right between my legs. Shaking and shocked from what I had just done, the most embarrassing thing in my life, I wept even more.

'Don't worry, baby, we are almost home,' John said with a much softer and quieter voice.

Upon our arrival, I lay my shaking body on the white sheepskin in front of the fireplace, decorated with pictures from our travels and candles. I curled up, facing the hot fire which caressed my face, and I closed my eyes. 'Please, God, help me,' I prayed, unsure of what was happening.

'Rest, baby. I'll clean the car and then make you some tea,' John said, kissing me on the forehead.

'I don't need anything,' I whispered, staring at the flames, slowly warming up my body.

John came back an hour later and cuddled me from behind. What was happening to me? What was happening to us? Why was that love so painful? We were supposed to have an easier life here. Would this divorce ever finish? How could someone who loved me so much also hurt me so much at the same time?

CHAPTER 52 - LADY OF LEISURE

Ants ran around the house with their tiny little legs, as if getting ready for an emergency meeting, and every time I thought I had got rid of them, they came back the next day.

I used salt, as my mama had recommended, but it didn't seem to work on Dutch ants.

'Maybe it only works on Polish ants. They seem to be some Dutch mutant ants!' I said to her on the phone and she burst out laughing.

They were in the living room, in the kitchen and the hallway, driving me crazy, only a few weeks after we had moved in. 'There are ants everywhere!' I called the landlady a week later, unable to protect our castle from the invasion.

'That's strange, there have never been ants in there. I'll bring you a special ant repellent,' she replied.

They appeared shortly after I had bought three mini palm trees from the local greenhouse as the space in the house was so big that we needed a few plants to make it more cosy. But as it turned out later, I also got free ants in the pots! Part of the Dutch package! And they were my only friends in the house. Maybe they just didn't want me to feel lonely.

One day, John bought me a beautiful white city bicycle with a straw basket so that I could go shopping, just like the Dutch ladies did. The only problem was that it was always windy. Always. Every day. Ok, maybe every other day. But it seemed like every day. Now that explained why there were so many windmills in Holland.

The open spaces around the village were to blame as well, so when John had finally bought his dream super car, I could then drive to the shops. The black beast was loud like a Polish tractor, or at least, that's how it sounded to me, and it made guys in the street cheer at us every time we drove past, shouting and showing thumbs up. The car was so fast that as soon as I had lightly pressed my foot on the clutch, it was already driving 70 miles per hour! And it also drank petrol like a fish and the moment the red light went on the dashboard I had to quickly drive to the nearest petrol station before it ran out of fuel or I'd be having to push it back home, asking tall Dutch men to help me. Dutch people seemed very tall to me. Both men and women. It was great for me though. Being a tall girl myself, I felt I was part of this Gulliver's land.

I decorated the house with luxurious furniture and accessories from a local designer shop where everything matched the interior of our house perfectly. When John was at home, we often went shopping there, spending a little fortune and leaving with so many bags that we had to drive to the store to load them into the car. Every single porcelain cup had a 'Happiness' or 'Joy' sign on it. We also bought a silver cake stand with a glass dome like from a Viennese cake shop, a coaster with an 'I love you' sign and a rattan bread storage box with 'Good Morning' on it. They were so beautiful that we wanted them all in our villa.

The large crystal wine glasses, square plates, cutlery with embroidered silver handles, luxury white leather bar stools, a silver wine rack and a Champagne cooler soon found a new home in our kitchen. A white rattan table right in the middle of the entrance hall was brought to life by a Roman vase with the largest amount of artificial (but real-looking) flowers I could find. It had always been my dream to have a hallway like this and a tall white French mirror that any guest could see the moment they walked in—even though we never had any guests visiting us. When John was at home, we enjoyed having meals and a glass of wine, sitting and hugging on comfortable black cushions of our new rattan furniture on the patio and listening to the relaxing sound of a three-layered water feature that John had installed after our visit to the garden centre.

I tried to be the perfect woman, lady of leisure, a housewife, a girlfriend, a partner or whoever else I had become. It was my first time in such a role and I wanted to show my gratitude and appreciation to my beloved man, looking my best with styled hair and make-up, most flattering clothes and sexy heels, cooking tasty meals whilst waiting for him to come home from work every day he worked in the local office. But I soon realised that John had more to talk about that had happened in his day and in his new job than in mine.

'I talked to the director of our Australian division today,' he said, having finished his lasagne.

'Oh that's great. How was it?'

'Oh, very good. He wants me to see him, so I will need to plan for a visit to Sydney soon.'

'Wow, that's amazing!'

And how was your day, baby?' he asked.

'Well, I saw this amazing mop in the supermarket today. It has got some fantastic features. I think I will get it! Oh, and I cleaned all the windows upstairs before it started to rain again,' I replied, but none of it seemed to be as impressive as John's day.

I was happy for him because he seemed much more relaxed in his new job and he didn't call me crying on the phone that he hated his job like he had done in England, glad that he was happy in his promotion.

I, in return, liked to surprise him by lighting candles around the house, putting our favourite Strauss music on and serving delicious dinners. One night, dressed only in black underwear and his navy blue silk tie, I waited for him to come home, resting my long crossed legs with black heels on the kitchen marble top. When he walked in, his large hazel eyes lit up.

'Hello, I've been waiting for you!'

'Wow, and I'm happy to be back home!' he replied and came up closer, running his fingers along my smooth, shiny legs, covered in shea butter lotion.

'I like your tie!' he said in a husky voice, kissing me tenderly.

'It's pure silk. I got it from the most sexy man on Earth, my boyfriend,' I replied, with a smirk.

Days like this were just another way to show how happy I was for all that John had done for me and our new life, and I also made sure that we had the best Valentine's Day ever. I decorated our marble dining table with romantic accessories from our favourite shop, silver candelabras, flowers and love notes, scattered red rose petals on the floor from the main door and put on a red dress. The note on the table said: 'Dear John, thank you for being the love of my life, I love you with all my heart and soul. No words can express it properly. Thank you for bringing the biggest blessings to my life. Monika.'

When John entered the house, followed the red rose petals to the table and saw me in a red dress, waiting for him, tears came to his eyes.

'Happy Valentine's Day, my love,' I said, wrapping my arms around him, smiling and unable to stop staring at the most lovingly decorated dinner table he had probably ever seen. 'And another surprise awaits you at the weekend!' I added mysteriously, as I had one more thing planned for us.

'I love you so much, baby,' he said, and squeezed me, taking my breath away.

After having enjoyed fresh oysters with lemon juice, prawns in garlic and ice cream chocolate desserts, John took my hand and danced with me, swaying to our favourite blues songs. I was happy. Finally happy. We had achieved our goal. This had been our goal. To make our dream come true. And it did. Dreams did come true after all.

CHAPTER 53 - ARCADIA

Being naked for a day in a spa seemed like a perfect Valentine's present for my sweetheart!

When I heard about this Paradise, where relaxed and naked spa lovers could enjoy over 20 different kinds of saunas, including outside wooden huts and hot tubs, swimming pools, steam baths and whirlpools, I knew it would be our Arcadia, the idyllic setting in the middle of the Dutch countryside. Perfect for that special day.

When we arrived, we were given crispy white cotton robes that we could change into, in the common lockers' area. Excited and jumping from joy like little children that were about to get some sweets, we walked into the outside area and saw a garden with naked men and women, hairy, not hairy, with saggy boobs, small boobs, fat, skinny and every shape of the body one could imagine, getting into the pools, having showers together and relaxing on sun beds to cool down. I tried to stay calm and not to laugh at the most unusual sight I had ever seen in my life. After all, it was not something I could call a reality, seeing strangers walking around naked in public.

'Oh my God, this is a bit embarrassing!' I murmured.

'Oh, wow,' John exclaimed. 'Ok, let's do this! Come on, baby, take your robe off!' he added, grinning in a frolicsome manner, ready for the antics in this surreal environment, and then he ran back to the building to hang his bathrobe, showing off his firm bare buttocks and sculptured athletic body.

I followed him and did the same! That was it, there was no turning back! We were both standing there naked, just as God had created us and looked at each other's eyes.

'It's cold!!!' we both exclaimed simultaneously and ran to the closest hot tub, looking like a giant oak wine barrel, except instead of being filled with mulled wine, which could have been interesting, it was filled to the brim with the most delightful hot water, making us sigh from the unexpected pleasure as soon as we had submerged our cold bodies in it.

Yes, this is Heaven, I thought, watching the hot steam dancing with the cold February air in perfect harmony.

It was not something I would have ever done in winter back in England, especially with the snow still lying on the ground. Or ever, really. It was a cultural shock, seeing naked people who smiled and said hello, not worrying about anything. But it was an unexpectedly freeing experience, diving into hot bubbles with my beloved man, holding his hand and sneakily kissing him on his wet neck. I had missed his closeness and affection. John had been away more than I had anticipated, and it felt as if something had changed between us since we moved to Holland. He seemed a bit more distant, we didn't talk as much and his calls became less frequent. I tried to ignore that unpleasant worrying feeling creeping in, but I didn't want to bother him with my feelings or mention the slight boredom in the house, left alone whilst he was travelling around the world, meeting new people and following his dream career. It could have sounded very ungrateful and after all, before we had moved, he had promised that he might take me with him to some of his trips—even though so far he hadn't. Saying goodbye to him early in the mornings, standing at the doorway in my silk white nightie, I thought, *I wish I could go with you,* but quickly dismissed my silly, unreasonable expectations, wanting to be grateful for living a life that many people could only dream about, our Dutch Dream.

Our day in Arcadia turned out to be wonderful, running around naked, trying out all the different saunas, followed by a relaxing couples massage and a healthy lunch, but this time wearing robes, as it would have been too strange to eat in a restaurant as God had created us. Entering one of the biggest sauna huts, full of naked women stretching on the hot wooden benches, a quick thought of regret had popped into my mind that maybe I shouldn't have taken John to this naked-women paradise, making it probably the best Valentine's present he had ever received! But knew I shouldn't feel threatened by any of these women, as John loved and adored me as the most wonderful woman on Earth. When we submerged into a hot, open-air, dead sea floating pool, surrounded by colourful Spanish style walls, I felt a glimpse of freedom. Freedom from the cold, winter air at twilight, but also a taste of freedom from worries, which were lurking in my mind, day and night.

Will we ever be free from his ex-wife? Will the divorce ever end? Will he have to work hard only to give away half of his salary because she doesn't want to work for the rest of her life? Will there always be the three of us in this relationship or will we have a clean break? I thought, but quickly reminded myself that it was supposed to be a relaxing time and I shouldn't worry about the future.

Floating naked in the hot sea water, feeling weightless, gazing at the deep blue sky sprinkled with luminous stars, being surrounded by the Spanish walls and palm trees, being gently moved around by John holding my head whilst massaging my scalp, was the most liberating experience of my life. I felt close to him again and I knew he felt the same.

After this surreal experience, we scrubbed each other's bodies in the low light of the *hammam* area. John lay on the blue marble surface with closed eyes as I scrubbed his arms, legs and belly in a gentle way with a soap and loofa, removing all the dead skin cells, making his sexy body smooth and soft. After washing it all off with water which I had brought from the taps in copper bowls, we swapped places and it was now my turn to relax and be pampered by my man. A true relaxation heaven. Scrubbing each other's bodies with fragrant sea salt during our showers the whole day was our ultimate loving act. That's how we had always shown our affection back home, taking showers together and lathering each other's bodies with our favourite aromatic shower gel, with exotic scents of rose, jasmine and sandalwood, which had left our skins beautifully fragranced and soft. We loved washing each other's hair whilst massaging the scalp with conditioners both for relaxation, and simply because we wanted to spend every minute together.

'It's a waste of water if we shower separately and we can't wash each other's backs, right?' I said to John as a perfect explanation.

'Exactly, you are right,' he agreed as it was a sensual and intimate daily ritual which had only made our relationship stronger.

CHAPTER 54 - BABY SLOPE

Our relationship changed.

At least, that's how it felt to me now. Maybe because the country changed. We were not in England anymore where we could do the usual things we loved, such as dancing, visiting historic houses, castles, beautiful gardens and having romantic picnics in the countryside. We had found ourselves in a new reality. It was supposed to be better for us, but was it? To my own surprise and genuine annoyance, I realised I actually missed England. But why? We'd hated it when we were there and couldn't wait to leave it. Perhaps because the Dutch seaside had always seemed very cold and windy and we didn't want to venture out there. Moreover, there weren't too many historic towns nearby and that was something we had always appreciated back in England. But luckily, we had an amazing trip planned to Innsbruck, the Tyrolean capital for my birthday in March, the perfect destination for winter sports and trying out skiing for the first time. I had never been skiing before and I was very excited to finally give it a go. The highlight of our trip was to be a visit to a crystal shop, not too far from Innsbruck. Every time John had returned from working abroad, the first thing he did was to open the suitcase and shower me with gifts, such as necklaces and earrings with crystals sparkling like diamonds, designer perfumes, make-up and local souvenirs, probably trying to make it up to me that he had left me at home while he was travelling around the world.

Our Innsbruck hotel in the town centre, overlooked the Tyrolean Alps, covered by the freshly fallen snow, glistening in the morning sun against the contrasting deep blue sky. After we had checked in, the concierge booked a dinner for us in one of the finest restaurants in town on the night of my birthday. I was very excited to hear that and simply couldn't wait. The lovely gentleman also recommended a few traditional places for us to visit. The picturesque town sat in a valley, surrounded by mammoth snow-capped mountains, with endless vistas. No matter what street we went to, it felt as if we had stepped into a postcard.

'Wow, wow, wow,' I said with astonishment every time we'd turned into a different street.

'Close your mouth, baby. You will catch a cold,' John replied, humorously.

The Altstadt, the medieval Old Town, with the Habsburg palace, was full of Renaissance and Baroque style buildings in various pastel colours of green, yellow, blue, turquoise and pink which only added to the idyllic scenery, perfect for a stroll hand-in-hand. We then enjoyed *Cafe Mozart*, full of warmth and aroma double espresso with whipped cream and a shot of sherry brandy on the side, whilst we were sitting on chairs covered by sheep skin, marvelling at the backdrop of scenic Nordkette mountains. We couldn't resist the traditional warm apple strudel, the most succulent chunks of apples, cinnamon and raisins, wrapped in a flaky pastry, also called 'Apple Whirlpool', topped with whipped cream. The oldest recipe, in a handwritten cookbook, dating back to 1696, was supposedly held in the Vienna National Library. Now that was something I should have seen last time we were in Vienna! Just, I hadn't known about this interesting fact then. One good reason to go back there, to see the original recipe for this heavenly dessert.

Later, we walked past the famous 'Goldenes Dachl', or the 'Golden Roof', slated with 2,657 fire-gilded copper shingles. The Gothic bay with the roof was built for Emperor Maximilian I around 1500 AD, for his wedding, but the main purpose was to put a stop to the rumours, regarding the imperial financial difficulties.

'Look at that shining gold!' I gasped.

'It's stunning!' John replied, opening his mouth this time from astonishment.

'Come on, I'll treat you to a birthday perfume,' John said, pulling my hand as we were walking past a perfume boutique.

'What kind of perfume are you looking for?' a tall blond lady asked with a strong Austrian accent, before I had even had a chance to look at anything.

'Umm, I think I like warm, sensual type of fragrances,' I replied.

'Ok, let me show you a few from this exquisite French perfumer using Arabian oils,' she replied, and sprayed the perfume from different coloured bottles, placed in a row on the shelf in front of us.

'These are the best quality perfumes we have in store, with great longevity and sillage. Which one is your favourite?' she continued, as I was smelling five different testing strips.

'I think, this one! I love it! How much is it?'

'A hundred and fifty euros,' she replied and John just asked her to pack it for me.

'Thank you so much sweetie, you are so kind!' I exclaimed, happy for my birthday gift.

'You are welcome! There is more to come! You smell like an Arabian queen now!' he replied, inhaling the intense scent of femme fatale, with sweet notes of French and Arabian roses and musky Guinean hibiscus, accompanied with spicy oud, patchouli and leather.

The luxury perfume in a golden bottle had become my favourite one, making me feel like a strong, sensual and powerful woman. It also worked like an aphrodisiac and a sexual tonic, turning John into a wild animal, obsessed with kissing and hugging me every time I had sprayed it all over my bare neck. The unspoken power of fragrance over men!

'You mean I smell like a Polish princess,' I replied, winking. 'We also had princesses in Poland, you know, and they could have worn such exotic perfumes!'

The next morning, we changed into our skiing outfits. My white set consisted of padded trousers with black braces, a matching jacket, white gloves and a hat, with ear flaps making me look a bit like a dog. We now had to get our skis and skiing boots from a hire shop nearby, which were so stiff that I could hardly walk in them, but apparently, that was the way they were supposed to be. Wearing our boots and holding skis, we got into the lift which took us to the top, in order to meet our ski coach for the next three days, waiting for us on top of the mountain. We saw him standing by an igloo, smiling and ready to greet us.

'Hey guys, nice to meet you! So first time, huh?' he asked.

'Yes, first time and ready to go,' John replied, smiling.

The views from the mountain were breathtaking and I was thrilled about the lesson on the 'baby slope'. It was called a 'baby slope' because it was for… babies or total beginners like us, who had never skied in their life and suddenly decided to just do it on the very top of the Tyrolean mountain. Our teacher, a young Austrian man with very good English, spent the first two hours to teach us how to stand, move in the right direction rather than backwards, and stop, by touching the front of both skis. It was quite a big challenge for us, but once we learnt the basics, we went up the 'baby slope', using a cute narrow belt lift. It was fun standing on it but the moment I turned around to look at John, I got dizzy and fell off it, with my skis stuck on it and me sitting next to it, watching John passing me by, waving and laughing his head off. That was a bit embarrassing, but not as much as when he later forgot how to break, smashing into the igloo with full force, like a funny cartoon character.

'Sweetie, please try not to kill yourself! I want you to live!' I said when he got back up the hill, with me grinning from the silent satisfaction that at least I knew how to break!

The scenery was splendid. The sky had the deepest hue of blue I had ever seen, due to the crisp white snow reflecting its beauty. I felt as if we were on top of the world, feeling the warm rays of sun on our faces and it wasn't even as cold as I had thought it would be. We could eat our *Wiener Schnitzel* and a beer on the wooden terrace of the restaurant. Having finished for the day, after attempts to jump over small hills, we had a beer in the igloo bar, carved out of ice, just like the ice bar in Prague. The seats were covered with sheep skin and dimmed colourful lights, and gave it a romantic atmosphere, but we decided to sit on sun beds, right by the edge of the mountain, marvelling at the most amazing views of Innsbruck, perfectly nestled in the middle of the valley.

'What a view! I'm so happy we've tried this!' I exclaimed, kissing my skiing champion, looking incredibly tired.

'Me too!' he replied with a visible relief that it had finished.

The next day, our coach decided we were ready to try the more difficult slope. The so called 'blue slope', which we had to get to on a ski lift. I sat with the coach and John was alone, right behind us. When we jumped off it, at the very top, I turned around and I couldn't see John. I then noticed him right in front us, trying to stop by the wall of snow.

'Jesus,' I said to the coach, laughing, 'and you think we are ready for the next level!'

When we set off down the slope, I quickly realised that it was a huge mistake. It was so steep that I ended up falling on my backside in the middle of it and not really knowing what to do next, afraid to get up and only hearing other skiers, swishing right next to me on both sides at high speed.

Oh my God, what now? I thought, being left there alone, as John could hardly stand and move, holding the coach's hands and looking completely terrified.

Right, I thought, *I need to do something to get out of here. I can't go back up, obviously, which would have been the best option, but it's impossible, so the only way, is to go down on my own.*

'You can do this,' I said to myself, lifting up slowly and trying to get my balance without flying off like a cocker spaniel on skis.

We didn't even have our sticks with us for balance because the coach had decided that we didn't need them and they would only distract us from skiing. So, I started to move in a zig zag style, as taught by the coach. As long as I moved closer to the bottom of the hill, I knew I would be fine. I conquered my fears, knowing that it was either do or die situation, and I managed to do it! I was so proud of myself. The only thing I had to do now was to wait about half an hour for John to ski down with the help of the coach and when he did, I didn't even say a word about it.

'Well done!' I said, gazing at him, looking red, with sweat dripping down his cheeks and breathing heavily.

Maybe that was enough of skiing for us this time in Innsbruck. Happy that we were still alive, we went back to the hotel and dozed off on the bed.

'What a day, huh?' I said, hardly able to lift my hand from exhaustion to put it on top of his.

'We did well!' he replied.

'We should do it again!' I said joyfully but seeing John's unamused face I dropped the subject.

I knew it was the last thing he would ever want to do again. But why? I loved that I'd taken this enormous challenge and conquered my fears. I felt courageous and the feeling of winning in the end couldn't be more rewarding. I had to find my internal strength and I did it. By myself and without anyone's help. Unlike John. But who said that men were stronger than women in conquering fears? Sometimes the difference was only in attitude and frame of mind.

CHAPTER 55 - CRYSTAL LADY

I couldn't feel more ecstatic, being driven to get my birthday gift in the crystals shop, just outside of Innsbruck the next day.

I gazed at the picturesque views of the mountains, squeezing John's hand in disbelief that it was really happening. I looked at him saying a silent gratitude to God for having such an amazing man in my life. Since I had started taking antidepressants in the last few months, my muscle pains were almost gone and I was full of hope for our future, avoiding talking and thinking about the endless divorce.

The shop was like a world of fantasy with artistic displays of the most unique objects, purely made from different size and colour crystals. The first thing we admired before we even went into the shop was a fountain in the shape of a giant's face, made from crystals and gushing water from his mouth and eyes. The inside of the building was a magical show of art and human imagination. Everything in there was made of crystals: the walls, miniatures of the Taj Mahal, the Pyramids and the Empire State Building, trees, giant statues and rings bigger than us. It was a bizarre but exciting show of human creativity and once we went past it, we were in the busy and lively shop, full of customers. We walked around it, staring at the most beautiful pieces of jewellery. Seeing a limited edition, celebrity-style chunky chain necklace with matching earrings, we both gasped. It was the most sparkling, glistening and stunning piece in there. The shop assistant, in her late forties, with short brown hair, and a bit plump, looking a bit like John's soon-to-be ex-wife, took it out of the display cabinet, wearing white cotton gloves, and put it on my bare neck. It glistened with millions of crystals against my dusty pink, merino wool V-neck jumper. I felt like Queen Victoria, trying on the crown from the Crown Jewels collection, just before the coronation.

'It's Monika's birthday today and we are looking for something special,' John explained to her.

'Oh, in that case, this is a perfect piece! There were only three necklaces like this made in the world and it looks just gorgeous on her!' she replied, grinning at John with an exaggerated enthusiasm.

'Do you like it? John asked.

'Oh I love it, but how much is it?' I replied, blushing, thinking that it must have been expensive.

'The whole set, both the necklace and the earrings, is €1000, but it's one of a kind and there are only three of these in the world,' she replied confidently.

'We'll take it!' John replied without hesitation.

'Oh that's lovely, let me pack it for you,' she said, looking at both of us with astonishment.

'So where do you live?' she asked as she was putting it in a lovely box.

'We live in Holland. This is our long weekend away to celebrate Monika's birthday,' John replied.

'Why don't you come to our VIP area for a glass of Champagne. It's Monika's birthday, after all. Would you like that?' she asked, surprising us with such a generous offer.

'Yes, that would be very nice, thank you,' John replied, looking at my grin.

'Great, follow me,' she said and after a few steps, she told us to wait and went on to talk to the security guard by the door.

'Wow,' both of us gasped simultaneously, looking at each other and kissing tenderly from excitement.

The VIP Champagne bar was chic, with walls covered in shelves full of all types of Champagne and glasses. Georgina, as that was the lady's name, sat down with us on an armchair at a small round glass table and continued with the conversation, explaining that she was originally from Canada and had decided to live in Austria for a while, after having travelled around the world. In return, John told her about his new job and the different locations he now had to travel to for work. I silently wondered why she was so nice, spending her working time to chat with us.

Why didn't she just take us to the table and leave us alone so that we could enjoy this experience for ourselves? I thought, feeling a bit annoyed that she had joined us.

'Anyway, it was lovely to meet you,' she finally said to my relief, stood up and left the VIP bar.

Finally! I thought, continuing to sip Champagne and not believing our luck and such amazing treatment, but after a few minutes later, she came back.

'Maybe you can give me your email address so that we can stay in touch?' she asked in a direct manner, looking at John.

I could not understand why she was so forward. I gazed at John, feeling my blood starting to simmer in my veins, wondering what he was about to say and to my huge surprise, he gave her his own email address, which she wrote down in her phone.

Why didn't he give her mine? I thought, feeling that it just wasn't not right.

'Thank you, let's stay in touch as I may be visiting Holland soon. Maybe we can meet up again!' she concluded, assuming that we would want to be her new friends.

For a while, I couldn't believe what had just happened. John had given his email address to a woman that we had just met, right in front of my eyes. Just like that. I knew he loved me and I had nothing to worry about, but it raised my internal alarm bells. Would he so easily give it away to a woman he met on his work travels? I thought. But then: Oh, stop it! He loves and adores you, Monika! He is your soulmate! said another internal voice, trying to calm me down.

In the evening, we dressed up for our pre-booked dinner in the finest restaurant in Innsbruck town centre. I put on my special dress with a jacket that I had worn for the concert in Schönbrunn Palace and, of course, my new crystal necklace and earrings. John, looking suave, wore his tuxedo with a bow tie and a crisp white shirt.

'You look stunning!' he said, kissing my hand like an English gentleman.

'You too! You are the most handsome and sexy man I have ever met!' I replied, making him pull his signature sweet, innocent face.

'Come on, I have another surprise for you,' he said, kissing me tenderly and a few minutes later, we were walking up the wide stairs of a casino. 'You do it, baby. It's your first time playing so it should be lucky,' he said when we stopped by the roulette table.

I chose a red number and... I won €200! A big improvement on my lost €1 coin in Monaco years before!

'You are amazing,' he said, kissing and squeezing my waist from excitement. 'Let's go for dinner now,' he added.

The restaurant was in the style of an Austrian castle where everything was made of wood, including the wood-panelled walls, tables and chairs. Through the windows, we gazed at the flickering lights of the town, sitting at a table covered with white linen, feeling like celebrities sipping Champagne and eating fresh oysters with herbs and lemon. Having finished our starter and the mains, the waiter came to our table singing 'Happy Birthday', carrying a chocolate cake with a sign: 'Happy Birthday Monika!' and lit up sparkles on top.

I instantly blushed and smiled, completely surprised and flattered that John had thought about such a special gesture.

What an amazing thing to do! I thought, feeling like the happiest woman on Earth!

'Thank you so much!' I said with gratitude, eating the most delicious flaky chocolate cake.

'You're welcome, baby!' he replied, placing a gentle kiss on my hand, making it the most magical evening yet, spending all the time and effort to make me feel so loved and special.

I couldn't have asked for a better man if I had tried. He was the man of my dreams.

The man of many women's dreams.

CHAPTER 56 - COINCIDENCE

As soon as we had returned from our trip to Austria, we already wanted to go back there again.

But it was not because of the amazing time we had skiing. After John's passionate igloo-kissing accident at full speed and struggling to ski down the 'blue slope' for over an hour, John was not so keen to do that again. Male pride! Men always seemed to only like doing what they were good at. We also didn't want to go back to Austria because of our visit to the amazing crystal shop, nor to the fairytale Neuschwanstein Castle near Füssen in Germany on our way back to Holland, a truly magical castle, surrounded by low-hanging gloomy clouds of mystery, built on a rugged hill by Ludvig II of Bavaria in the 19th century, when I wore my new necklace over my bare neck on top of a white jumper and a hugely oversized grey furry hat, making me look like a Russian princess. I was fascinated by the story of the castle told by a funny sounding tour guide with an unrecognisable accent, making him sound like a chipmunk, causing me and John giggle at the back of the tour. He told us that King Ludvig II had been obsessed with more traditional, medieval times but unfortunately, he was declared insane before the building of the castle was finished and was taken away. The next day, he and his doctor were found drowned, supposedly after an evening walk.

'Umm, it sounds a bit suspicious to me! Did anyone force them into the river because he was inconvenient?' I whispered to John.

As a result, only a third of the rooms were actually completed and the King himself was said to have only lived in the castle for 170 days. We loved the King's bedroom as our favourite room in the castle, with the night sky built into his bed. Apparently, the

King only slept during the day and perhaps that was one of the reasons why he was doomed to be called 'crazy'.

John and I actually wanted to go back to Austria because of another reason, the fabulous five star hotel that we had stopped in for a couple of nights ,with a heated infinity pool and the most spectacular view of the Alps. Moreover, having tried the healing Tibetan bowl massage, we knew we had to go back there again soon. It had been an extremely exhilarating experience to be lying on the floor, surrounded by various size Tibetan bowls which were made to 'sing' by a man running around, striking them one after another, creating a vibration concert with waves of energy, penetrating the smallest molecules of my body, clearing energetic blockages. It was a treatment for the mind, body and spirit which we both needed, releasing any negativity and tension that had been stored in our minds and bodies for months.

But only after a few days from our return home, something strange happened. I was using the computer and because John and I had nothing to hide from each other, we shared our email accounts, and I saw an email coming from Georgina. My heart started pounding fast as it was a reply to a previous email.

Why didn't he tell me about the correspondence with her? I thought.

'Oh, I forgot to tell you!' John exclaimed, trying to brush it off as if it was nothing when I confronted him, but this made me worried as we had never had any secrets from each other.

'You should've just told me. And why does she want our home address?' I asked, getting more and more annoyed.

I had met women like this before. Zosia was a perfect example. Slowly creeping into my life and a happy relationship, stirring things up so that I would end up like her. Miserable and lonely, without a man by her side who would love her. Just because she wasn't happy herself.

'She is just being friendly! And wants to send us a postcard from her travels!' John replied, clearly defending her and making me feel like there was something wrong with me not him.

I tried to forget about the whole conversation but it stayed at the back of my mind, popping up now and again and letting me know that it was wrong.

'Do you want to meet up for dinner with her when we are back at the hotel?' he asked a few days later.

'Are you serious?' We are going for a relaxing romantic break and you want to spend an evening with her? No, I don't want to meet her for dinner,' I replied, feeling annoyed even more, seeing that he wasn't happy with my response.

Why would he want to meet up with her again? Maybe he organised this next trip, to the exact same place because... he wanted to see her? It couldn't be the reason, surely. He only loves me. He is a faithful, genuine and loving man. My thoughts started to go in circles, trying to find a logical explanation.

***

When we arrived at the hotel a couple of weeks later, the scenery looked slightly differently to the one three months before. It was a warm spring day and most of the snow was gone from the mountain tops. Every morning, we took a yoga class in front of the hotel, admiring the perfect postcard view. We then relaxed in the spa and enjoyed the Tibetan bowl massage, followed by a swim in the infinity pool, filled with pleasantly warm water and the best view of the mountains one could imagine. One morning, after our yoga class, we stood on the sunny terrace and I noticed Georgina, talking to two other people. She turned around and having recognised us, she waved.

'Hi, how are you? I didn't know you were here!' she said, giving us both a kiss on the cheeks.

I was furious. *How dare she come over, asking why we didn't announce our arrival to her? What did she want from us?* I was so consumed with anger that I didn't say a word to her. I couldn't. I was speechless, feeling my blood reaching maximum temperature before boiling like in a kettle. John looked uncomfortable, smiling nervously and replying to her interrogative questions. After a while, she finally sensed that we were not interested in having a conversation.

'Well, enjoy your stay!' she said, and walked away a bit confused.

Why was she trying to get into our lives? She is so pushy, I thought.

We went back to the room in an awkward silence and without holding hands. I didn't want to have an argument but I could clearly sense that John was upset. He seemed to like her and wanted to go out with her, having drinks and dinners. But why would he? Wasn't my company enough for him? I tried to convince myself I shouldn't feel threatened. I knew John loved me. But I found it very strange that we met her again. Was it a coincidence?

'Did you tell her we would be here?' I finally asked John whilst having dinner on the restaurant terrace at twilight.

'Of course not!' he replied, and continued to eat his grilled sea bass nervously, avoiding looking into my eyes.

What was this all about?

***

The next day, we stopped at a boutique hotel on top of the Italian Alps. Standing next to each other on the viewing terrace, looking at the magnificent views of the valley surrounded by tall mountains, I felt that John was a bit distant towards me. He wasn't as affectionate as usual, hardly holding my hand and staring at the distance without saying a word.

What is he thinking? I wondered as it wasn't the first time I had felt it.

After his return from Canada two weeks before, I had also sensed that something was wrong. He wasn't as enthusiastic and happy to see me as he had always been. Having spent another two weeks alone in the house, I was desperate for his affection. But he didn't give me many hugs or kisses. He welcomed me with a not-so-passionate kiss when he woke me up, having entered the bedroom in the morning and didn't even want to jump into bed with me. It was his third trip to Canada in the last two months. It must have been an important direction for him. Moreover, during his trips abroad, he was getting more and more busy, so our daily calls turned into every-other-day calls and then every three days or more, a significant change to our communication from when he had been stuck for months in the Middle East, hating it and wanting to be out of there, sobbing a few times a day on the phone. When he got back from Canada this time, he was mysteriously quiet.

'I'm going to do some more shopping for dinner, ok?' I said when he was sitting in the sauna, reading a newspaper, without much reaction to what I had just said.

Maybe he is just tired, I thought, riding my bike to the local shop to get my favourite white asparagus, creamy sauce and sea bass.

***

This hotel on top of the mountain was famous for a state-of-the-art Michelin star restaurant, so having dressed up for the occasion, we sat by the window, or rather, a tall glass wall with stunning view of towns and villages in the valley at twilight. But we did not talk much. The dinner included an array of gustatory little dishes, paired with white wine. The first one was the smallest portion of peas and sprouts in a tiny little cup with an artistic glaze on top. It reminded me of the first meal I had in England when I had counted the 15 peas on my plate, but that was something else!

This was the tastiest, greenest, tiniest little gem of healthy peas and sprouts I had ever tasted, and I only appreciated it once I tried it, but not when the waiter had first uncovered it on my plate, making me ask: 'Oh, that's it?' He did not find it funny, and neither did John. Was I the only one in that restaurant with a sense of humour? The cute, tiny dishes that followed were absolutely mouthwatering, slowly filling up my empty stomach. I loved the thin, delicate ravioli with sheep's milk ricotta, spinach, tomato sauce and basil. The dessert, a honey tart with camomile which melted in the mouth as if it was a tango of flavours, was an unusual and beautiful combination.

'When we go into town tomorrow, I would love to get a copy of a designer bag. I heard that they are only €100 in Italy. What would you like to get?' I finally asked, trying to break the awkward silence.

'Nothing, I think I'll save my money,' he replied with cold voice, making me suddenly felt guilty that I wanted to get something for myself.

But why should I feel guilty? True, I wasn't working anymore, but he'd told me I didn't have to. Moreover, he planned to help me find a job in his company. But it felt to me that John wasn't happy that I wasn't working now. After all, he'd fallen in love with me being impressed by my independence and admiring my achievements in England. I was a different person to him now. Without an identity or work achievements, and completely reliant on him.

After dinner, I took a quick shower and wrapped in the thick crispy white towel. I curled up on the bed and sobbed. John lay down next to me, till it got really dark. I tried to reach out to him but he pushed me away.

What's wrong with us? If only I knew, I could do something about it, I thought.

The next morning after breakfast, I decided to go for a walk on my own, seeing him staring aimlessly at the wall, I couldn't take it anymore. I walked out of the hotel and found a tourist track. I walked and walked, not knowing why I was feeling so bad. I noticed a small charming lake in the middle of the forest and I sat on the bench, listening to the birds singing. I closed my eyes, trying to meditate but I couldn't calm my mind. It all seemed too strange and painful to me.

Why am I alone here? Why can't we communicate properly? What's wrong with us? I thought with desperation.

Two hours later, I went back to the hotel room and sat in an armchair in front of John, but we had nothing to talk about.

'What's wrong? Can you tell me, please?' I asked but he did not say a word, just kept staring at the wall, and none of my efforts to get through to him worked.

Driving back home, we hardly spoke. Halfway through our journey, John had another outburst of anger, shaking and crying, so I told him to stop as soon as I saw a petrol station.

'Calm down. What is it? Is it the divorce? Tell me! Please!' I asked, not knowing what was happening to him but he didn't reply, only cried, staring at the window.

'I'll drive from now on. Come on, let's change the seats,' I commanded, feeling responsible for our safety and silently praying for us to get back home safe.

If only I had known what was wrong! But I could only guess. The divorce.

CHAPTER 57 - ONE-WAY TICKET

I just wanted to get away for a while.

On my own. Go to Poland, spend some time with Mama, whom I greatly missed, and return to Holland once the divorce nightmare was finally over. I started to feel resentful towards John that it had been taking so long, the opposite of what he had promised before our move to Holland. I knew it wasn't his fault, but after two years of dealing with it, our lives were still affected by it on a daily basis. Even here, in a different country, building a new life. John said that it was almost over but deep down, I knew that the worst was still yet to come, in the final round of the battle. I knew he was going to soon realise he had lost almost everything, but I didn't have the strength and energy to watch him anymore, slowly defeated, in this money-grabbing war. This divorce had affected my health and I needed to get better once and for all. My muscle spasms were almost gone, but I had still felt pains all over my body, feeling lethargic and sleepy all the time. I realised it was time for John to take full responsibility for his life and deal with it. On his own.

'Why don't I go to Poland for a while and you can come and get me in the car once it's over. I think it's best for us. Plus, you are going away to Canada for two weeks again so I would be alone here anyway. What do you think?' I asked one evening, not having spoken to him all night, as he had been watching TV.

'Ok,' he replied after a long silence, as if absorbed in his own thoughts, and booked the flight for me from Frankfurt to Bydgoszcz. It was a one-way ticket.

Before I left two days later, John asked me to leave the keys to the car, which were attached to the house keys, and I left them all. Having a last glimpse at the villa, which I had decorated beautifully with so much care and love, making it look stunning, I didn't know then that I would never see it again. I gazed at its grandness, surrounded by the mini moat, when we were driving off, with only one travel bag in the boot of the car.

We had decided to drive to Frankfurt so that we could visit my sister before my flight, and also because John really liked driving our super car on a German motorway with no speed limits. Well, only in some places, but other than that, there were none.

'Do you want to drive? The car can do 350 kilometres per hour but I don't want you to drive that fast. That would be a ridiculous speed and even I wouldn't do it. But you can still get a good feel of it,' John said, when we were approaching the German border.

'Ok, I'll give it a go!' I replied, excited and we swapped seats at the petrol station.

'Come on, baby, you can do it! Faster!' he exclaimed encouragingly when I was getting a feel for the car.

'Jesus Christ, look, it's 250,' I said, glancing at the dashboard a few minutes later, 'I can't believe it! This is crazy!!'

I was driving so fast that both sides of the road, started to blur into a one indistinguishable stream.

'Look! How can they go faster than us!?' I exclaimed, seeing another car, zooming next to us on an empty road.

'Uhuuuu, this is amazing!' I said, smiling, but feeling tense from the sheer stress and adrenaline rush, in charge of a car at such a ridiculous speed, and most of all, our lives. One wrong move and we would be dead. In a split second, our lives on planet Earth would have been over and it would have been very tragic, indeed. Thinking about such a scary scenario, I slowed down and stopped to swap seats again.

'It was unbelievable! I can't believe I did it!' I said, hugging John tight, having got out of the car, feeling my heart pounding as if it was about to jump out of my chest.

'Well done! You are a fantastic driver. I'm proud of you!' he replied, kissing my forehead.

'Ok, let's go. My sister is waiting,' I said and got back to the passenger seat.

My sister and her partner, welcomed us with a true Polish feast and John ate so much that his belly started to hurt and she had to give him some herbal tea for digestion. We then went for a walk along the river in the city and a coffee in the Old Town.

The next morning, John drove off after giving me a not-so-passionate kiss. Was he suddenly upset with me for going to Poland? But if he was, why didn't he stop me by saying, 'Please don't go, I want you to stay here, with me.' If he had said it, I wouldn't have gone. I assumed it was the best solution for us in these circumstances, so that we could stop arguing and hurting our relationship because of the never-ending divorce. We needed to do something to make things better. I needed to make things better and return home when John was finally an officially divorced, free man.

The first two days back at home seemed strange. John didn't call me even once. He didn't even ask if I had arrived ok. It worried me a little bit but I thought that maybe he just needed a rest to get his thoughts together. When he did call me a few days later though, he sobbed on the phone, mumbling through the tears, and I couldn't understand what he was trying to say.

'What is it, sweetheart? What's wrong? Tell me,' I asked, desperate to make any sense out of it.

'It's horrible, baby,' he mumbled through his tears.

'What's horrible? The divorce? You need to stay strong! It will be fine,' I replied, trying to give him the remains of my own confidence in any reasonable outcome, but deep down, I was losing the conviction in my own words.

Moreover, I wasn't sure whether he had meant the divorce or that he was there without me. Or maybe both. But he was going away again for three weeks and I also felt lonely in that house for four months when he was constantly travelling, meeting people around the world whilst I was… cleaning windows and fighting salt battles with the ants, spreading it along the walls and windows as if protecting our fortress from the Ottoman invasion.

I felt sad for him, like I had been for two years, but he needed to deal with it alone from now on. I had to stand up for my own sanity and health. I had no mental strength to cry with him, feeling completely exhausted and depleted, as if I was dying inside from the lack of energy that had been sucked out of me, constantly tired and sleepy. I sometimes lay on the sheep skin by the marble fireplace, staring at the ceiling with tears falling and I didn't know why I was feeling like this. But I felt I was losing my sanity and I needed to do something about it. I had to change something. And take drastic action. Even if it meant leaving my luxury villa where I was supposed to be happy but felt strangely empty instead.

I had read one of John's emails to his mother, saying that the divorce wasn't actually my business, making me feel hurt and… well … betrayed. I felt betrayed because, after all, it was me who had been supporting him every single day for the last two years, encouraging him and suffering his pain. Now he said that it wasn't my business. A paradoxical statement about someone who had gone through that hell with him. And an ungrateful one. I didn't expect a medal, recognising my sacrifice, both health and career wise but a simple 'Thank you' would have been enough.

The beautiful, hot and sunny Polish weather in May made it propitious for sunbathing with my mama in the garden, making the emotional burden I had been carrying with me slowly melt away.

'I finally had the guts to say to John: This is your divorce, your life and you need to deal with it. I feel so exhausted as if I was getting a divorce myself! A strange feeling, especially since I've never been married,' I said to Mama whilst sipping my cold apple juice.

'Of course, darling. It's out of your control anyway, let him deal with it once and for all. It's not your divorce and not your problem,' she replied with full understanding of my decision to remove myself from that situation and take care of my own sanity and health.

'I want to have a new and fresh start with John and not a relationship built on constant despair, crying and misery,' I continued.

This statement, of taking responsibility for my own wellbeing and feelings, and letting John do the same, freed me, in every possible meaning of the word. We both had to feel whole and happy as individuals, rather than unhappy and incomplete and trying to make one whole happy union. After all, we were separate individuals, but we had merged so tightly and completed each other's love that we forgot about our own separateness of being two human beings, with our own hopes and passions. I completely lost my own identity for the sake of being part of his. And it didn't feel right anymore. I had to feel full and complete myself. I just didn't know how, yet. I knew that moving away from the situation a bit was the first step to figuring out what I actually wanted and not only what he wanted. But in that moment, I didn't yet realise that the desire to feel 'free' would turn out to be so—in every sense of the word.

CHAPTER 58 - ALL OR NOTHING

'Only a crystal clear question yields a transparent answer.'
-Zen Proverb

There was that relationship advice book I had read years ago, written by a German female psychologist and a relationship expert.

She explained that if a woman wanted to get a full commitment from a man, she should simply ask him for it and if he said, 'No', leave him. Yes, simply walk away and if he truly loved her, he would be back within two months. But there was obviously a risk and the small print. Once a woman had challenged the man and left him to give him time to decide, there were only two possible outcomes. Either he would realise how much he loved her and come back, wanting to spend the rest of his life with her, or he would decide that he didn't want to get married and never come back to her. I realised that once I decided to leave him, in hope of his quick return, the risk was I could lose him forever. But I needed to know, once and for all, what our future would bring. I had to be brave. My soul couldn't let me settle for an endless uncertainty.

So, two months, according to the studies, was a necessary period of time for a man to realise if he wanted to fully commit. It seemed like an eternity to me but since it was a tried and tested formula, giving a crystal clear answer, I knew had to do it. I needed to know the truth about John's plans for the future, right here, right now. Why wait another year or two? We were almost two years together already, dealing with his never-ending divorce. That had been our goal. To deal with HIS divorce. But what about

MY dreams? What about OUR future together after the divorce? Was marriage and family possible? I still wasn't sure if I would ever want to have children but one thing I did know, I wanted to spend the rest of my life with my soulmate, the man I loved with all my heart, John. I was 99 per cent sure that he wanted the same but the only way for me to find out about the remaining 1 per cent was... to ask him.

And I did.

'I would like us to get married one day, obviously once you get divorced,' I said calmly and with confidence on the phone, having gathered courage for days.

'I'm broke. I've lost everything. I can't do this to you,' he mumbled, being lachrymose on the phone again.

'I don't care if you lose everything. We can work together. We can build our life together from scratch. We have each other, that's all that matters. I love you with all my heart and I want to spend the rest of my life with you,' I replied.

John did not give me the answer, which was fine. I knew he had to think about it. It was an important decision after all, to commit to one person forever. A scary thought for me too. A huge unknown, as it would mean I would always have to have that person in mind when making any significant decisions in the future. I knew I would lose some of my independence and it would not be just about me, anymore. I would always have to consider him and it was a big step for me too, after being independent for so many years in between relationships, gathering strength and living my freedom, deciding what I wanted to do with my life. Once we got married, I would have to follow John to different countries, as we were only supposed to live in Holland for three years before he would be moved somewhere else in the world for another assignment. And it could be anywhere: Africa, the Middle East, Australia. It would mean leaving my friends and family and moving even further way, only relying on him. Hoping he would always love and care for me, making sure that we were fine. It was a huge thing for me to surrender to a man this way. With my whole life. But I was ready to commit. Only to him. I wouldn't have done it for anyone else. But I would, for him, because I trusted him with my whole life.

Unfortunately, soon after my question, our text messages had quickly turned into power struggle of him saying what he wanted and me saying what I wanted. One day, I received a text from John which I would never had expected to receive, not in a million years. 'I'd rather pay for a prostitute than to get married, ever again.'

Having read it, my heart started pounding really fast, as if I had just received my final answer, but I tried to understand why he would say such a horrible thing. His divorce had been hell and the last thing he probably wanted now was to get married again. But he loved and adored me so much that he could have at least given me some hope that it would happen one day. In a year or two. I needed that hope. We needed that hope. Something positive and happy to look forward to, rather than just a divorce settlement, not a natural scenario for a couple, with this as the only goal in a relationship, rather than looking forward to getting married. I wanted to change our sad focus into a joyful one. Moreover, our engagement wouldn't mean we would get married straight away. I would wait.

Our texts became more and more heated. I kept going back to my book, over and over again. It clearly explained that if the man said 'No' to the commitment (and it was likely to happen according to her, because men didn't want to be confronted about it) then I had no other choice but to leave him. My values and dreams as a woman to be in a fully committed relationship for the rest of my life were to be stronger than the man himself. John was the only man I had ever wanted to marry. I had never wished to be a wife of any of the men I had dated before. I had walked away from them, not wanting to settle for something that didn't feel like true love. I kept looking for the right person and finally, John was the right person. I knew he loved me and that he would be back. I just had to wait for a short while, in order for him to realise that he wanted to spend the rest of his life with me. But the fear of pain that this waiting period would bring, was overwhelming, especially when he stopped calling me and texting. I felt sick at the very thought of us not being together. He was my soulmate and I knew I was his.

'I'm sorry, I can't give you what you want. I only made you ill,' John said on the phone, weeping.

'Ok, I understand, but since you say you could never marry me, it's over then. It really is. Send my things to Poland. I can't be with you anymore. I don't want to give up on my dream to get married one day, something I had been yearning for, since I was a little girl. You want to deprive me of it? Of making my dream come true? You also said that you don't want to have more children. I'm not desperate but what if I did want to have a child in a few years' time? Would you deprive me of that as well? I can't let you destroy all my dreams. It's not just about you and the divorce. It's also about what I want. I'm sorry, but it's over.'

CHAPTER 59 - QUEEN IN EXILE

'Silence the angry man with love. Silence the ill-natured man with kindness. Silence the miser with generosity. Silence the liar with truth.'
-Buddha

Once I had made my decision that I couldn't be with John without commitment, there was no way back.

I had to stick to my principles. I had to say 'No' to being just his 'lover', 'girlfriend', 'lady of leisure,' or whatever else he wanted to call me. I realised perfectly well that he would not like the fact that I wanted to stick to my values, because he wanted to control my life his way and according to what he wanted. But my values were strong and I had to stick to them, regardless of the consequences. And the consequences could have been dramatic. I took a huge risk. A crazy risk, to do it, to challenge John when I was on a holiday in Poland, with no job or money and at his complete mercy, depending on his good will. And in that moment, he had that power over me, like a king of his castle, to let me live or to let me die. I was afraid. I was petrified. But deep down I knew I had to be strong and find out the answer. I couldn't betray my soul and stop my willingness to love him forever. Because I was ready to love him, till I die. And I knew he felt the same.

'I sent you an email,' John texted me, a few days after my 'standing up to myself' and letting him know that I was ready to leave him, unless he wanted to marry me.

My Internet wasn't working, so I quickly got on my bike and rushed to the neighbours' house. 'Can I just quickly check my emails, please?' I asked Daria's grandma who had opened the door, with a pounding heart from riding my bike like a lunatic, but mainly from the sheer panic of what he might had written. I opened my inbox and saw the email. It wasn't very long.

'Hi Mon,

Firstly, I would like to thank you for everything that you have brought to my life. We have gone through so much together.

However, I think we have too much history and I can't give you what you want. I don't want to get married again. I'm also worried about my sons and because of all that's happened, I worry I may not have a good relationship with them. I'm really sorry. Please apologise to your mama.

I wish you all the best in life,

John.'

Tears came to my eyes and my heart was pounding as if it was about to explode.

What does he mean? What is he saying? That he doesn't want to be with me or just doesn't want to marry me? That it's over? Like, forever? I thought frantically, not believing my own eyes, quickly filling up with tears, trying to process it in my head.

I switched the computer off and left before Daria's grandma could notice me crying. I rode back to my house 100 miles per hour and ran into the kitchen, breathless.

'What happened?' Mama asked me with a worried voice, looking at me as if she had seen a ghost.

'It's... over.'

'What do you mean, it's over? John said that? Really?'

'Yes, he said he can't marry me and be with me, and I should say to you that he is very sorry,' I replied with a shaky voice.

My mama's face turned pale staring at me, shaking her head with disbelief, trying to understand what I had just said. I ran out of the house, got on my bike again and cycled to the chapel by the lake where John used to run to whilst I rode my bike next to him. We had often held hands there, saying a little silent prayer, as if it was our vow to be together forever, as if it was an unspoken wedding vow, right there, by the chapel, overlooking the lake at sunset. I sat on the very same steps we had used to sit on, in front of the calm, glasslike surface of the lake and stared at the sky that had turned red from the setting sun and the mammoth red clouds, bleeding, just like my heart. Tears cascaded down my cheeks and I submerged in the biggest grief and sorrow of my life.

How could it be? He is just saying it in anger, surely, it can't be over. He loves me! More than anything! It's only his first reaction. I'm sure he will soon realise how much he loves me and wants to be with me. He will soon understand it. As the book says, he will be back within two months but I'm sure it will be much sooner than that. He wouldn't leave me like this, would he? He wouldn't do such a horrible thing. My mind bombarded me with thoughts from all directions, as if grenades were thrown into a war field and wounding every hope that was still alive.

I then kneeled in front of the statue of Saint Mary, surrounded by pink rose bushes, the same one I used to kneel in front of with John.

'Please, give me the strength and help us. Please, let him realise how much he loves me and come back to me, I know he will—he loves me and I love him with all my heart. Thank you.'

***

'The transport is very expensive. With your furniture, it will cost over €5,000,' John texted me a few weeks later.

Surely he is just saying it out of anger, he doesn't mean it, I thought, knowing that the two-month separation period hadn't been over yet.

'Well, in that case, keep the furniture. You lost yours in the divorce, so keep mine,' I replied with angry pride, confident that he would never do it to me. I just knew it.

'I sent your things. The lorry will be with you tomorrow,' his text said a few days later.

I dialled his number but I only heard voicemail.

'Noooooooooooooooooooooo! Why did you do it??????? Why??????' I cried out in despair, crumpling onto the sofa and sobbing into the cushion. The anguish was so great that if I were alone, I would have finished with my life right there and then, but Mama entered the room and tried to calm me down.

'Please, leave me alone! 'I mumbled, not wanting her to see me crying, seeing the same pain in her eyes, hugging and weeping with me, without saying a word, as nothing she would have said would ease my pain.

That was it. The man who I believed was my one and only soulmate had left me. He had abandoned me. Just like that. With cold blood, he had packed all my belongings in boxes and sent them to me, like the unwanted baggage that shouldn't have been there in the first place. I could never go back to Holland now. I became like Vashti, the Queen of Persia, exiled by the king when she refused to fulfil his request to appear in front of him at a banquet to show off her beauty in front of other men. She knew that there could be severe consequences for saying 'No' to the king, but she still stood up to her values, what she believed as right or wrong, and respected herself as a woman, for which, she was punished. I was not banished from my native country but I was put in exile from my home in Holland. Because it was my home—up to this one moment, this one decision, that had changed my life forever.

CHAPTER 60 - REBIRTH

'The wound is the place where the Light enters you.'

-Rumi

'Let's redecorate the house!' I said to Mama one morning, forcing myself to eat my favourite soft-boiled eggs, which now didn't taste as good as before.

I knew I had to do something to survive this nightmare. My mind kept telling me to just do something, anything that would help me get out of my cave, lying on the heated mat on my bedroom floor, feeling the agony of losing John's love.

'Mama, I want to paint the walls and the ceilings. I want to do something useful, or I'll go mad,' I continued and after some consideration, she agreed, hoping that it would help me get out of the state I was in.

Over the next few months, we redecorated most of the house. A local builder plastered the walls and ceilings so that I could paint them white afterwards. Each time a roller covered another grey area, I felt an immense sense of achievement. I was painting the old, replacing it with the new. We chose new wallpapers with palace-like designs, inspired by all the historic buildings I had visited, where walls were covered in damask and tapestry. We also bought new sofas, tables, chairs and wardrobes which stretched along the whole wall on one side. One half of it was mine and the other was for Mama. I now had the space to put all my clothes and shoes that John had sent me in boxes. I put all our souvenirs and pictures deep in the boxes and hid them in the attic so that I would never see them again. This was my sanity project, helping me in the darkest moments of the biggest heartbreak of my life. The immense love and care from my mama, who had supported me all this time, helped me heal a little bit more each day.

In those months, I tried calling John, even though I had no idea what I would have said, but he never picked up. I never heard his voice again. He was gone. He disappeared from my life, even though I still hoped that it was just a nightmare I would soon wake up from and that he would be back any time.

Once the house was redecorated, I retreated back into my new bedroom, numb and betrayed by the man whom I had considered to be the love of my life for two years. He betrayed my heart. He betrayed my soul. His love for me stopped, as if he had a little black switch on top of his heart that could do it in one move, turning me into being non-existent. As if we had never existed, as if we had never experienced the most wonderful moments of our lives together. I didn't know what to do now and how I ended up in a state of a complete mess and failure. I only had three options; finish with this unbearable pain and give up on life, or… embrace the 'failure' and stay in Poland and perhaps teach English or find a job in a big city, or… I could go back to England and start all over. From nothing. From zero. I just didn't know if I had the strength to do it. And I didn't understand why God would have wanted me to go through another test like this. After all that I had already proven, years ago. Why would I have to go through this again? Maybe there was reason why, but I didn't know it then. When I went to the job centre in my town to register as unemployed, I couldn't do it.

'You worked and paid taxes in England for the last few years so unfortunately, you are not entitled to it in Poland. Honestly, if I were you, I would go back there to find a job. It may still be much easier than here, but have a look at the job board outside!' said an official-sounding lady with a not-so-compassionate voice in the job centre, but the only jobs advertised on the empty board in the corridor were: one for a painter, and one for a builder, probably because they all had gone to find a job abroad, which was better than being unemployed and unable to have a decent life.

Eventually, I realised I didn't want to stay in Poland. I felt that my life in England wasn't over yet, that I had been deprived of it in the most cruel and horrible way and it was not what I wanted. Never, not in a million years, would I have expected John to leave me like this, not caring about any consequences of his decision over my life and what would happen to me from now on.

One day, I emailed my good friend Mike back in England who was retired but still young in spirit, in his fifties and with a caring and friendly nature. We had been friends in the gym, even before I had met John, and he knew I had moved to Holland. When I told him what had happened, he called me straight away. 'What? I can't believe it! I thought he was your soulmate! You were so in love with each other! And he just sent you your stuff because you said you can't be with him without getting married? Why did he take you to Holland then? Wasn't that the purpose anyway? I can't believe it! How could anyone do such a horrible thing? I am so sorry, Monika, it's really awful,' Mike said.

'John has lost his mind. He compared me to his lazy ex-wife and I became a projection of his frustration. He couldn't do anything to her because of the law, but he could do anything he wanted to me because we were not married. He had more control and power over my life and perhaps it made him feel better to be able to treat me like this or it simply had given him an opportunity to show what kind of a man he truly was,' I replied, 'John said, "I'm not who you think I am" in one of his last texts and I don't really understand what that means! What does it mean, Mike? Do you understand it?' I asked, desperate to make sense out of this nightmare.

'No, I don't understand either. Well, who is he then? Maybe he knows he has some personality disorder. It seems to me he is a narcissist and only used you for his own gratification. As soon as you were at his complete mercy, he lost interest and moved on,' he replied.

After months of repeating John's words in my head, I had finally understood what he meant. John had simply been pretending all this time. He had never truly loved me. None of what we had experienced together was real to him. He had lived in a fantasy world and when I had confronted him about the reality and our future together, he had suddenly woken up from his imaginary world, having taken me to Holland without much thought of the consequences on MY life and enjoying his new promotion and travelling, but when it had come to dealing with the earthly, financial problems, not so much. Especially after I had presented him with a spreadsheet of our outgoings against our income, taking into account the costs of the divorce and the impact it would have on our future, including paying thousands for his marital debt, which had made his face go pale. I told him that it would be a challenge, but we could do it. John had to face the harsh reality but he didn't like it.

'Come back to England and start all over,' Mike suggested.

'How can I go back? With no money, no job?' I replied with resignation about any successes in my life.

'Don't worry, you can stay in my house till you find a job and get independent again. I believe in you,' he replied encouragingly, so that I regained faith in my abilities.

The last thing John ever did for me was to buy the plane ticket to England which I asked him for because he had left me with no money. I flew back from Bydgoszcz to the same Stansted Airport, exactly a year after I had moved to Holland. Having come out of arrivals, standing in the exact place when I had arrived years before, I looked around, still desperately hoping to see John's face, waiting for me with flowers, coming up to hug and kiss me and saying, 'Baby, it was a one big mistake,' but... he wasn't there.

'Hello, darling!' Mike exclaimed, walking up to me, with visible sympathy on his face, expressing both happiness to see me and sadness about what had happened.

'Hi,' I said and hugged him tight, trying to stop tears falling down my cheeks. I can do it. I need to be strong. I have to do it, I thought.

CHAPTER 61 - UNFINISHED LIFE

'What if you realised Today,
that Yesterday never existed?'
-Monika Wiśniewska

I was back in England again, with only £100 in my pocket and two suitcases, just like 10 years before.

Well, almost. I had two suitcases with me this time, instead of one, which was some kind of progress.

'You will not survive without me. You will not achieve anything if you leave.' John's words haunted me, punishing me for sticking to my values.

But I couldn't betray my own soul. I was ready to fully surrender and give my life-long commitment to him. But as I had found out, in the most cruel and unexpected way, he wouldn't have done the same for me. John's words hurt me to the core of my being but at the same time, they triggered some internal strength, an even stronger desire in my spirit, to pick myself up and prove him wrong. I had been a successful and independent woman before I met him but he had taken that away from me, cutting me off from the rest of the world with one clean move of his sword, depriving me of the right to contribute something valuable, making a difference and having a purpose as a fulfilled human being. From now on, I was on a mission to get my life back. But I knew it was not going to be easy. I knew that, because I had already done it once before and it wasn't pretty. I also knew it because of my emotional state. I was in a complete and utter mess, still unable to understand what and why it had happened.

Will I ever understand? I thought, over and over again.

All I knew was that that I couldn't let John break my spirit. I couldn't let John defeat me in this cruel way, taking away his love and leaving all alone. Just by myself. Unloved. Unwanted. Unappreciated. I knew I had to keep going. No matter what. No matter where. I wanted to live. I wanted to live my life to the fullest and be happy again. Even if it meant being without him. And I was determined to do it all over again, by putting my life to the biggest test yet. In England.

Mike turned out to be an amazingly compassionate friend. He gradually helped me restore my faith in myself and life. I was grateful for his help. If it wasn't for him, I wouldn't have come back to England. I would have had nowhere to go. Nowhere to stay. I didn't want to bother any of my friends and their families who had other things to worry about, too embarrassed that my Dutch Dream hadn't worked out. I had taken a huge gamble with my own life, and I had lost. Or was it the contrary? Perhaps I had won? After all, I had finally learnt the truth. Even though it was a very painful truth, surely it was better to know the truth now, rather than find out years later that it had been a lie all this time? When John had told me he wouldn't marry me, he must have known before I had asked him that he would never want to marry me in the future either. And if so, why had he taken me to Holland with him in the first place? And how many more years would I have wasted for a dead-end relationship if I hadn't challenged him to tell me the truth? Two? Three? Five? And how much harder it would have been for me to recover?

I chose the TRUTH.

I chose my LIFE.

***

I didn't know that pina coladas had such miraculous healing powers, until the darkest times of my life, trying to accept the sad reality and starting all over in England. I was a mess, a complete mess. But I knew I had to keep going and keep living day after day, hoping that one day, life would get better again. Mike was very kind, but he soon realised that we both needed a cocktail or two to survive together, me emotional and stressed about the trauma I had gone through and looking for a job again. He let me stay in his spare bedroom, which became my new cave where I had unpacked my two suitcases.

A year ago I was in a Jacuzzi with John in our home in Holland. Why am I here now? I thought, standing at the job centre queue, desperate to get a job, together with other unemployed people.

After a few interviews, I had a choice of two temporary jobs and I took the one closest to Mike's house, with a nice company car and a laptop, trying to enjoy it as much as I could in those circumstances.

'Finally, my own money,' I said, smiling at my first pay slip after a month.

Mike's house was just round the corner from where I used to live in our 'nest'. One snowy afternoon, I went for a walk along the familiar streets. The icy snowflakes hit my face in the cold wind, and as much I was petrified to face the reality, I stopped outside the flat. The lights in the living room were on, indicating that someone else was living there now. Only a year ago, it was me and John, dancing to romantic music in candle light, hugging and kissing and laughing. Only a year ago.

'Tell me, why did it happen? Why did he do it? I thought he loved me. He told me he did, 20 times a day. He showed it to me by the way he cared for me. All I wanted was to spend the rest of my life with him. But how could I have given up on my dream of getting married one day? Why should I have given up on my dream?' I asked Mike, weeping, over and over again, sitting on his brown leather sofa.

Since my return to England, I had never heard from John again. Not even, 'Are you ok? How are you? Do you need any help? After all, we were together for two years.'

I had stopped existing to him.

In his emails he had sent to me when I was back in Poland, he had even tried to accuse me of having lovers in England and tried pushing me into Alexander's arms. Yes, Alexander that I was supposed to visit by the sea but I never did, because I stopped on the way in sunny Weymouth and decided to be with John, my true soulmate. 'You would have a better life with Alexander. He's got a house. I have nothing now,' John had often said jokingly during our relationship, which I had found very annoying, but I had never thought he had actually meant it, as I hadn't cared whether he was going to lose everything in his divorce.

Living with Mike for the first few months was not easy for either of us. I cried a lot and I became a loner. After being cocooned in the safety of my bedroom for the last year, I still liked to hide under the duvet in the bedroom. I could only spend short periods of time in Mike's company, not because he wasn't nice, but because I wanted to retreat back to my anguish and the painful thoughts piling up in my head, overtaking my whole being.

'Do you want to watch a movie? Or if you like we can go for a walk?' asked Mike, having knocked on my door, not understanding why I wanted to be alone so much.

He tried to help me as much as he could. To bring me back to life. But that's how I dealt with my pain. Retreating back to my cave. My mind couldn't take too much at that time. As if it was getting overloaded quickly. Especially when the new job became a bit more stressful. I was not my normal self. I kept wondering where John was, and what he was doing. I couldn't stop thinking about him. I didn't know if he had eventually got divorced or maybe he had changed his mind, having realised that he had too much to lose, and eventually went back to his wife.

If only I could know the truth, I thought, because not knowing was worse than living day by day in the uncertainty and unanswered questions.

The way he had abandoned me, deleted me from his heart with one flick of a switch, leaving me in dismay and disbelief, had been killing me inside ever since. I blamed myself for my decision and that if it hadn't been for my question about commitment, we would be together now. The guilt, the blame, the shame and the sorrow had overtaken my whole being, leaving no space for any happiness, joy and love because I had promised myself, I would never love anyone again.

CHAPTER 62 - MARRIED

A month since my return to England, a quiet voice inside told me to look for John online and see if I could find out what he was doing, alone in Holland and whether he was as devastated about the end of our relationship as I was.

I found him.

And I also found someone else… his wife. His NEW wife. My heart rate and pulse sped up rapidly because my eyes couldn't believe what they were seeing. He had married another woman who looked just like… his ex-wife. She seemed to be in her fifties, plump, with big boobs and short dark hair and glasses. She couldn't be more different to me. They had married in South Africa, posing and grinning for the camera, looking overly happy and in love but with a visible effort to make it all look perfect. But what struck me most was John's smile. It was the exact same smile he'd had when he was with me. He just looked much older and fatter now, as if he had grown ten years older in only a few months!

'He got married!!' I exclaimed, rushing up to Mike, sitting on his sofa in complete and utter shock.

'What do you mean? Who?' he asked, astonished by my sudden announcement.

'Him! The Bad Guy! He married another woman—look—after he had told me he would never get married again! Never!' I replied, feeling I was falling into a dark cave head-on.

'Oh, him? Really?? Well, he had to marry a rich woman in his financial situation, I guess, having lost his house, pension, savings and everything else he had. Just proves he never loved you and it was all a big fat lie. A fantasy world, which unfortunately, you fell a victim of, as I know you truly loved him. After all, you wanted to marry him. What can I say? You are better than that. At least, you have learnt the truth about who he really was and you can now move on,' Mike replied, shaking his head with disbelief but with a calm reassurance in his voice.

'He told me he had to let me go, and that he couldn't do this to me! I assumed that the divorce outcome must have been really bad,' I continued frantically, trying to talk it through and under-stand it all.

John—or The Bad Guy, as I had agreed with Mike we would call him from now on, to avoid painful feelings every time his name was mentioned—had told me that he couldn't do this to me but only three months since he had sent the lorry to Poland, he'd married another woman for money! Or at least, that was what it looked like. Three months! What also seemed weird to me was that she was Canadian. Canada was a frequent destination for him in the five months I had been stuck alone in our Dutch house, waiting for him to come home like a good housewife. Did he meet her then? Could that be possible? I thought I could trust him with my life. Could he have met her in a hotel bar one night and never told me? Maybe I only made it all easier for him with my decision to go to Poland? Maybe he knew he would never bring me back from there when he had bought my one-way ticket? Maybe once he felt he became strong emotionally and healed from the divorce, he didn't need me anymore? My unspoken mission to help him get through the most painful period of his life was over. And as he had said in his goodbye email, we had too much history and bag-gage because of it, which seemed like he blamed me for the two-year divorce nightmare I had gone through with him, somehow turning it against me and that was the reason why we couldn't be together. Maybe. But I would never know for sure.

The shocking realisation that he had married another woman gave me the only conclusion. Once he had turned me into a woman at his complete mercy, he lost interest. I hadn't had my own car, my own money or my own bank account. I hadn't even had a job in Holland. My only job was to wait for him patiently to come home, once in three weeks, and live for HIM. It had always been only about HIM. My needs, my own desires and my mental and physical health had not been his priority, and as soon as I had removed myself from suffering with him daily, he'd revenged in the most cruel way. He had lost his unlimited energy supply to fuel his narcissistic ego, meaning me, feeling sorry for him all the time and suffering with him.

'I'm not who you think I am, I'm like Jekyll and Hyde,' said one of John's last text messages.

These words had haunted me persistently, as if trying to give me the clue that I needed so much, to understand the biggest mystery of my life. I hadn't known what they had meant for a long time but they had finally become clear to me. He had been perfectly aware of being a liar and only needed me to achieve his goal, to get a promotion and leave England. However, his dual personality of Jekyll and Hyde had not allowed him to suppress his dark side for much longer, because it was hard for him to keep up with something that was all fake. That explained why he had been able to switch his emotions off, with one clean move, making me nonexistent to him, because I had never truly had existed for him. Once he got what he wanted, he didn't need me anymore. But what he did need was to find another naive fool who quickly fell for his charm and married him three months later, having believed in his fake persona. No emotionally healthy man could do that. As Mike had always said, most men would take even more time than a woman to heal their emotional wounds and mend their broken heart. But the reality was he had no wounds and his heart was not broken. Because he had never truly LOVED me. John had turned out to be a liar, my soulmate who had never existed. It took me a long time to heal from the biggest betrayal of my life. My bleeding wounds in my heart didn't want to heal easily, though. No matter how many stitches I put on them in form of alcohol, denial, anger, suppression or medication and it was only by facing my demons head on, feeling them, crying with them and acknowledging their existence, I was finally able to work through them and release them back to the universe, leaving me lighter and free from the suffering. But it was a long process that took years.

I tried different types of spiritual healing rituals like cutting etheric cords with John, as one of the energy healers had told me that he was still sucking energy from me, even though it had been a long time since the breakup. I also tried relaxing to yoga nindra and doing a daily ten-minute meditation which eventually resulted in positive changes in me. I finally faced all my pain by exposing it to the light of God, even though it was a very scary thing to do. I closed my eyes and I looked straight into my pain's nasty eyes and said: 'We are done here, your time is up, it's high time to say goodbye and move on, to start a new life and live it to the fullest,' but it took me much more time and effort to deal with all my baggage from the past relationships.

***

'My dream is to live by the sea. But I would need to sell this house to be able to get a nice flat there,' announced Mike one day, to my horror.

The moment I had returned to England, he'd started contemplating moving house which would have left me in a vulnerable position again, with nowhere to live.

'Well, if that's your dream, then you should follow it. Nothing keeps you here anyway.' I encouraged him to do what would make him happy.

The only problem was selling the house. After a lot of viewings, he still had no offers.

'It's because you need to de-clutter it and present it to the potential buyers in a more attractive way,' I advised him. 'Look!

What's with that picture? And why do you keep those chairs over here?' I asked, pointing at things which my intuition was telling me didn't help.

Mike had lived alone for over 15 years after his divorce and the house had become his man pad, so initially, he was stubborn to any of my suggestions but after a while, he began removing unnecessary furniture and accessories from all the rooms, one by one.

During that difficult time for me, I was probably not the most agreeable person on the planet, even quite argumentative I would say, even though I was not consciously aware of it. One of the emotional reactions to my pain was anger. I was angry about everything. During one big argument with Mike, I ran back to my room and shut the door with a big bang. Having noticed an envelope which he had given me for filing my documents, I opened the door and threw it high up in the air till it landed on the floor.

'Ok. That's it! You're moving out!' Mike shouted, having opened the door, and closing it right after.

'I will move out and I will not stay here any longer,' I shouted back, knowing that I had to keep my word now.

My pride would not let me back out. I had a new job now and I could rent a room somewhere else. I found an advert for a lovely en suite bedroom in Ascot and I arranged to view it the next day. It was very expensive but when I saw it, I fell in love with it. The room was in a brand new apartment of a gated building and had its own beautiful white bathroom. It was just perfect for me. Nick, the landlord, was a bald, fat, short man, in his late forties.

'Let's take a seat in the kitchen. Tell me about yourself,' he said as if he was starting some kind of job interview.

'I really like the room but I need to think about it because it's obviously quite expensive,' I replied, wanting to make sure I make the right decision.

'Have you eaten dinner yet? I haven't. Do you want to go to a local Spanish restaurant and have a chat? You can then see that I'm a normal guy,' he asked.

'Ok, sure,' I agreed, thinking it was a good idea for me to get to know him a bit more before I moved into his place. When we sat at the bar area where I also met the Spanish manager of the restaurant and his lovely Polish girlfriend, Kasia, I felt that I could trust Nick's genuine hospitality.

The next day, I packed all my belongings, put them in my car and drove off. I felt sad that it had to end like this with Mike, but I was ready for a new chapter of my life. At least that's what I thought after four months of living with him. Things change and I had to move on with my life. Nothing could last forever.

CHAPTER 63 - VIVE LA FRANCE

'Memories follow you everywhere.'
-Monika Wiśniewska

Standing alone on top of the Eiffel Tower at midnight, looking at millions of twinkling lights in the most romantic city in the world, with the cool breeze touching my face and eyes, drowning in the pool of tears, was not something I would have ever expected to happen, less so being without John after moving to Holland.

Flashbacks of how we had met dancing tortured my soul, which was now overflowing with pain, trying to break through my skin, as if parched by the hot sun on a desert in the hope of release from the prison of its own confinement. To escape. To be free. To be alive.

'Where are you now, John? Are you happy with her? Do you ever think about me? Why did you abandon me like this? Why didn't you love me like I loved you? Why did you lie to me for so long?'

I tried to convince myself that I'd done the right thing by leaving John. I couldn't have stayed with a man who didn't want to marry me and commit to building a solid future. How could I have betrayed my own soul and agreed to something I wouldn't be happy with for the rest of my life? Marriage would not guarantee happiness. Oh, no. From what I had heard, it required some effort to keep the love alive. But it would have shown his commitment. In my eyes at least. That's what I had always believed in. That's what many other people had accomplished. Obviously, some didn't. Even John, himself. But some people were happily married for years, thriving in their love for each other. Some were unhappily married for years, too but it was everyone's choice to live either live a happy or an unhappy life. As my mama always used to say:

'Marriage is like winning a lottery. When you buy the ticket you will either lose or you will win. And some people do win, so it's possible. Just because some don't, it shouldn't stop anyone from trying. After all, how can you know if you win if you don't try?'

The spectacular light show of millions of sparkling lights on the Eiffel Tower itself, a few minutes after midnight, had helped me forget for a split second that I was there on my own. And I was alone because Nick, my landlord, was back in our hotel room. I'd left him there, because I couldn't stand him anymore and his violent outbursts. Earlier in the morning, he shouted at the waiter that his soft boiled egg wasn't runny enough so he commanded him to make another one, with exactly four and a half minutes' boiling time. I was embarrassed to be sitting with Nick at the table, watching him treat people with such arrogance and his hubristic belief in his own self-proclaimed superiority. He noticed my dissatisfied look and he didn't like it, just like he didn't like that I had rejected his advances earlier this evening, after our visit to see the most spectacular show in Paris, Moulin Rouge, with half-naked women, dressed in most stunning colourful costumes and feathers, singing and dancing while we were drinking Champagne.

Nick had been asked to come to Paris to work on a conference for three days, so he had invited me to join him so that I could see this magnificent city whilst he was working. Had I ever wanted to see Paris on my own? Not really, but it was a good opportunity for me to see a few major attractions. I knew Nick liked me but I didn't think he would try anything inappropriate, especially, after I had clearly stated that we needed two single beds in the room and he was fine with it. He had agreed that we were only going to Paris as friends. I was wrong to have trusted his word. Nick got very angry that I didn't want to be with him.

Ever since I had moved into his apartment, he had been always been nice and businesslike when it came to things like signing tenancy agreements and payments. We often had dinner together as it was nicer to eat with company. I had sometimes shared with him what I'd cooked or he'd sometimes brought a take-away in with him after work and we ate it, watching TV. Nick had always made the effort to create a nice atmosphere and often lit candles in the tall, silver candelabra in the corner of the kitchen, whilst telling me about his day. He considered himself to be quite rich. Whatever rich meant! He kept bragging that his apartment was worth over half a million pounds and he considered himself to be upper class. But… he also had habits.

'Put your glass on the coaster,' he'd say, in case a few drops of water would end up on his black marble table, shining as if licked by a dog all day. 'Oh, no, Monika, this is how you should be holding a fork. Like this, you see?' he'd also say, teaching me how to use the cutlery properly, even though, in all my years, I had never been told that my table manners were unsatisfactory.

Until now!

***

After our argument in the hotel room for not keeping his part of the deal, I'd tried to stay away from him. The next day, I could see Paris, even though all I had with me was a day train pass and a map. I couldn't speak French, except the common '*Merci*', '*Bonjour*' and '*Je t'aime*'—but being able to say 'I love you' in French, was definitely not useful for me at that time.

First on my list to visit was the Louvre, which I entered through the glass pyramid and the first thing I rushed to see was one of the most valuable paintings in the world, Leonardo da Vinci's Mona Lisa, where a crowd of people, separated by a silver railing, were taking pictures as if she were a celebrity. But then, she kind of was. The painting was protected by bullet-proof glass and to stop hateful people's acid, paint or even coffee attacks. Why anyone would ever want to do that was beyond my comprehension but she also had a lot of fans and received hundreds of love letters and flowers, and supposedly, she even had her own mailbox! Another interesting fact was that Leonardo had painted it on poplar plank, rather than canvas, which was less accessible in those times. Looking into her beautiful, mysterious eyes and gentle smile, it seemed as if it was a picture taken with an HD camera. I could feel her soul, as if she were alive. The colours were vivid and the projection of the imaginary background, a new technique, were the proof of Leonardo's true genius.

Ok, I've seen her now—mission complete, I thought with great satisfaction.

It was impossible for me to see everything in the Louvre in one day. If I had wanted to look at each of the 70,000 pieces of art, it would probably have taken me four months. After all, it was the largest museum in the world. So all I could do in a day was to run through it, as if I were being chased by the French police for taking a prohibited selfie with one of the precious paintings. I quickly found the sleek, life-size statue of another famous lady, Venus de Milo or the Goddess of Love, Aphrodite, who had supposedly been found on a farmer's plot of land on the Greek island of Milos, hence the name. I felt that it was a real shame her arms were missing. Nobody seemed to know what had happened to them and nobody could be ever sure of what she was actually doing with them. Perhaps she was holding an apple, spinning yarn or just posing, showing off her nudity and as a result, starting a new portrayal of female beauty in Western Civilisations.

At the head of the Daru staircase, I gasped at the alluring, grey, marble statue of Nike of Samothrace, The Winged Goddess of Victory. With her dramatic wings, she looked as if she was fighting against a strong wind but unfortunately, she didn't have a head. That really upset me now. First Venus de Milo with no arms, and now Nike with no head. How come the male statues always seemed to have their bits perfectly preserved, including the famous

David, whose even most intimate jewels could be admired to this day. It all seemed like a secret conspiracy of jealous men, making sure women's statues were always missing something! But my favourite place in the Louvre was the opulent interiors of Napoleon III apartments, with antique furniture and the most gigantic crystal chandeliers I'd ever seen in my life—and I had seen many! He must have had the most ostentatious apartments in the world at that time, despite the French Revolution and the drive for non-decadence.

The next day I wanted to visit Versailles, so obviously I took the train to Porte de Versailles, but when I came out of the station, I couldn't see any signs to the palace.

'*Excusez-moi, madame,* where can I find Chateau de Versailles?' I asked a lady passing by in my broken French.

'Versailles? *Non*!! Train outside of Paris! Village Versailles, 16 kilometres outside Paris,' she replied with a strong French accent, smiling at me as if I were a crazy person who hadn't done her homework on the location of the most ostentatious French palace.

So there I was, travelling from one station to another, looking for the place I had really wanted to see, the former royal residence up to the French Revolution, where King Louis XVI and Queen Marie Antoinette, born in the very Schönbrunn Palace I had visited with John, were brought to Paris, found guilty of treason and executed by guillotine. Her famous saying: 'Let them eat cake,' referring to the hungry people who had no bread, did not help while she received justice. When I finally got there, I stood awed in front of the humongous, gold leaf, 'Gate of Honour', with the crown on top of it. The afternoon sun beamed through it, accentuating the craftsmanship of the gilding, made of 100,000 golden leaves. Behind it, I saw the architectural grandeur of this Baroque palace and I couldn't wait to go inside to see the state apartments but having entered through the gate, entering the grounds of Schönbrunn Palace with John had come to my mind. Walking through the magnificent Hall of Mirrors, with over 300 floor-to-ceiling mirrors, reflecting the daylight, coming in through tall windows and by hundreds of candles at night, I marvelled at this masterpiece of the imagination of Louis XIV, or the 'Sun King'. Again, I was haunted by sudden flashbacks of the Strauss concert, imagining dancing with John on the shining wooden floor, swishing my white long dress to the rhythm of 'The Blue Danube'.

Why aren't you with me now? Hugging, kissing and enjoying the grandiose apartments, stopping in each of them, marvelling at their opulence and gazing at me, without the need to say words? I thought, looking through the tall window, overlooking the de-signed-to-perfection Gardens of Versailles, a true wonderland of fountains, statues and trees, cut in the shape of an umbrella.

Once I sat down in the middle of the wide stairs outside the palace, I didn't have the energy or a strong enough will to stroll through the quaint gardens on my own. Feeling physically tired from having run through the tree-shaded Champs-Elysees, baking in the summer sun, admiring the luxury shops, theatres and restaurants, where I had a moist, flaky croissant and the most fragrant *café crème*, close to the Arc de Triomphe but still, not as tasty as if I had shared it with John, it wasn't the same. I was alone. How could I enjoy any of it without the man I loved? Why couldn't I appreciate it? Why was I still hurting?

I stretched my aching body on the steps of Versailles Palace and gazed at the clear blue sky, without even one white fluffy cloud in sight, asking God: 'Why?'

I wonder what Nick is doing right now. And what is going to happen when I return to the hotel? I thought on the train back to Paris city centre.

'I changed our train ticket reservations. We are going back home tomorrow,' he announced, lying on his bed, when I walked into the room.

We didn't say much during our trip back. Actually, we didn't talk at all. I ran behind him on the way to the train station, like a dog trying to catch up with his owner, as the last thing I needed was to be left alone in Paris, trying to figure out how to get back to England. Sitting in front of him on the train, I looked at the cold expression on his face and unhappy demeanour, as if he was boiling inside. I prayed that I would not have to pay for my decision to say 'No' to him but my intuition was already preparing me for it. I knew I had to pay the price for sticking to my values again and not going against my feelings.

CHAPTER 64 - HOMELESS

'Courage isn't having the strength to go on-
it is going on when you don't have strength.'
-Napoleon Bonaparte

The following day, Nick strangely didn't go to work, even though it was Wednesday.

I took a quick shower and stayed quietly in my bedroom. Half an hour later, Nick knocked on my bedroom door.

'Have you decided that you definitely don't want to be with me?' he asked angrily, as soon as I had opened the door, wearing a white bathrobe and a towel over my wet hair.

'Yes, I have, now please just leave me alone,' I replied and shut the door.

'I want us to be together,' he exclaimed from behind the door, half an hour later.

'Well I can't be with you. I'm sorry. I don't feel that way towards you. I like you but that's it. I want to be alone now!' I replied, having opened the door again.

'In that case, I want you to move out! Right now!' he shouted with fury as if I had just refused to give him power over his imaginary kingdom.

'Listen, I will move out as soon as I find somewhere to stay. I've already started looking,' I exclaimed with a pounding heart and shut the door again but a few minutes later, he walked in without knocking this time.

'You have two hours to move out. Pack your stuff and I want you out immediately!' he shouted with a cold voice and the eyes of a wild animal that had lost its way in the woods.

'What do you mean, move out now? I can't. I have nowhere to go. I haven't found anything yet. Please don't do this,' I begged, feeling that my world was falling apart again.

'You have two hours and I want you to start packing now!' he shouted mercilessly, opening the wardrobe doors and throwing all my clothes and shoes on the floor as if he had been a burglar, looking for precious items in a victim's house and soon after, he dragged my suitcases out of the storage and threw them in the middle of the bedroom with a loud bang.

'There you go. Pack and get out! Now!' he shouted and walked out of the room.

I started crying. What am I supposed to do? On a Wednesday afternoon! I have nowhere to go! I thought in horror.

'I paid for the room till the end of the month. We have a tenancy agreement. You can't just throw me out because I don't want to be with you! It's unlawful!' I shouted in despair, having walked into the kitchen where he was sitting like a policeman ready for the trial of a criminal.

'I can throw you out! I can do what I want! This is my house, not yours! And I will give you the money that you have overpaid for the rest of this month!'

'I don't believe you! I don't trust you! I've already trusted you with Paris and you didn't keep your word!!'

'I'll give you the deposit and the rest of the payment you made for this month the moment you pack your stuff and give me the key back,' he replied with vicious eyes, full of anger so I had no other choice but to start packing, even though I didn't know where I would go now.

Before we had gone to Paris, I'd accepted a new job offer to work for a German company. 'With your experience, you should be earning more money!' Nick used to say encouragingly. My current job had not been bad and was similar to what I had been earning before leaving England, but I had known it would have been good to earn more, especially since I still couldn't afford living on my own, being forced to rent rooms from people like him.

The recruitment consultant who had helped me get my first job in England since my return had called and said, 'How are you Monika? How is the job going? I have this amazing opportunity to work for a German company whose owner is looking for someone with experience like yours.'

'Well, I've only just started, why would I want to change jobs?' I asked.

'The salary would be much higher and an opportunity to be a UK sales manager!' she replied.

'Ok, let me think about it and I'll get back to you,' I said, but two days later I accepted the new offer and gave up my current job.

The company had booked my flights to Frankfurt, where their head office was, and I was excited about the new opportunity that would give me a better financial independence. Packing my belongings now in the middle of the day, not knowing where I was going to go, I was in between jobs and without the company car, so I couldn't just put my things in the car and drive off, with dignity and pride.

'Where am I supposed to go now?' I asked Nick one more time, weeping but he was intransigent.

'I don't care! I want you out. Now!' He shouted and walked to my room, checking if I was packing, staring at me with hateful eyes as if he was the devil himself.

I went out of the house and I called the only person I could think of.

'Can I please come back? 'I asked Mike, weeping on the phone.

'What happened?' he asked, worried.

'I just can't stay here any longer,' I replied, avoiding a straight-forward answer.

'Ok, come back, but you have to wait till Friday as I'm away.'

'Thank you, I will,' I replied, both relieved and horrified as I was now facing being homeless for two days.

It was only Wednesday. Where was I supposed to sleep for two nights? There was only one person I could call and ask—Kasia from the restaurant.

'Nick is throwing me out in the street! I'm packing now. Can I please stay with you for two days till I can move back to my friend's house? Please??' I begged her, embarrassed, with no time to pretend I was ok—I was not ok and had to swallow my pride.

'Sure, George will pick you up in an hour,' she replied and I went back inside to finish packing and start taking my belongings outside.

Nick was sitting in the kitchen, watching me with a look of a madman. 'Give me the key and I'll give you the money back,' he demanded when I had finished my most humiliating experience yet.

'You give me the envelope first, then I'll give you the key back,' I replied.

'No, you do it first!' he said and after five minutes of this ri-diculousness, we finally agreed we would do it simultaneously.

He grabbed the key and gave me the money back. I stood in the street in front of the gate to one of the most expensive houses in Ascot, surrounded by all my belongings, some of which I had quickly thrown into bin bags, still scattered on the pavement. Why is this nightmare happening? It's only getting worse. Now I'm in the street, homeless, I thought.

When George arrived, I could see in his face that I was not a pleasant sight. After all, I had been evicted onto the street, with only two hour's notice, standing there surrounded by bin bags filled cutlery and pans, red-eyed and lachrymose.

'What has got into Nick? Why did he behave like this?' Kasia asked at dinner later that night.

'Well, he was an angry man who didn't get what he wanted' I replied. 'Thank you so much for rescuing me—I will be eternally grateful,' I added, appreciative that there were still good and generous people in the world, glad I would never have to see that nefarious man again in my life.

CHAPTER 65 - PERSEVERANCE

'Going up the hill, the strong gale blew in my face but I put my hat on and said: 'Bring it on! I'll keep going anyway!' When I'd reached the top, the sky was blue and the air was still. I sat on the rocks and said with a smile: 'I told you I can do it, didn't I?'
-Monika Wiśniewska

'Hello darling! Aww, I've missed you!' Mike greeted me with a big hug at the doorstep, after two days of me being homeless and living on my friends' sofa.

We never talked about what had happened. It seemed better that way. All I wanted to do was to forget about it all and move on. I wanted to forget Nick, Paris and constantly moving from one place to another, like a homeless dog looking for a new owner. We knew our friendship was going to survive this—even though it had changed and evolved over the years, it did pass the test of time and turbulences.

'I'm going to Frankfurt next week for the new job training and I will be able to see my sister again,' I announced, sitting on his sofa again and drinking my greatly-missed mojito.

'Oh, fantastic! Well done, I hope you enjoy it,' he replied. 'You always amaze me with the ability to get a good job,' he added.

In Frankfurt, when the job training was over, the lady from human resources asked to have a conversation in her office. 'Monika, would you consider being self-employed?' she asked with a strong German accent.

'Oh, no. The owner promised me a good salary and a company car, so I'd like to stay with that offer,' I replied, surprised by her question.

After saying goodbye to everyone, including the owner herself who had invited us to dinner, a traditional German schnitzel and a beer, I flew back to England. As soon as my plane had landed, I received a text message. I thought it was from Mike, letting me know about the pick-up point. But it wasn't him. It was the company owner.

'Hi Monika, we are really sorry but since you don't want to be self-employed, we cannot offer you employment with our company. All the best and good luck!'

My heart sped up rapidly. How could she do this to me? I gave up my current job to work for her. She knows that! How could she be so deceitful? I thought.

I was jobless again. Before I had gone to Frankfurt, I had thought that this job had been secured by the recruitment consultant, but I later realised that the consultant had never sent me a contract to sign. Signing a contract for a new job turned out to be a necessity before quitting the existing one! No matter what any company owner promised or said, counting on people keeping their word, even in business, turned out to be a huge mistake.

Being without a job now meant that when Mike went away for two months to Bulgaria's sandy coast of Sunny Beach to stay in his flat, I could visit him for relaxing beach holidays. Bulgaria in August was extremely hot. Mike's flat, situated in a holiday complex, overlooked a pool area, the picturesque Black Sea and long sandy beaches. It reminded me of the Spanish coast, but less crowded. Every night we had sampling sessions of cocktails, tasty Bulgarian wine and *rakia*, the Bulgarian traditional drink of fruit brandy with a similar strength to Polish vodka. And all this was accompanied by a bit of a cry. From me. Not him. But then, he probably felt like crying himself, listening to my never-ending wallowing upon the misery of my broken heart and no luck with the jobs, silently praying for this 'broken record' to 'get unstuck'.

'Don't worry. Everything will be fine. Your life will get better,' he said to console me in my sorrows.

He was right. A month later, I was offered a new job in a well established company which gave me valuable experience for my future career. After months of Mike's welcoming me at the doorstep with a pint of freshly made cocktail to calm my nerves, and a Champagne Christmas, when we drank 20 bottles of this wonderful juice of Gods, there came a time to say goodbye.

'I sold the house!' he announced one day and I was both happy for him and sad for myself because I had to move out again.

Since my return to England, I had to move six times over the period of four years until I was finally able to get my own place and regain the full independence which I had lost because of John. At one point, my whole life fitted into my small baby blue car, with pillows and duvets pressing against all windows, making it almost impossible to drive to the next place which I would call 'home' for a while. I once had to live on my friend's sofa for a month when I was in-between jobs. I will always be grateful to Viola for showing me so much kindness in one of the worst times of my life.

My come-back to England was even harder than my first leap of faith in 2004. But I did it. I did not give up. Over the whole 13-year adventure, I had to adapt to new circumstances very quickly. I had to fight for survival on every level. Physical, emotional, financial. I had to change jobs to get a better salary. Having started at just over £4 per hour, at the very bottom of the career ladder, I quickly realised that I couldn't live like this for a long time and I challenged the status quo. I challenged myself to get better jobs, sometimes completely different to what I had done before and without much experience in that specific area. But I had learnt quickly. I adapted and learnt new skills, in order to progress even further.

Breaking the glass ceiling had always been hard and being a woman didn't help. Most of the senior management had always comprised of men wearing tuxedos meeting for a cigar, whiskey and gossip in the billiards room after dinner, or at least that's how it felt sometimes. It was never an easy option for me, a woman, to join their special club of top management champions. How could I drink with them after work? But that was something I could certainly try to match up to. After all, I wasn't born Polish for nothing. In the eyes of the British, Polish people had a reputation for good drinking abilities, meaning vodka, together with a few other favourites. 'Oh, you're from Poland? Lovely, so you like cabbage, potatoes and vodka. And it's always cold in Poland, isn't it?' they would say, showing off their extensive knowledge of my country.

Oh, yes, you are right, sometimes it's so cold in Poland that we have polar bears running in the streets of Warszawa. And when it comes to cabbage and potatoes, well who doesn't like veggies? And I guess you like five o'clock tea with milk, followed by fish and chips with peas.

Stereotypes. All one can do is love them. But fresh, white, flaky cod, melting in the mouth, eaten by the English coast, had indeed become my favourite English food. Also, bread and butter pudding and, of course, the quintessential experience of Champagne high tea in Waddesdon Manor or at hotels in London was a true feast for the soul, consisting of a three-layer plate structure, of freshly baked scones with strawberry jam and cream on the top plate, then French macaroons—colourful meringues with delicate jam fillings—placed in the middle, and tiny chocolate cakes with blueberries and lemon tart at the very bottom. All this accompanied by tantalising little sandwiches of smoked salmon, herb *crème fraiche* or cucumber and watercress, together with freshly brewed jasmine leaf tea and a glass of bubbly. A true ceremonial hour of gustatory heaven.

When I found out that according to studies in 2017, women in 21st century England still earned less than men, even in the same positions, it made me reflect that it wasn't just them. What about many in the Eastern European workforce accused of being 'cheap labour'? If a friend had told me he was earning less than his English colleagues, I always got upset.

'Why don't you ask for better pay? Why don't you believe in yourself and that you are worth more?' I asked.

'Oh but my English is not that great and I'm happy to have a good job, anyway.'

'But your skills are just as good, and the fact the employer offers you less is because he knows he can, and that you don't know how much you should be paid. But now you do know,' I would reply, 'and in the end, you will be blamed for working for less, because it's your fault that you are so naive, and an English person can't get a job because you work for less. A true paradox. It all comes down to your self-worth and self-confidence,' I added.

Moreover, what many people never liked to admit was that in spite of earning more in England, they also spent more on the living costs. I'd felt it, being single for half of my time in England, without the ability to share the costs with a partner. It was a huge challenge for me to live on my own from the salaries I had earned. Being single in England was not easy financially. It was always better to split costs in half but I was never a woman who would want to share a house with a man, just to make living cheaper. I had never blamed anyone for my struggles of living in England. I always took responsibility for my own life. I decided how much I wanted to earn, and worked on getting new and better paid jobs, even though I still ended up earning less than many of my English girlfriends who had often earned twice as much.

'Oh Monika, I wouldn't get out of bed for your salary. You need to know your value. You have amazing skills and you need to believe you are worth it. I must tell you that I've just doubled my salary. I said at an interview that I would work for them if they gave me what I'm asking for' said Laura one day.

Now that was a confidence I had never exuded. I had to learn, slowly, to appreciate my value as an employee.

'We are offering you *this* amount of money,' the employer would say.

'How come? Someone else has just offered me *that* amount of money, and it's much more, so I will take their offer' I would reply.

In the end, I realised it was me who decided how much I was worth and wanted to earn, which was way above the national average, even though I later realised that earning more money but not living life purposefully was not the way forward, either. I set out to find my purpose and passion in life, doing something that made me really happy, rather than earning more money at the cost of stress. It took me a long time to become fully independent in England again, but John's prediction that I would never make it without him didn't come true. I was proud of what I had achieved. Without him. Even though it turned out to be an extremely hard journey. But on that journey, I found out more about myself and the world than I would have ever expected. I had to wait for my 'die before you die' awakening a few more years after the arrival of the Dutch lorry in Poland. But it eventually did come.

CHAPTER 66 - SYNCHRONICITY

'Would you like a lift?' asked a young bearded man, grinning from a car window when I was walking past the Eton College Chapel, on a hot summer evening.

'Oh no, thank you very much, I actually like walking' I replied, smiling, surprised by his offer, which would have more likely happened in my town back in Poland, rather than on Eton High Street.

It must have been obvious to him that I would say 'No'. It wouldn't have been wise for me to get into a stranger's car, regardless of his charming smile, which I had actually found endearing.

Two weeks later, on a Saturday afternoon, I felt a sudden urge for a slice of chocolate cake. I jumped in the car and drove to the supermarket to satisfy my sudden desire. On the way back, I stopped at the petrol station to fill up my lovely baby-blue car with some superpower juice.

I heard a familiar voice just as I was leaving the till, having paid my bill. 'Hey, do you remember me? I wanted to give you a lift the other night'

'Oh, yes, of course, I remember you!' I replied with disbelief, having turned around and seeing the same bearded man, grinning.

The universe was obviously very determined to help us meet again. Was it just a coincidence or a mysterious synchronicity, joining our two souls together? I instantly knew that there must have been a reason for it.

'I knew you would say 'No'. I was just practising my confidence, offering help to such a beautiful woman like you. I knew you were walking to the nearby town and it was still a long way to go,' he replied, showing off his white teeth from underneath his beard.

'Oh, thank you, don't get me wrong, I did think it was very kind of you. You certainly have got confidence and you have done well, but I really do like walking,' I replied, amused by the whole situation of talking to him again in the most unexpected moment—at a petrol station.

Somehow, I found him fascinating. His name was Peter and he was from Hungary. He asked me for my number but since he had nowhere to write it down and I didn't have a phone with me either, I quickly said it out loud. Only once.

He'll never remember it, not in a million years, I thought.

But he did.

A few weeks later, Peter was sitting in front of me at a small wooden table by a window of an old English pub, on a rainy autumn evening.

'I've just moved into a flat with views of Windsor from the balcony. It's really nice,' he said, staring at me with his piercing blue eyes sparkling from candlelight.

'Don't tell me it was from a landlord called Edward?' I exclaimed.

'Yes, Edward, how do you know?'

'Because I wanted to rent that flat myself but when I contacted him, he said I was too late. He had already rented it to someone else. So it was you! You nicked my perfect flat!' I replied, astonished by the amount of synchronicities from the universe which had really brought us together for some unknown reason.

'So, how old are you? It's hard for me to tell because of your beard' I continued.

'Umm, 26,' he replied, with a bit of hesitation.

'Oh my goodness, you are a bit younger than me,' I replied, thinking I had already dated a younger man before and it had only ended in Greek tragedy.

But on the other hand, I had also dated older guys who in the end had told me that they were too old for me. I was now in my mid-thirties and started to wonder if age had anything to do with love and relationships. Just because society imposed certain stereotypes of what was right or wrong, allowing for the judging and criticising of others, especially in the new era of social media where anyone with a nasty streak could write nonsense, any time of the day, fearing no consequence from their new-born eloquence, just to show how brave they were. What had happened to deeper understanding, tolerance, acceptance and compassion for other human beings?

Peter walked me back to the car park and hugged me tight to say goodbye. He then kissed me, without even asking for my permission. I was not expecting it—neither the kiss, nor that I would like it. I loved it. He didn't know what he had just done. He had woken up a sleeping volcano. In the four years since my tragic breakup with John, I had tried my best to get my mojo back, the confident and happy self, looking at the mirror, trying to feel attractive again as a woman. But my heart was still surrounded by a thick wall which I had built around it, in order to protect it from pain. I couldn't just let any man suddenly sneak into it and risk being hurt again. Not now. Not after what I'd gone through.

'Let's stay friends,' I suggested in good will, thinking it was the best solution to my dilemma.

He agreed with a mysterious smile, which could only mean that this would be a huge challenge, considering the chemistry that we were feeling. Being with Peter turned out to be one of the most incredible relationships of my life. The intensity of various feelings from huge fascination, to feeling overwhelmed by the energy of just being together every day, not understanding the force that was pulling us towards each other, turned out to be verging on suffocation. The perfect juxtaposition of emotions. All my trapped emotions of anger, anxiety, sadness and self-loathing from the last four years, and probably many years before, secretly suppressed at the back of my mind, inconveniently and simultaneously surfaced to the light of my consciousness, exploding like hot lava in the most unexpected moments. The massive bricks I had chosen so carefully to build the thick wall around my heart started falling off my shaky building structure one after another, as if the weak foundation could not hold them in place any longer. I was flooded by a sudden build-up of stimuli which left me completely petrified, I was crying for no reason in one minute and laughing in the next. Peter didn't know what was happening to me. I didn't know what was happening to me.

I saw a reflection of me in him.

And I reflected back what he was giving me. We were mirrors to each other's souls. What I was so afraid of, he was afraid of even more. Whatever I didn't want in my life, he didn't want it either. Was he my twin flame, the other part of my soul which was once split in half, to help us both grow in unconditional love until we were ready to meet and live a happy, enlightened life? Or was he just incompatible and a man that I was simply not supposed to be with?

'Do you want to go dancing with me? It's great fun. I used to dance years ago,' I suggested one day, hoping that I was now ready to face one of my biggest fears of dancing again, but I was wrong.

As much as I tried to enjoy dancing with Peter, it just didn't feel right. My subconscious mind expected the same experience and the same exhilarating feeling that I had felt when I danced with John. It was a disaster. As much as my lovely Peter tried to learn the moves and swirl me around, and as much as I tried to enjoy it, I still felt the pain deep down which I couldn't get rid of. It had only made me feel worse, reminding me of the past. The past—that was gone. Why was I still suffering because of it? After four years? Why couldn't I just enjoy the present moment? Why couldn't I just move on? How much longer was I to be haunted by the torturing memories of my biggest heartbreak of my life.

'Thank you, you can dance with others now. You know, you don't need to dance with only me. It's ok to dance with other people,' I said after another dance.

'Alright, I'll go,' he replied coldly, leaving my embrace and walking off in the opposite direction over the dance floor.

I sat down on a chair by the wall and watched him, standing by the stage, staring at his phone. He didn't dance with anyone else. I couldn't believe we were sitting on opposite sides of the hall, with people dancing in the middle, separating us, while we were supposed to be a strong and loving couple. Some man asked me for a dance and when I was spinning around, I noticed Peter rushing out of the hall, dressed in his black leather jacket.

How could he just leave me like this? Walk out and not care about what would happen to me? I thought, feeling hurt to the core.

When my dance had finished, I changed my shoes, put my blue trench coat on and left the building, prepared to walk home, now that he had left me.

'Where are you going? Wait!' Peter exclaimed in the car park, running behind me and trying to keep up.

'I'm going home. Alone.' I replied, feeling as if my heart was going to explode from fury.

'Come on, why? I only went outside to make a call. Come on, let's get in the car,' he continued, but I was determined to stick to my decision.

Wearing my dancing dress underneath the coat and warm boots, I could easily walk two miles at ten at night. I had done it before. Many times. I didn't need him.

'Please, get in the car,' Peter exclaimed, pulling up next to the curb in his green sports car.

'No, thank you. I'm walking back home!' I replied, determined, but since I could not get rid of him driving alongside me on the road, making a scene out of it, I decided to get in the car.

We never went dancing again.

'Let's visit the horses. I know a place where we can see them. I've done it before' he suggested one day.

Walking up towards five gorgeous horses along the public footpath of an open field covered in lush grass, touching them, talking to them and gazing at their big sparkling eyes as if they could see more than we know, was a beautiful experience which put my guard down even more.

'Let's go up that hill. You just need to jump over the fence. Don't be scared, I've done it many times before' Peter suggested half an hour later, reaching out for my hand.

'I will not jump over the fence into some field. It's inappropriate. I won't do it!' I replied, upset that he had asked me to do such an outrageous act.

How could it be right? Having a date with a man telling me to jump over the fences and run through the fields? Or eating pistachios on a summer evening in secret gardens and risk being put in prison? I had never wished to end up as a criminal for smelling pink peonies and roses. Or, how could it be right, climbing into a WWII submarine capsule through a narrow round opening just to see what being in a submarine could feel like, not caring if it was dirty, old or rusty and at the same time, a crazy thing to do— something that would have been more appropriate to do as a teenager? Or going for a ride in the wooden carriage of a famous cartoon train, with kids screaming from excitement at the sight of the cows in the fields, and doing three rounds of going backwards and forwards over a one-mile distance? But then men and trains seemed to always go together. And cars, of course. Or, anything that would move, more precisely. But Peter was also a man I could always rely on, with fixing my head lamp on my 'vintage' baby-blue car or picking me up at one in the morning after my work Christmas party at Madame Tussauds where I was waiting for him, a bit drunk, sitting in my long red chiffon party dress and a fur coat outside on the pavement, talking to passersby who worried that I would fall asleep.

'Hey, come on, let's go.' Peter lifted me from the ground whilst I was laughing at myself, sitting in the street at night, and made sure I get back in the car.

'I've missed you' I said, wrapping my arms around him whilst he was trying to concentrate on driving in central London.

'I can see you've had fun' he replied, kissing me quickly back and telling me to rest.

Whilst stopping in traffic, a taxi driver in the black cab started saying something to me so I opened the window. 'Your dress! Look, it's stuck!' he shouted, smiling.

'Oh, thanks,' I replied and opened the door to release the trapped red chiffon, thinking that it was very nice of him to let me know about it.

Peter's childlike enthusiasm started to wake me up from the sad, miserable life of grief and mourning that I had been living because of John. He wanted me to live without boundaries, without limitations, trying new and—in my opinion—crazy things, but I was too scared to let go. I was not that carefree girl, running through the fields of barley at sunset back in Poland, eating apples from the local farmer's orchard and then confessing it as one of my sins to the priest's surprise during the Sunday mass. Living an independent and adult life in England had made me lose that childlike exuberance and Peter's crazy ideas didn't match to what I had considered a proper behaviour. How could he be the One? My Prince Charming. Telling me to jump over fences on a date? My mind could not comprehend why God had wanted me to meet him. Someone who was completely different to the soulmate that I had thought I had already met, years ago. John. And who had betrayed my soul by betraying his. There was only one soulmate I was meant to find in my lifetime. One. That's what everyone had said. That's what movies had shown ever since I had remembered.

That's what friends and aunties had said. That's what everyone seemed to have believed in and strive for. The one and only soulmate I was supposed to spend the rest of my live with. But the problem was, if John had been my soulmate, why hadn't he married me then? He'd married someone else. Would my TRUE soulmate had ever done that?

Logically thinking, no, he wouldn't have. It was obvious to everyone else. But not to me and not to my heart, clinging to the belief that he was the one and only and I would never meet anyone who could make me happy again. It was very hard for me to explain it to my heart that: *No, he was not my soulmate after all. Can't you see, Monika?* Why did my heart not want to listen to perfectly formed logical arguments and choose to live in its own conviction, making this emotional hell from my life? Could I just blame my heart for not letting go, unable to forgive and forget, and if I should, would it also indicate that I was essentially blaming myself?

My whole being was still feeling guilty for what had happened and for having been hurt, unable to heal my broken heart. But who could heal it? If I had found an expert in mending broken hearts with a one-hour session, I would have paid him all my money. To be free again. To be happy again. To live life to the fullest, instead of existing in my half-dead soul, dragged in my body over the surface of the Earth, wasting every single day and night on feeling incomplete without love. Without my heart. Without John who had taken it and never given it back to me, so that I could take ownership of it again. I had given him back the keys to our house in Holland. But he never gave me back the keys to the safe in his heart so I could remove mine and put it back where it belonged.

In ME.

It was My Heart, after all.

Not his.

CHAPTER 67 - BREXITPOCALYPSE

'To understand everything, is to forgive everything.'
-Buddha

'I was afraid to speak to the lady in the supermarket today, in case she could recognise from my accent that I'm not British,' I said to Peter, cooking dinner one evening, shortly after the Brexit vote.

'What? Are you serious?'

'Yes, I am. I may be getting a bit paranoid but since that vote, having been reading about all the racist comments and hatred towards immigrants, especially Polish people, I'm starting to be afraid to speak to strangers, in case they voted for Brexit. What if they are horrible to me and tell me to leave?' I replied, before stirring chopped tomatoes into the mushrooms and onions in the frying pan.

'Come on, not everyone voted Leave, only 51.9 per cent. The others are not like that, and not all who voted for it did it because they want us out—maybe only half of them. I don't know, the Remainers probably like us,' he replied, trying to comfort me.

'I know but that means every other or every third British person I speak to may have voted against ME, against my life here, against US being here. Do you know how it makes me feel? Unwanted and unwelcome,' I replied, pointing out that Peter, being Hungarian, was in the same situation.

'I've been so stressed about the UK media promoting hatred towards us, as immigrants from Eastern Europe, even though Poland is technically in Central Europe, as if we were all guilty of some horrible crime against humanity for wanting to come to

England in search of a better life, being resilient and working hard. I'm so stressed, I can't sleep at night,' I added.

'I know, I feel like this too, to be honest. That's why I want to leave England one day and never come back. I'm considering going back to Hungary,' he said, hugging me. 'We should just leave. Let's leave this country, as they are telling us. Why stay here and feel unwelcome, like an intruder, taking up a parking space or seeing a doctor? If they don't want us, then we should go,' he added.

'No, why should I leave after 13 years of working so hard in this country, contributing to the economy and making Great Britain richer by paying taxes and spending all my money on bills, food and flights. Everyone has benefited from my professional skills and working in this country: the landlords, the car sellers, the supermarkets, the local hairdresser's, the restaurants, everyone, except Poland, which lost a young hard-working professional like me,' I replied, frustrated and feeling more and more angry at his suggestion. 'But what I don't understand is how my neighbour, who hasn't worked for years, living off God knows what, smoking some smelly grass as I leave for work in the morning and as I come back in the evening, can decide about my personal life and my future?? How is that possible? With his SAY, he can tell me to pack my stuff and leave, just because he says so?? I feel like I have lost control of my own life, being able to make a decision as a human being. Surely, if I decide to leave because I don't want to live in this county anymore, it should be because I say so, not HIM! I feel hopeless, not knowing if we will even have the right to stay here, if I should plan to get a better car, or if I should get another phone contract. What if I'm forced to pack my stuff in a lorry that they have sent and deport me to where I belong, according to some horrible people on social media, full of hatred? Where does so much acrimony come from?' I added, feeling more and more upset.

'Stop panicking,' he kissed and hugged me to comfort my shaking body.

'I feel blamed for everything, for being different, blamed by people who cannot solve their own unhappy lives and can only attack others, blaming, criticizing and judging. I had never thought I would come to live in twenty-first century Britain where I am hated by some people, just because of my nationality. I feel like I shouldn't have come back here. I should've stayed in Poland when John sent me my belongings. It was all for nothing, coming back here, trying so hard to get my life back, only to face another disaster—political this time. How much more can I take? My only reward for the pursuit of the English Dream is this Brexit Apocalypse,' I added.

'Oh, stop it, please. Is the pasta ready? Come on, let's eat, relax and have some wine,' he replied, seeing me falling into pieces over the new situation we had found ourselves in, which was affecting my personal life so greatly.

'One of my English friends said he voted for Brexit but not because of me. I'm good and I'm nice. He voted to stop the new ones from coming. How am I supposed to feel when he describes part of my nation as bad, categorising and putting labels on me, saying where I belong and where I don't belong? I go to work now and I don't know how many of my colleagues voted against me being there, working alongside them. They just never had the courage to say it to my face before, but they have said it now, behind my back. I feel betrayed and stressed about this new reality that has changed overnight. It's so distressing and disappointing,' I continued, having another sip of Merlot.

Ever since the Brexit vote in June 2016, I'd been seriously considering if I should just leave. I didn't know if I would want to stay in a country where I felt like an 'immigrant', something I had never felt before the vote. I had not experienced any nastiness from horrible people, just because I was... Polish. Yes, I did hear some sarcastic comments like, 'Oh, so you are Polish? So, do you like to polish?' from people who thought they were clever.

Yes, I was also asked by a drunken, nefarious Englishman in a pub whether me and my friend were prostitutes just because we were Polish. 'Polish? Do you work at night? How much do you charge?' he asked, having another sip of ale.

'Come on, we are leaving,' I shouted in Viola's ear.

'Why? We have just got here,' she said, looking confused and enjoying her chat with another man at a bar.

'We are leaving, Now! He has just insulted us, calling us prostitutes,' I replied and having put her glass on the bar, I pushed her out of the busy pub.

'I am wearing jeans and a warm jumper and he dares to insult me like this? No way, I will never go back to that pub again!' I exclaimed, furious about such an abrupt end to our night out.

And yes, I did also experience race discrimination in a company I worked for after my return to England, but I sought justice and I received justice. My fighter spirit had always had the courage to stand up for myself and for what was right. When people asked me where I had taken so much courage, strength, resilience and determination from, I always replied: 'Umm, from God, I guess, or maybe because in my previous life I was a Polish winged hussar— one of the two.'

However, I came to the conclusion that no nation was perfect. Eureka! Idealising the British people and their way of life was not a good thing to do, but then Polish people were not perfect either, nor the Germans, nor the Italians. After all, we are all just human beings, full of flaws, imperfections, easily judgemental and critical. But deep down, I still came to believe that people were good and as much as there would always be horrible people out there, I hoped there would always be more good ones who would stand up for justice, kindness, compassion and love.

In all those years, I had found the British people to be polite and friendly. Maybe some had never had the courage to say anything bad to me, even though they had thought it, but I had never felt like I was a second class citizen and 'just an immigrant with a number to identify myself with.' I felt I was part of the community that I had tried to integrate into and an overall part of humanity. I'd met some amazing people, like Thomas, the taxi driver, Adam, who had let me rent his flat after our breakup and Mike, who had helped me get back on my feet.

I also experienced many acts of kindness from strangers. Once, after a job interview, I was sitting in a cafe in Henley-on-Thames, waiting for the wall of sudden rain to pass, when an older English lady came up to me and said: 'Here, take my umbrella!'

'Oh, no thank you, I can wait,' I replied, surprised by her unexpected, kind gesture.

'It's ok, you need it more. Here, take it,' she replied with a warm smile and left it on my table and walked away.

'I will bring it back to you,' I said, but she only shook her head, indicating that it was a gift.

Another time, having left the house at half past seven in the morning for work, I noticed that my front tyre was flat. I didn't know who to ask for help at such a crazy hour, so I knocked on my neighbour's door. Michael had just woken up but he eagerly went downstairs with me and spent half an hour changing the tyre so that I could go to work and then a tyre shop. The next day, as a thank you, I bought Polish chocolates in the local Polish shop for his children, which he was really happy to receive.

I had always loved that about England, that I never knew who I was going to meet and speak to: 'Oh, you are from Spain? *Ola!*' or 'Oh, you are from Italy?! *Bella!*' I had also liked additional days off in England such as the national Snow Day when a few flakes of snow on the ground would bring the whole country into a standstill, and me and my colleagues didn't have to go to work. It was perfect for Fridays.

I would call my boss in the morning, having woken up to the joy of seeing the white dust on the driveway. 'I don't think it would be safe for me to drive on a motorway today. Can I please work from home?'

'Oh, that's fine. It's the same here—we can hardly dig ourselves out, so I'm staying home too!' he would reply.

I had always loved being part of this British multicultural society, appreciating the fact that I could live alongside the British people on their land because the European Union had given me that choice and freedom. Especially after having had so much history together. During WWII, 200,000 members of the Polish Armed Forces in the West had fought under British High Command. The Polish Fighter Squadron 303 in the Royal Air Force, one of 16 other squadrons, had fought relentlessly, shooting down 126 German planes in only 46 days, fighting for the freedom of both our countries. Unfortunately, Poland didn't take part in the London Victory Parade in 1946 and we had to wait for 'full freedom' from Communism until 1989, but we did it. I believe this spirit will always stay in us Polish people, including me. To never, ever give up and fight for what is right. Even if it means risking it all. Having stopped once at the Polish War Memorial in Northolt, I prayed for all the souls of the Polish pilots who had died so that we could live in free countries now. As free people. Enjoying lives that those brave pilots had not been able to live, able to travel the world and decide our own fate.

Brexit had a huge impact on my life. It forced me to think about my life. I started to ask myself questions such as: 'Why am I here?' Especially after hearing this exact question from English people more and more.

'Oh, don't you know why I'm here? Don't you know about the economic situation in Poland, our history and why I would want to come to England in search of a better life?' I would reply, irritated, having to suddenly justify why England had been my HOME for over 13 years, 'Why have your parents got a house in Spain? Why did they move there? We all have reasons why we move to a different country.'

But pondering on this question a bit more, I started to seek a deeper understanding. Actually, why am I in England? What is keeping me here? It is not the paradise that some people back in Poland might think is. It can be great and it can be bad. Just like anywhere else. It all depends on being able to use the opportunities, I thought and asked myself another question: 'Well, who am I? I am Polish, that's my nationality. I am a woman, that's my gender. I am a professional, that's my identification with a job. But I am also a human being, with the free will to live the life I choose to live, whether it's in England or Spain or Poland. Whether it's in the city or in the countryside. I am still free and have the power to decide about my own life. No other person, nor circumstance. Only me. That's my true internal strength which gives me control over my life.'

These sudden reflections on my life turned out to be a precious, unwanted present for my 37th birthday from a friend, called Brexit, wearing a bowler hat who had been gathering his courage to hand it to me for a very long time. But just like with any gift, I choose what to do with it now. Because it is in my hands.

CHAPTER 68 - AWAKENING

'Self-love, my liege, is not so vile a sin, as self-neglecting.'
-William Shakespeare, 'King Henry V'

'Is this love? Tell me, Moni. I have never loved before, I have only been with one woman before,' said Peter, stretching out his muscular torso by my side on the grass, still warm from the midday sun, a few months later by a river bank, overlooking Windsor Castle.

'I don't know. I'm the last person you should ask,' I replied with full sincerity and honesty. After all, I still hadn't figured it out myself, and who could say what true love really was? It was not an easy concept to define, even for many philosophers and mystics.

'Fancy visiting the castle?' he asked.

'Yes, I would love to. Let's go on Sunday, shall we?'

Walking around the ostentatious State Apartments, holding hands and kissing at every corner, flashbacks of me and John in Schönbrunn Palace years ago haunted me again. Why do these sudden, unexpected and unwanted pictures of the past still torment me? After four years! I thought.

Marvelling at the giant white carved marble fireplaces, paintings of kings and queens, colourful Italian tapestries on the walls and meticulously painted ceilings, it was easy for me to imagine the Queen herself, wearing a long blue chiffon evening gown and a diamond tiara on her silver hair, walking through the tall white wooden door, embroidered with golden carvings, and sitting down on a red, damask sofa by the roaring fire of the fireplace, in a calm, composed manner. She would sip a freshly-brewed cup of traditional English tea and admire the peaceful view of the perfectly designed gardens, visible from the tall, wide windows, decorated with draped, red curtains and gold tassels whilst gathering her thoughts before the gala ball.

Climbing up the grand staircase, covered by a soft, thick red carpet, I looked at the two knights in shining armour, majestically seated on black stallions, and wondered if Peter could be The One for me. The man I had always been searching for. But the medieval armour on display was obviously empty, with no real knights inside which, on reflection, made me think that they had probably never existed at all. Had they ever rescued damsels in distress? It must have been just another fairytale told for centuries. Walking around The Doll's House, built for Queen Mary in 1920s, I gasped with admiration at the superbly designed miniatures of furniture, books, fabrics and cutlery, showcasing the atmosphere of each room as if it was a real house but for very tiny people in Edwardian England. The house had running water and electricity, which made it even more of a masterpiece, instilling me with appreciation for the skilled craftsmen of that time.

After the excitement of watching the ceremonial Changing of the Guards, dressed in black and red outfits with massive, black, furry bearskin hats, marching in perfect harmony and making a loud bang every time their black, shiny shoes hit the ground, we sat down on a wooden bench inside St George's Chapel, in awe of the carved stone ceiling. We then stepped onto the tomb of Henry VIII, which was built into the floor of the chapel.

In only a few months of our relationship, Peter had challenged my whole world, my whole existence and my whole way of thinking and being. I knew deep down that what he was seeing and feeling was exactly what I saw and felt. How life could be lived to the fullest. All my limited beliefs of what should and shouldn't be, crumbled away. But I was too scared to admit it. Too scared to look at the world from a different perspective. To break away from the boundaries that society had put on us small insignificant human beings, only to keep us under control. Breaking free had always been my dream. My TRUE dream. The dream of feeling fulfilled by living with a purpose and not suffering in circumstances which had made me unhappy, including a job or relationships, every single day, no matter how crazy or unrealistic it would seem at the time, no matter how scary it would be to even begin. But then, courage had always been my forte. The blind unwavering courage to deal with all internal demons and thoughts which had whispered in my ear that I couldn't do it. I realised that my 13-year journey in England had only been a preparation for the next phase of my life, that these experiences had shaped me into who I was eventually to become.

If I had died now and God had asked me: 'If you knew what your life was going to look like after choosing the path of living in England, would you have done it again?'

'Yes, of course,' I would reply.

'Why? You would know how tough that path would be, in every sense,' God would continue.

'Yes, but was I ever meant to have an easy path? And what would I have learnt if I had chosen an easy life, feeling half-dead inside, denying who I really was and not living My Truth of what I believed in? Not much,' I would explain with confidence.

Perhaps I had never been meant to be rescued by my knight in shining armour. Perhaps I was to understand, finally, that nobody could rescue me from pain, sorrow, fear, suffering, feeling unloved and suffocating from internal unhappiness, until I finally rescued myself. Because the solution was always there with me. All the time. I just had to go through my battles to finally see it. It had taken me a while but it was worth it. Forgiveness, compassion, acceptance of *what is* and unconditional love for myself freed me from everything that I had wanted to run away from all those years. Not a different country, not a different location, for nothing could cure the internal turmoil of emotional baggage I had dragged with me like a weight chained to my leg, everywhere I had gone. Because the clue was not in the external world.

The clue was in the internal world.

Peter, my lovely bearded man, seemed to have been on a secret mission from God to bring me back to life. He was meant to come to my path. Literally. Driving along it and catching me at the right place and the right time of my life, after I had shut my heart four years before, somewhere between England, Holland and Poland, becoming half-dead inside, having decided not to love anyone again. But not again, not in this lifetime at least, knowing that I could not survive another heartbreak. I couldn't risk my life like this again.

'I can't do this anymore. Please leave me alone. Now!!' I commanded him, weeping one day, feeling totally overwhelmed with my unexplainable emotions as if my head was a volcano, about to erupt with the lava of all my demons.

I didn't really want him to leave me, as contradictory as it might sound.

I wanted him to stay.

But he left.

The next morning, I was sitting in my car before going to the office when I heard a knock on my window. It was Peter and I let him in.

'I've just gone to work to tell my boss I quit my job. I'm leaving this country. I'm going to Tenerife. It has always been my dream. I can't be here in England any more. Not without you. I just can't,' he explained.

'How could you do it?? I helped you get this job! It's a good job! What do you mean you can't live here without me?' I flooded him with frantic questions, feeling my blood thumping through my ears.

'I hate England, especially now with Brexit and feeling unwelcome! I don't want to live here anymore. And not without you. I came to say goodbye,' he continued and left me alone in the car.

I'm sure he is just saying it in anger, I thought, wiping my tears before entering the office and gathering strength to face another day at work.

I received a text message from him two days later. 'I am at Heathrow Airport, flying to Tenerife in two hours.'

'I love you. Please don't do it. Don't leave me. I didn't mean it. I was just angry,' I confessed on the phone, hoping that he would change his mind, having heard that I'd finally opened my heart to him. It felt so liberating to say these words again. After four years.

'I'm sorry, Moni. I'm feeling sick from all this. I don't know why but I feel I need to do this. For myself. To change something. I can't live like this anymore. Let me do this. Please. I'll be back,' he replied, asking for my compassion and understanding when all I wanted to feel was hatred. I hated him for what he had done. Leaving me all alone.

Will he ever come back? I thought, as I had heard these words before from someone who had promised the same—but he had never came back for me back in Poland.

In the next weeks, I felt all the possible feelings a human being could feel, just simultaneously. Anger, hatred, fear, frustration, grief and something that felt like… LOVE again. After four years, my heart seemed to have finally opened, together with all the wounds of the past, and Peter smashed all the walls I had built around it, despite my efforts to protect it. After a month of endless weeping, waiting, trying to make sense of what had happened and random communication, I finally texted him:

'Do you love me? If you do, please come back and let's finish with this madness.'

'I met someone. She is nice. From Holland,' he replied a few minutes later, and I my heart stopped for a second.

'Oh, that's great! I'm happy for you! Me too, I met someone too. He is a very nice man,' I replied, trying to hide my anguish.

Holland? Could the universe be more cruel? The very name of that country had made my heart sink, under a heavy stone, pressed on top of my chest. It was bleeding again, cut into a million pieces. But why? We were not even right for each other. We were so different. And he had always driven me mad. So why did my heart say something else then?

'I hated and I loved,
I grieved and I overjoyed,
I cried and I laughed,
I judged and I accepted,
I resented and I forgave,
I cursed and I complimented,
I feared and I ventured,
I starved and I prospered,
I lost and I won,
but most of all,
I have been a human being,
I have experienced it all
and I have lived.'
-Monika Wiśniewska

CHAPTER 69 - DÉJÀ VU

'Your task is not to seek for love,
but merely to seek and find all the barriers within yourself
that you have built against it.'
-Rumi

Peter's sudden disappearance from my life helped me find what I had been so desperately looking for all those 13 years in England.

I found LOVE.

But not just any kind of love. During one of my daily meditations, when tears were flowing down my cheeks as if I had been watching a horror movie, with all my pain, suffering and demons, playing main characters in the story of my life, I had felt an inexplicable warmth in my heart. I felt something that I had never felt before. An unconditional love... for myself. I felt that I was more than just a human being. I felt I was part of the surrounding universe. I was a spirit. And in that moment, I felt as if nothing else had existed or mattered. No worries. No problems. There was no past. There was no future. There was only ME and there was no... suffering any more. No more pain, no more heartbreak. I didn't need anyone else to love me because I BECAME love. I became who I had always been so desperately searching for, whole as a person. I realised that only when we are whole as a spirit, filled with unconditional love for ourselves, that can we truly find and share an immense love with another human being, the one that is right for us and who is also whole as a person.

Life turned out to be a never-ending chain of events, bringing constant changes. Nothing, I mean nothing, stayed still throughout my journey. Nothing seemed to last forever either. People would come and go. Men would come and go. But every person that came to my life was there for a reason. People showed up on my path to bring the necessary changes I needed to make in order to grow. To learn. Even if it meant through pain and disappointment. Or maybe *especially* because of that.

In all my years in England, my circumstances had changed daily, weekly, sometimes from one minute to the next. Day always turned into night. Summer always turned into autumn. The wheel of fortune spun restlessly, rattling me inside, making sure that what went up, also went down. Sometimes literally. Every goodness had a seed of badness in it, and every happiness turned eventually into a form of misery. There were always two sides to every coin. Constantly chasing after tomorrow and not fully appreciating the present day was the main reason for my suffering. Constantly dwelling on the past and not on the present moment made it impossible for me to feel happy. Every ending was just an illusion because it was just a beginning of something new. The only thing that had always stayed with me was ME—the love for myself which was all that I had ever needed, the love that would never leave me and it was with me all the time. I was born with it and I would die with it. It would be the only thing that I would probably be in the next dimension, just like other human beings who also believe they could be more than just a physical body, which essentially comes down to the only difference between us; our experiences during our time here on Earth.

The moment I had realised that this unconditional love was the only force that I could ever be sure of in my existence, everything else seemed meaningless. I stopped waiting for validation from another human being and I didn't feel like dying when that validation stopped. Only by feeling the unconditional love for myself could I have enough to share with the world, without feeling depleted and resentful that I was not getting enough in return. But in my physical dimension, the belief in a better day was what really kept me going and not allowing me to ever give up.

In the precious moments of solitude, I had also found something that I had not expected to find, but deep down had always wanted and needed—the gratitude for all that I was, the gratitude for all that I had. In all those years, I had always strived for more. More money, more success, more material things, more love, more pleasure. There was a never-ending dissatisfaction with what I already had, because I was constantly aware of what I did not have and paid too much attention to it.

And when I had lost everything again—Peter's love—I saw how much I did really have. I saw how much of this world belonged to me already, making me feel like the richest person on the planet. Walking along the Great Walk of Windsor Great Park, I could see the most spectacular gardens in England and I realised that even though I didn't even own it, because the Queen owned it, I could still walk around it and appreciate its divine beauty. It was free and no garden or lawn of my own could be greater than this, which in the old way of thinking, would have only made me feel worse. So instead of feeling sad at such a strange realisation, I felt gratitude. I could see what the Queen could see from her windows, and I could admire what the Queen could admire.

I felt the universe had given me so much for free already and instead of feeling miserable that I could not afford visiting Asia or Africa this year, I could enjoy the hot sun caressing my face wherever I was, the wind cooling my skin, the birds singing for me, the green grass allowing my body to rest and all these gifts of the Earth were at my doorsteps all along. And it was free. Yes, absolutely free. For me and everyone else to enjoy, every single day. How could I not have seen it before? How could I have walked the same path a thousand times and only worried about things which I shouldn't worry in that moment, unable to see what I should be seeing. This new reality hit me like a big slap in the face, as if I had finally awoken. Not only from the inability to love my inner child, but into loving the world around me. Feeling grateful and saying 'thank you' to every beautiful thing I had noticed, the sweet smelling pink rose, the bench I could sit on to admire the deer at the distance, the fresh air filling my lungs giving me energy, the exhilarating feeling of being connected to all the things in the universe, and most of all, the feeling of overwhelming beauty inside and out, forgiving the past and trusting the future. It all turned me into a new person, reborn, awakened and excited about every single new day, gazing at my reflection in the mirror every morning saying a simple 'I love you' and giving a wink to myself, despite the sexy bed hair and sleepy eyes.

I fell in love with myself and I fell in love with the world. The world which was beautiful, whether drinking Champagne on a boat in Cote' D Azur, or drinking just a cup of most fragrant coffee, gazing at the majestic Windsor Castle. I was finally able to enjoy everything, without imposed judgements, without imposed standards, without any limitations that society had been telling me to have or not to have.

I decided to cherish my new-found enlightenment, thrilled as if I had finally solved the enigma of life. In my moments of greatest loss, I had found the greatest gain. By losing, either emotionally or financially, I gained something more precious. And it was not money that made me happy—the additional zero in my bank account. It was the experiences of what money could buy. Because it could buy a lot of experiences, no doubt about it. But paradoxically, money could not buy gratitude and appreciation for the smallest things in life. Despite many people saying that nothing was free in life, I had discovered that many things were free and available to everyone already. The wealth and beauty of the Earth had always been there for me. I just had to open my eyes to see it. And I did it, surprisingly, by closing them in moments of meditation. By listening to my thoughts and sounds around me, I learnt to discover more about myself, asking the right questions and receiving the answers to what truly mattered in life. Unconditional self-love and gratitude transformed my life and made my journey in England worth all the pain, struggle and sacrifice. Would I have done it anywhere else? Possibly. Was I glad that I did it in England? Yes.

'I closed my eyes to finally see.'
-*Monika Wiśniewska*

***

I heard a knock on the door. Peter was standing there, grinning from ear to ear, tanned head to toe and with a head full of the lightest hair, bleached from the Canary Islands sun.

'What are you doing here? I asked, opening the door, embarrassed to be only wearing my white, silk dressing gown which I had just put on after a shower straight from work.

'Hi!' he replied cheerfully as if nothing had ever happened.

'Wait till I get dressed!' I ordered him, feeling shocked, and shutting the door when he walked into the kitchen.

I hid in the bathroom. My heart was pounding fast. *Why is he back? What for?* I thought, looking at my stunned face in the bathroom mirror.

I couldn't bear the closeness of his energy, standing in front of him in the kitchen a few moments later, now dressed in jeans and a yellow top. He hugged me awkwardly with a smile, as if trying to show me he had actually missed me.

'Let's go for a walk by the river. I can't breathe, there is no air in here,' I said with a deep sigh, pushing him away.

We were walking fast in silence, passing the thick grey stone walls of Windsor Castle, which looked similar to the walls that had surrounded my heart until recently. The setting sun, reflecting dancing rays of hope, bounced off the calm surface of the river when we were crossing the bridge. Peter sat on a narrow, wooden bench by the river bank, facing me. The air was still pleasantly hot, despite it being after nine in the summer evening. I looked at the Royal Standard flag, gently swaying on top of the castle tower, indicating that the Queen was in again. *What could she be doing now? Is she relaxing in her gardens?* I wondered, trying to distract myself from the unexpected situation. And then: What is he going to say to me?

Peter had been texting me for two months that he had planned to stay there forever. To leave England and enjoy a new life in Tenerife. Lying down on top of a mountain, gazing at the clearest, darkest sky, sprinkled with millions of luminous stars, deeply inhaling the freshest air. But he knew how tough it had been for me to get my independence back, since my return to England four years before. He knew how much the decision to follow my Dutch 'happily ever after' Dream with John had cost me in the end. And that I would never do that for any other man again. I just could not.

He hugged me tenderly and I could feel his heart beating fast, close to my chest. Inhaling the familiar scent of his skin made me dizzy from its sweet, warm intensity. I ran my fingers through his thick wavy hair. My cheek brushed against his, hurt by the roughness of his short stubble. When he released me from his strong arms, I couldn't look into the depth of his soul. His eyes. I would drown in them if I did.

'It was great!! I'm going to live there. I love the people, the weather. I can't be here in England anymore,' he confessed whilst I was listening in silence, looking at the boats passing by under the bridge and swans diving in, hiding their long necks under the water, leaving only white triangles sticking out on top of the water surface. 'I hate it here. This isn't living. It's just existing. But I can't be in Tenerife without you,' he continued, with his eyes sparkling with little diamonds and his hand reaching out for mine, connecting us in an eternal bond.

I had dreamt to hear these words for so long.

'I came back to ask you a question,' he said.

My heart stopped at the eerie familiarity of experiencing déjà vu, and a question I had once heard from a man I used to love so much. 'Would you like to... move to Tenerife with me?'

CHAPTER 70 - KARMA

'You don't need to believe in karma to know it works,
just like you don't need to see the air, to know it is there.'
-Monika Wiśniewska

Having given the obvious answer to Peter the night before, I couldn't concentrate in front of my computer at work all day.

How could he have come back and asked me such a ridiculous thing? He must have realised I wouldn't do it, knowing I had a chance for a career in England after finally getting my life back. How could I have left everything for him next month, pack my belongings and follow him to live the Happily Ever After, on a beach in Tenerife, hoping for a better way of living? I had done it once before and it only ended in the biggest disaster of my life. I could not make the same mistake again.

Tenerife—true, the Paradise. Indeed, I had always dreamt of living by the sea, waking up to the warm breeze blowing through the white veil, revealing a glass balcony overlooking the turquoise sea, glittering in the morning sunrays and being kissed good morning by my true soulmate, embracing him with my whole body under the warm bed sheets, inhaling the intoxicating, alluring scent of his skin and remains of his woody aftershave from the day before, running my fingers through his hair and welcoming another day in heaven on Earth. Another day in the Gardens of Eden.

Yes, his dream to live in Tenerife would have certainly matched my dream. The universe might have finally manifested the dreams both of us had. After learning so much through my life lessons and synchronicities, it would have finally made the dream of two people come true.

But I wasn't ready.

'Are you crazy? I can't just leave everything and move to Tenerife with you next month. I can't. I wish you all the best though. I hope you will be finally happy there, without me.' So I had finished our chat on the river bench that night, but I couldn't stop thinking about it the next day.

I needed to see him again, to try to understand why he would want to do that. *Maybe he will want to stay in England when he sees me again, maybe he will change his mind from this most stupid idea I've ever heard in my life, to just leave everything and go,* I thought.

'Let's meet tonight. To talk,' I said to him on the phone when I got back home from work.

Dressed in my short blue skirt, black leather jacket and black heels I got into his car parked outside.

'I'm going to Croatia for two weeks and then I'm moving to Tenerife. That's my plan. Are you coming with me?' he asked, piercing me with his hypnotising blue eyes when we were sitting in an old country pub.

'You know I can't. I've worked so hard to get my life back here in England. I can't just leave it all. I can't. Why can't you stay?'

'Because I don't like it here now.'

'Ok, I want to go home now—we have nothing else to talk about. I won't go to Tenerife and you won't stay here, so I want to go now,' I replied with a pounding heart, and ran out of the pub into the darkness and the pouring rain, waiting for him to catch up with me and open the car door. 'I hate you! You are such an egoist! You only think about yourself! You know I can't go and you still ask me! How dare you? You think my heart is made of steel?? That nothing can ever destroy it? That it's indestructible? How much do you think I can take in life? How much pain and betrayal? How much more? Tell me! I have my limits too! I am only a human being! I never want to see you again in my life. Never! I swear to God!' I shouted in a fury, watching him driving more and more nervously, cutting corners on the dark country road, hardly visible in the wall of pouring rain.

'But you told me to leave you alone! Remember? You told me to go away!' he shouted back.

'Yes, I did tell you to leave, because you were driving me mad! But I didn't want you to go to Tenerife and bugger off to the sunset forever! Don't you understand? I changed my mind. I can change my mind. Which part of it do you not understand?' I replied.

I knew I had to end this suffering once and for all. I knew I couldn't take it anymore. It was the end. Truly. I had to end it right there and then.

'Please, wait, don't go,' he begged when I tried to open the door to the pouring rain outside my house. 'I'm sorry, I don't know why I am the way I am. I'm scared of what will happen if I stay, I'm not ready. I can't believe I will never see you again. This is the worst day of my life,' he added, sobbing into my shoulder as we hugged in our last embrace.

I cried too. We both did. The heavy drops of rain on top of the car, as if the heavens had opened in despair, made the whole world cry with us, in the darkest moment of our lives.

'Why can't you let me go?' he asked through tears, as if he couldn't understand and believe that I could love him.

'I don't know why,' I replied, wiping my tears, taking a breath from squeezing him in a tight embrace. 'I tried to let you go, but I just can't. As much as I try. It's like you are part of my soul,' I added, 'but if you want to go, go. I need to let you do it. Do what will make you happy. I don't want you to give up on your dream,' I said, opening the car door, feeling the cold rain drops hitting my hand.

'Good bye,' I whispered.

'Good bye,' he whispered back.

I rushed upstairs to my flat. I turned on the dim, side lamp in the kitchen and looked through the window. Peter was there, looking through the car window, making sure I got back 'ok' like he had always done. His tears were not visible now, as millions of tears were falling from the sky, hitting the kitchen window with a loud bang.

'Please, park the car and come to me. Change your mind and stay in England,' I prayed with the last remains of hope.

I knew he loved me. Why couldn't he just admit it? He had told me he had not been able to cry for years, that nothing had ever made him cry, and now he wept as if the dam had suddenly opened. For those few moments, which seemed like an eternity, we stared at each others' eyes as if they were connected with an invisible thread, uninterrupted by the thunderstorm between us.

He drove off.

I sat on the floor and covered my eyes, hoping it was just a bad dream, the nightmare I had hoped I would never have to experience again.

Two weeks later, I was with my beloved Mama in Poland. She had fallen down on wet tiles and broke her knee cap in half, two days before my arrival and three days before my nephew's wedding in the south of Poland, where we were all supposed to drive to.

I felt incredibly sorry for her when I was picking her up from the hospital, seeing her unable to walk with a straight, immobilised leg, which made it a big challenge to pack her into the front seat of the car. I looked after her the best I could. It was my turn now, after years of her looking after me and being the best Mama ever, even though we had spent so many years apart, only seeing each other once or twice a year for a short period of time, because of the life I had chosen. Because of my choice 13 years ago to stay in England.

Our new German Shepherd, Bruno— Cezar had unfortunately died of cancer and had been buried under a plum tree in our orchard—didn't help with the challenge of looking after my mama. On the contrary, he took a puckish delight in teasing me, running around the house and the garden like a lunatic, a battery-charged, unstoppable toy, impossible to control, biting everything, grabbing my cosmetics bag and dragging it right into the middle of the field, scattering all my expensive make-up as if planting seeds, and stealing sofa cushions, making me chase him ten times around the house before I could catch him, which was not easy. Oh no.

Unfortunately, Mama had to stay at home and couldn't go with us to the wedding of her beloved grandson, whom she couldn't see very often, ever since he had moved to work in the middle of picturesque Scotland. Looking at my tall, handsome nephew walking into the church with his beautiful bride, I had tears in my eyes. I was happy for him. But I was alone again. At a wedding. *Will it ever be me? Will I ever meet the man I want to marry and he marry me? Will I ever get married, even if I do meet him? Is this the only way? Maybe I will not want it anymore. Maybe I will be happy with whatever life brings, regardless of the outcome,* I thought.

Having returned to my mama, walking around the garden in the evening, I deeply inhaled the fresh country air, saturated with the scents of barley and lilac. Listening to the crickets playing their goodnight serenade, I could also hear the horns of trains passing across the fields, gazing at the huge vastness of the sky at twilight, turning dark blue and preparing for the night performance with luminous stars as main characters. I suddenly heard a message sound on my phone.

'Do you believe in karma?' Peter asked mysteriously.

'Yes, I do. Why? Why do you ask? What happened?' I replied, feeling my pulse quickening, not knowing what he was about to say.

'I've done something stupid. I'm in a hospital. In Croatia. I fell off a five-metre cliff that I tried to climb onto. I broke both of my legs and seriously hurt my lower back.'

'Nooo, why did you do it? Why did you risk your life like this? Why are you so stupid? Why can't you just be a responsible man? Do you want to kill yourself?' I asked, feeling more angry than compassionate, but adding, 'Will you… be able to walk again? Will you be ok?'

'Don't worry, I'll be fine. I will walk again but I need an operation and months and months of rehabilitation. I have to stay in Hungary once they transport me there.'

'I understand. I wish you all the best. Please look after yourself. I will pray for your quick recovery,' I replied tearfully, thinking how life would never stop surprising me.

'Thank you, and you look after yourself in England too,' he said. 'And I want you to know something, I love her and as soon as I get better I am moving to Holland.'

'Oh that's fantastic! I'm happy for you! Holland? You couldn't have chosen a better location! I'm sure you will both be very happy there. See? We were never meant to be anyway—God wanted you to find your destiny and soulmate in Holland!' I replied, holding off my tears in the most unexpected turn of events I could have imagined.

I thought I had seen it all. But obviously not. I would have never imagined meeting a man who would move to Holland for the love of his life. A man I fell in love with, wanting the exact same thing as I had, years before. This full circle of my life had made me realise one thing.

The universe truly had a cruel sense of humour.

EPILOGUE - I WILL ALWAYS LOVE YOU

'Listen to the wind, it talks.
Listen to the silence, it speaks.
Listen to your heart, it knows.'
-Native American Proverb

Standing on Eton Bridge five months later, gazing at the majestic tower of Windsor Castle and the Union Jack flag swaying in the breeze, I pondered on my 13-year adventure in England which turned out to be my soul's journey to self-discovery and spiritual enlightenment. *What will happen now? How will my life unfold?* I thought. But wasn't it the mystery of not knowing what would happen tomorrow that made life so exciting? If I had known what every decision, every encounter and every relationship would end up as, maybe my soul wouldn't have enjoyed it so much after all. It was life's never-ending surprises that made my human experience so unique, so human. Gazing at the boats passing under the bridge, and handsome swans peacefully floating on the river, which glittered in the afternoon sun, I felt I was finally enjoying BEING. More than I had ever in my life.

I was alone.

But I was at peace.

Because, regardless of all the turmoil around me, I still had ME and the true, deep, unconditional love for my own physical form. Having walked from one side of the bridge, I realised I was standing right in the middle of it, leaning against the railing. It had always been my favourite place to stop at. In a few minutes, I was about to walk to the other side and go up the hill towards Windsor Castle. The bridge was like my life. I walked on it from my Past. I stood in the middle of it, which was now my Present, and once I would cross it over to the other side, it would be my Future.

Standing in the middle, I could either look back at the road I had just came from. Or I could look at the river in front of me, flowing effortlessly, just as my breath and thoughts did in the present moment. I kept looking to the other side, not knowing what was waiting for me when I continued walking. All I knew was that I enjoyed the sun and the gentle breeze on my face and that everything else did not matter, and I had no control over either the past or the future. Only a decision made right now would move me into a new direction. The unknown future was good enough reason for taking another step forward, in the anticipation of another unique and unrepeatable moment. That was the beauty of being a human and living the everyday adventure of life with gratitude, love and faith.

I took out my phone and read again a recent message from Peter:

'She can't replace you. I showered her with the affection that I was feeling… for you. I tried to replace you but you cannot be replaced. You are the woman I should have been with but I was scared to admit it to myself. I am not scared anymore to admit it. I am sorry it took me so long to realise that

I LOVE YOU. I WILL ALWAYS LOVE YOU.'

The End

My name is Monika Wiśniewska.
I am Polish and this was my story.
I will always be proud of who I am and where I come from.
I will never be embarrassed of my life experiences and being HUMAN.
Are you ready for your own journey to self-discovery?